D0521348

The Northwest Best Places Cookbook

VOLUME 2

THE NORTHWEST BEST PLACES®
COOKBOOK

VOLUME 2

More Recipes from the
Best Restaurants and Inns in
Washington, Oregon, and British Columbia

CYNTHIA C. NIMS

SASQUATCH BOOKS
SEATTLE

Copyright ©2003 by Cynthia C. Nims

All rights reserved. No portion of this book may be reproduced or utilized in any form, or by any electronic, mechanical, or other means without the prior written permission of the publisher.

Printed in the United States of America
Published by Sasquatch Books
Distributed by Publishers Group West
10 09 08 07 06 05 04 03   6 5 4 3 2 1

Cover photograph: E. Jane Armstrong
Cover design: Kate Basart
Interior design: Stewart A. Williams
Indexer: Miriam Bulmer

Library of Congress Cataloging in Publication Data
Nims, Cynthia
The Northwest best places cookbook : recipes from the outstanding restaurants and inns of Washington, Oregon, and British Columbia / Cynthia Nims, Lori McKean.
    p. cm
    Includes index.
    ISBN 1-57061-075-4 (vol.1) / ISBN 1-57061-380-X (vol.2)
    1. Cookery, American–Pacific Northwest style. I. McKean, Lori. II. Title.

TX715.2.P32N56 1996
641.59797–dc20

                                    96-13187

Sasquatch Books
119 South Main Street, Suite 400
Seattle, WA 98104
(206) 467-4300
www.sasquatchbooks.com
books@sasquatchbooks.com

Contents

The Best Places®
Travel Series:

Best Places Alaska

Best Places Baja

Best Places Destinations California Wine Country

Best Places Destinations Central California Coast

Best Places Destinations Marin

Best Places Destinations Northern California Coast

Best Places Destinations Oregon Coast

Best Places Destinations Palm Springs and the Desert

Best Places Las Vegas

Best Places Los Angeles

Best Places Northern California

Best Places Northwest

Best Places Phoenix

Best Places Portland

Best Places San Diego

Best Places San Francisco

Best Places Seattle

Best Places Southern California

Best Places Vancouver

DEDICATION

To the chefs, farmers, bakers, fishermen, and all others in the business of bring-ing food to our tables. It is thanks to their passion for and devotion to what they do that we in the Northwest eat so well.

ACKNOWLEDGMENTS

Many thanks to those who helped with recipe testing: Erica Strauss, Cathy Sander, Michael Amend, Jeff Ashley, Paul Swanson, Anne Nisbet, and Sara Dickerman. Leora Bloom was also a great help with testing, as well as with copyediting and other fine-tuning details that come with wrapping up any cookbook. Her energy and focus were very welcome additions to the project!

INTRODUCTION

We're living in global times, which is perhaps why celebrating regionality whenever possible has been gaining momentum, food being one of the best vehicles for doing so. This is a delicious prospect in the Northwest, where the sheer array of foods–both wild and cultivated–provides a world of culinary inspiration. While we can now buy most any ingredient we want at any time of the year, the desire to seek out that perfect tree-ripened peach in August or first-of-the-season plump crabs in December is even more acute, as if in reaction to the blandness that gastronomic uniformity creates.

To help celebrate the culinary offerings of the Northwest, we invited restaurants, cafes, bakeries, and other dining destinations from the fourteenth edition of the Northwest Best Places® guidebook to participate in this collection of 123 recipes that serves up a snapshot of our regional cuisine.

A follow-up to the popular first volume that was published in 1996, this second volume features a wholly new selection of recipes, from both new restaurants that have opened since the first cookbook was published as well as long-time Northwest favorite dining destinations. Little surprise that there is a lot of seafood in these pages–Dungeness crab, halibut, salmon, oysters, black cod, mussels–the list goes on. Asparagus, hazelnuts, apples, cherries, pears, and cranberries play a role in our regional offerings as well. Wild mushrooms, which abound in a variety of habitats throughout the Northwest, and other foraged foods also contribute distinctive character to these recipes.

Luckily, we Northwesterners have good access to the best of these seasonal products. Farmers markets provide a wonderful farm-to-consumer direct exchange that makes a broader array of seasonal food available than we'd find in most grocery stores. Many chefs in the area have become passionate about exploring the offerings of local producers, whether farmstead cheeses, heirloom plums, or free-range chickens. The proximity of many of these farms to major metropolitan areas means consumers can even go directly to the source to learn more about these foods and how they're grown or made.

The regional hallmarks of the Northwest weren't simply dreamed up by savvy chefs or marketing gurus in the last few decades, though both certainly have capitalized on the extraordinary bounty of seafoods, produce, fruits, and other local offerings. Long before the major papers and national glossy magazines "discovered" the restaurants of the Northwest, residents were eating their summertime fill of just-picked berries while making jams to last through the year or were braving the dark, damp, and chill of late fall mornings to head for the foothills in search of wild mushrooms. The first hazelnut tree was planted here in the mid-nineteenth century, and sweet onions were introduced to Walla Walla just a couple of decades later. This is no Johnny-come-lately culinary trend we're talking about.

Some of the recipes presented here draw on influences from beyond the region, reflecting the inherent melting-pot component of New World dining, but the bulk of them reveal a distinctive sense of place. I hope you'll enjoy celebrating the seasonal and regional best of the Northwest in your own kitchen.

—Cynthia C. Nims

Breakfast

Crab and Havarti Omelet *Skagit Bay Hideaway*

Hazelnut French Toast with Orange Zest *Villa Isola*

Lavender Cream Scones with Raspberries *Groveland Cottage*

Caramelized Onion, Tomato, Basil, and Cheese Frittata
Portland's White House

Apfel Pfannekuchen (German Apple Pancake)
Ann Starrett Mansion

Granola *Rock Springs Guest Ranch*

Skagit Berry Oatmeal Muffins *The White Swan Guest House*

Baked Apples with Puff Pastry *Old Parkdale Inn*

Spicy Honey-Glazed Bacon *The Shelburne Inn*

Salmon Egg Bake *Skagit Bay Hideaway*

Inspirational Hash Browns *All Seasons River Inn*

Poached Eggs with Dungeness Crabmeat and
Chipotle Hollandaise *Etta's Seafood*

Oatmeal Spice Pancakes *Lefty's*

Cheese Blintzes with Blueberry Sauce
The Old Farmhouse Bed & Breakfast

Donna's Baked Pears *The James House*

Crab Strata *Cliff House Bed and Breakfast*

Blackberry Coffee Cake *First Street Haven*

Ham and Apple Frittata *Greystone Manor*

Orange Pancakes *Chestnut Cottage*

Salmon Kedgeree *Toad Hall*

Savory Torte with Spinach and Mushrooms *Turtleback Farm Inn*

Apricot-Cranberry Bread Pudding *Portland's White House*

Crab and Havarti Omelet

Skagit Bay Hideaway,
La Conner, Washington

One of the most iconic foods of the Northwest, Dungeness crab is caught along the ocean coast, in the Puget Sound, and in numerous bays such as Skagit Bay. Here the sweet crabmeat is paired with mushrooms, tomato, Havarti, and green onion for a savory breakfast dish. At the Skagit Bay Hideaway, they often garnish the omelet with nasturtium flowers from the garden.

MAKES 2 SERVINGS

⅓ cup Dungeness crabmeat (about 2 ounces)
3 tablespoons unsalted butter
3 to 4 mushrooms, wiped clean, trimmed, and thinly sliced
4 eggs
1½ tablespoons whipping cream
Salt and freshly ground black pepper
2 ounces Havarti cheese, thinly sliced
½ plum (Roma) tomato, seeded and chopped
1 green onion, chopped

PICK OVER THE CRABMEAT to remove any bits of shell or cartilage. If the crabmeat is quite wet, squeeze out the excess liquid. Set aside.

MELT 2 TABLESPOONS OF THE BUTTER in a small skillet over medium heat. Add the mushrooms and cook, stirring often, until tender and the liquid they give off has evaporated, about 5 minutes; set aside.

MELT THE REMAINING TABLESPOON OF BUTTER in a 10-inch omelet pan or skillet (preferably nonstick) over medium-low heat. Whisk the eggs and cream together in a small bowl and season to taste with salt and pepper. Pour the eggs into the omelet pan and cook until just barely set, 8 to 10 minutes. Cover the omelet with the cheese and cook until it is melted, about 1 minute. Add the crab, sautéed mushrooms, and most of the tomato and green onion (reserve a little for garnish).

FOLD THE OMELET IN HALF and cook for another minute or two to allow the filling to heat through, then gently slide the omelet onto the serving plate. Scatter the reserved tomato and green onion over the top, and cut the omelet in half to serve.

Hazelnut French Toast with Orange Zest

Villa Isola, Langley, Washington

Villa Isola is lucky enough to have the Langley Village Bakery nearby, where they get the hazelnut bread used to make this rich French toast. If you're unable to find hazelnut bread (and you don't live near the bakery), use another hearty artisan-type bread. To get that hazelnut crunch and flavor, add ¼ cup finely chopped toasted hazelnuts to the recipe, sprinkling them over the bread with the orange zest. You could also add a couple of teaspoons of hazelnut syrup or liqueur to the egg-and-milk mixture for even more nutty flavor.

Because the bread is cut in generously thick slices, one slice per person is plenty for most appetites. However, the thickly sliced bread needs to soak longer than in most French toast recipes, so plan ahead. The overnight option makes this a snap to fry up and serve come morning.

MAKES 6 SERVINGS

---

4 eggs
2 cups milk
⅓ cup granulated sugar
1 teaspoon vanilla extract
1 teaspoon ground cinnamon
½ teaspoon freshly grated or ground nutmeg
6 thick (1½-inch) slices hazelnut bread (or hearty country-style loaf)
Grated zest of ½ orange (about 1 tablespoon), plus zest curls for garnish
4 to 5 tablespoons unsalted butter
Powdered sugar, for serving
Butter and maple syrup, for serving (optional)

WHISK THE EGGS in a large bowl, then whisk in the milk, sugar, vanilla, cinnamon, and nutmeg. Whisk well for a minute or so to thoroughly blend. Pour the egg mixture into an ungreased 9- by 13-inch baking dish. Lay the bread slices in the dish in a single layer and let sit for about 30 minutes, so the slices soak up some of the custard. Turn the slices over, then sprinkle the tops with the grated orange zest. Cover the dish with plastic wrap and refrigerate until almost all of the custard has been soaked up by the bread, at least 3 hours or overnight.

JUST BEFORE SERVING, preheat the oven to 300°F.

MELT 2 TABLESPOONS OF THE BUTTER in a large nonstick skillet over medium heat. Add half the bread slices, orange zest side down, and cook until nicely browned on the bottom, about 3 minutes. Turn the slices and brown for another 3 minutes. Transfer the slices to a baking sheet and put in the oven while browning the remaining slices, adding more butter to the skillet as needed. When all the slices have been browned and are in the oven, bake for an additional 10 minutes.

ARRANGE THE FRENCH TOAST on individual plates, sprinkle with powdered sugar, and serve right away, passing butter and syrup if desired.

HAZELNUTS

Come October, it's hazelnut harvest time in Oregon's Willamette Valley. Oregon produces more than 99 percent of the hazelnuts grown in the United States, with growers to the north in Washington State making up the difference. An English sailor retired from the Hudson's Bay Company is said to have planted the first hazelnut tree in the region back in 1858, in southern Oregon's Umpqua Valley. Today there are literally millions of the trees in western Oregon producing tens of thousands of tons of the nuts each year. Many go into commercial production of baked goods and candies, but plenty are available for cooks to toss into salads, as a coating for pan-seared halibut, or made into addicting hazelnut brittle. The nuts also produce a rich and aromatic oil that is delicious in vinaigrette dressings and flavorful marinades. In these pages, hazelnuts show up in a topping for roasted oysters (page 41), in a morning French toast (page 4), paired with blood oranges in a salad (page 111), and in both a stuffing and a sauce for portobello mushrooms (page 140).

Lavender Cream Scones
with Raspberries

Groveland Cottage, Sequim, Washington

Sequim is known not only for being home to the Dungeness Spit, namesake of the distinctive Pacific Coast crab, but also for its many lavender farms. At the Groveland Cottage, owner Simone Nichols developed this scone recipe, with just a subtle hint of the aromatic flower in the dough, to coincide with the annual Celebrate Lavender Festival held in and around Sequim each July.

Note that the raspberries need to be fully frozen before starting this recipe, so plan ahead. You could also use prefrozen berries, though be sure to choose berries that are unsweetened and individually frozen rather than frozen in a block.

MAKES 12 SCONES

---

1 cup raspberries, fresh or individually frozen
1½ cups whipping cream
2 tablespoons fresh lavender flowers or 1 tablespoon dried lavender
3 cups all-purpose flour
½ cup sugar
3 tablespoons baking powder
½ teaspoon salt
Butter and jam, for serving (optional)

IF USING FRESH BERRIES, scatter them in a baking pan and freeze overnight.

COMBINE THE CREAM and lavender in a medium saucepan and bring just barely to a boil over medium-high heat. Take the pan from the heat, cover with the lid, and let sit for 10 to 15 minutes. Strain the cream and set aside to cool completely, then refrigerate until cold; discard the lavender.

PREHEAT THE OVEN to 375°F. Lightly butter a baking sheet.

COMBINE THE FLOUR, sugar, baking powder, and salt in a food processor and pulse a few times to blend. Drizzle in the cream, pulsing as you go, until the dough begins to clump together, adding the frozen berries with the last addition and pulsing 2 or 3 times just to incorporate them. (Don't overmix or the scones will be tough and the berries will be puréed; berries should remain in chunks.)

TURN THE DOUGH onto a floured surface and very gently knead it just a few turns to make a cohesive dough. Form the dough into 3 balls, flatten each ball with your fingers to a ½-inch-thick disk, and cut each disk into 4 wedges. Set the scones on the baking sheet and bake until lightly browned, 12 to 15 minutes. Transfer the scones to a wire rack to cool slightly, then serve warm or at room temperature, with butter and jam if you like.

LAVENDER

Lavender is so closely associated with the dramatic parched landscape of Provence in southern France, it seems unlikely that the same flower could thrive in the significantly different climate of the Pacific Northwest. But thrive it does, particularly in the northern part of Washington's Olympic Peninsula, where lavender farms now dot the landscape. A distinctive microclimate in the vicinity of Sequim provides an average annual rainfall of just about 15 inches, while less than 50 miles away the Hoh Rain Forest in Olympic National Park can get 150 inches of rain or more each year. Sequim is even home to the annual Celebrate Lavender Festival, held in mid-July to correspond with the height of lavender bloom.

There are many different types of lavender, some with a heavier, perfumy aroma and flavor and others with a more moderate scent. English lavender provides a good balance for cooking; Provence lavender is a bit milder but is also a good culinary lavender. You can use fresh lavender from your (or a friend's) garden if it has not been sprayed or otherwise chemically treated. Consider drying some of that lavender when in full bloom to use throughout the year, tying the stems into small bundles and hanging them upside down in a dark, dry spot. Dried culinary lavender is often available in specialty spice or tea shops and in some well-stocked grocery stores.

Among the recipes using lavender in this collection are Mussels in Lavender-Garlic Broth (page 53), Lavender-Crusted Free-Range Chicken Breast with Blueberry Habanero Chutney (page 130), and Lavender Cream Scones with Raspberries (opposite).

Caramelized Onion, Tomato, Basil, and Cheese Frittata

Portland's White House, Portland, Oregon

This frittata gets a load of flavor from red onion, fresh basil, and just a touch of balsamic vinegar. Feel free to use Monterey Jack, Swiss, or mozzarella instead of (or blended with) the cheddar cheese.

MAKES 6 TO 8 SERVINGS

---

2 tablespoons olive oil
2 medium red onions, thinly sliced
2 tablespoons balsamic vinegar
4 plum (Roma) tomatoes, thinly sliced
¼ cup chopped basil
1½ cups grated cheddar cheese
8 eggs
¾ cup buttermilk or whole milk
Salt and freshly ground black pepper
½ cup grated Parmesan cheese

PREHEAT THE OVEN to 350°F.

HEAT THE OLIVE OIL in a large, ovenproof skillet (preferably nonstick) over medium-high heat. Add the onion and cook, stirring often, until tender and lightly browned, about 15 minutes. Stir in the balsamic vinegar and continue cooking until the liquid has fully reduced, 1 to 2 minutes. Stir in the tomatoes and basil and cook until the tomatoes begin to soften, 3 to 5 minutes.

REDUCE THE HEAT to low and sprinkle the cheddar cheese evenly over the onion. Beat the eggs in a medium bowl until evenly mixed, then beat in the buttermilk with a good pinch of salt and pepper. Pour the eggs into the skillet and stir gently to mix the vegetables with the eggs, spreading the vegetables out into an even layer. Sprinkle the Parmesan cheese over the frittata and bake until the eggs are set and the top is nicely browned, about 30 minutes.

TAKE THE SKILLET from the oven and let it sit for a few minutes. Loosen the edges of the frittata and slide it onto a cutting board or serving platter. Cut into wedges to serve.

Apfel Pfannekuchen
(German Apple Pancake)

Ann Starrett Mansion,
Port Townsend, Washington

A great use for the region's outstanding apples, this recipe would also be delicious prepared with pears. "My *oma* [grandmother] used to serve this with her homemade applesauce or pear sauce, whatever fruit happened to be in season," recalls owner Edel Sokol. Quite rich, this puffy, oven-baked pancake is delicious with a simple complement of fresh fruit and crisp bacon.

MAKES 2 TO 4 SERVINGS

¾ cup all-purpose flour
½ teaspoon salt
1 cup milk
3 eggs, lightly beaten
6 tablespoons unsalted butter
1 tart apple, cored and cut into ½-inch slices
1 to 2 tablespoons sugar

PREHEAT THE OVEN to 425°F.

IN A LARGE BOWL, combine the flour and salt and make a well in the center. Add the milk and eggs to the well, and whisk just until the batter is smooth.

HEAT THE BUTTER in a medium, heavy ovenproof skillet (cast iron is a great option) over medium-high heat until bubbly. Add the apple slices and sauté until nearly tender and beginning to brown, 3 to 4 minutes, turning the slices once or twice; do not allow them to burn.

SLOWLY AND CAREFULLY pour the batter into the skillet, moving some of the apple slices if needed so that they're more or less evenly distributed in the batter. Bake the pancake until the edges are browned and crisp and the pancake is puffed, about 20 minutes. Take the pan from the oven and sprinkle the sugar over it right away. Cut into wedges to serve.

Granola

Rock Springs Guest Ranch, Bend, Oregon

Try varying this flavorful granola by adding 2 cups nuts (such as pecans, walnuts, pine nuts, and/or almonds) to the oat mixture before baking. Or for a fruitier twist, consider embellishing it with 2 cups mixed dried fruits (banana chips and/or chopped dried apricots, peaches, or pineapple), adding them at the end with the raisins. The granola will keep for 1½ months in an airtight container stored in a cool, dark place.

MAKES 6 TO 8 SERVINGS

---

3 cups rolled oats
½ cup sweetened shredded coconut
½ cup sliced almonds
¼ cup wheat germ
¼ cup hulled sunflower seeds
¼ cup plus 2 tablespoons honey
¼ cup vegetable oil
2½ tablespoons water
2 tablespoons packed light brown sugar
¾ teaspoon vanilla extract
¼ teaspoon salt
¾ cup raisins

PREHEAT THE OVEN to 350°F.

IN A LARGE BOWL, combine the oats, coconut, almonds, wheat germ, and sunflower seeds. Stir to mix, and set aside.

IN A MEDIUM BOWL, combine the honey, oil, water, brown sugar, vanilla, and salt. Stir to mix well, then pour this over the oat mixture, stirring well to evenly coat the dry ingredients with the honey mixture. Spread the granola onto a rimmed baking sheet and bake until golden brown and toasty smelling, about 25 minutes, stirring gently every 5 minutes so that the ingredients bake evenly.

LET THE GRANOLA COOL completely, then stir in the raisins. Transfer the granola to an airtight container until ready to serve.

Skagit Berry
Oatmeal Muffins

The White Swan Guest House,
La Conner, Washington

The Skagit Valley is a lush, fertile growing region in northwest Washington that is perhaps most famous for the spring explosion of tulips, though the culinary riches of the valley—including berries—are significant as well. "Don't wash the berries," warns owner Peter Goldfarb. "If they're sandy, brush away the sand or any other debris. Berries become waterlogged when washed, which would make the muffins gooey." Frozen berries can be used, but don't thaw them before adding them to the batter.

MAKES 12 MUFFINS

---

2 cups all-purpose flour
¾ cup granulated sugar
½ cup rolled oats
1 tablespoon baking powder
½ teaspoon salt
1 egg
¾ cup milk
¼ cup vegetable oil
1⅓ cups mixed berries, halved or quartered if large
1 to 2 tablespoons raw sugar (optional)

PREHEAT THE OVEN to 400°F. Line a 12-cup muffin tin with paper liners.

IN A LARGE BOWL, combine the flour, sugar, oats, baking powder, and salt and stir to mix well. In a medium bowl, lightly beat the egg, then beat in the milk and oil. Add the wet ingredients to the dry ingredients and stir gently, then add the berries and continue stirring just until the ingredients are evenly mixed. Don't overbeat the batter or the muffins will be tough.

SPOON THE BATTER into the muffin cups, filling each about three-quarters full. Sprinkle the top of each muffin with some of the raw sugar (if using), and bake the muffins until a toothpick inserted into the center comes out clean, about 20 minutes. Let cool slightly in the pan, then remove the muffins. Serve warm or at room temperature.

Baked Apples with Puff Pastry

Old Parkdale Inn, Parkdale, Oregon

"This is part of our signature breakfast served with Northwest smoked salmon, bagels, and cream cheese," notes innkeeper Heidi McIsaac Shuford. She suggests serving the spiced apples with vanilla yogurt. They would also make a great dessert, served with vanilla ice cream instead. Fujis are one of her favorite baking apples; they not only hold up well when baked but maintain a pleasantly crisp texture as well. The apples can be prebaked and topped with pastry up to 8 hours in advance and then refrigerated until ready to bake, adding 5 to 10 minutes to the final baking time to compensate for the apples being cold.

MAKES 4 SERVINGS

4 Fuji apples
⅓ cup packed dark brown sugar
2 tablespoons raisins
2 tablespoons dried cranberries
2 tablespoons Red Hots candy or other hard cinnamon candy
1 tablespoon unsalted butter, at room temperature
¼ teaspoon ground cinnamon
⅛ teaspoon pumpkin pie spice or a pinch each of ground ginger and nutmeg
1 sheet puff pastry, thawed

PREHEAT THE OVEN to 350°F. Butter a baking dish large enough to hold all 4 apples, as well as 4 individual baking dishes, each just large enough for 1 apple (or simply another larger baking dish that will more generously hold all 4 apples).

CORE THE APPLES from the bottom, stopping just before the stem end and being careful not to core them all the way through. Combine the brown sugar, raisins, dried cranberries, cinnamon candy, butter, cinnamon, and pumpkin pie spice in a small bowl and stir to thoroughly mix.

PUT THE APPLES IN THE LARGER BAKING DISH, stem side down, and spoon the filling into the cored cavity. Cover the dish with a piece of foil and bake until the apples are tender when pierced with the tip of a knife, about 1 hour. Take the apples from the oven and transfer them to the individual baking dishes, still with the stemmed side down so the filling stays in. Reserve the cooking juices from the baking dish; increase the oven temperature to 425°F.

CUT THE PUFF PASTRY SHEET into quarters. Drape 1 piece of pastry over each apple and wrap the dough snugly down over the apple. Set the dishes on a baking sheet and bake until the pastry is browned and cooked through (pull one edge up from the apple to check that it's no longer doughy), about 20 minutes. If the top of the pastry is becoming too brown before being fully cooked, cover the apples with a piece of foil.

TO SERVE, GENTLY TURN EACH APPLE UPSIDE down onto a plate, with the stem end up. Drizzle about a tablespoon of the reserved cooking juices over each apple nestled in its own pastry, and serve right away.

Spicy Honey-Glazed Bacon

The Shelburne Inn, Seaview, Washington

This is an unusual treatment for your morning bacon, but the spicy-sweet results are quickly addicting. The same process could be used with sliced ham for another breakfast treat. The recipe works best with thick-sliced bacon; if you use thinly sliced bacon the baking time will be significantly less.

MAKES 6 TO 8 SERVINGS

1 teaspoon cumin seeds
½ teaspoon coriander seeds
¼ cup packed light brown sugar
¼ cup honey
2 tablespoons dry white wine
1 tablespoon Dijon mustard
⅛ teaspoon dried red pepper flakes
1 pound thick-sliced bacon

PREHEAT THE OVEN to 400°F.

PUT THE CUMIN SEEDS and coriander seeds in a small skillet over medium heat and toast for a few minutes until aromatic, shaking the skillet gently. Let cool, then grind the toasted spices in a spice mill or clean coffee grinder.

COMBINE THE SPICES, brown sugar, honey, wine, mustard, and red pepper flakes in a food processor and process until smooth, scraping down the sides as needed.

ARRANGE THE BACON on a rimmed baking sheet and bake until beginning to brown, 15 to 20 minutes, turning the slices once. Drain the fat from the pan and brush the top of each bacon slice with some of the glaze. Return the pan to the oven and bake until the top is bubbly and glazed, 8 to 10 minutes. Turn the bacon over, brush the top with more glaze, and bake until the bacon is nicely caramelized, 5 to 7 minutes longer. Serve right away.

Salmon Egg Bake

Skagit Bay Hideaway,
La Conner, Washington

A luxurious way to start the day, the combination of thinly sliced lox-style salmon and fresh dill dresses up morning eggs in great style. This rich dish is a wonderful brunch-for-two option, though you could certainly increase the quantities to serve a larger group. If you don't have 1-cup ramekins, you can use another baking dish of the same volume, though keep in mind that a shallower dish will require 5 to 10 minutes less baking time.

MAKES 2 SERVINGS

---

4 thin slices cold-smoked salmon

4 eggs

½ cup crème fraîche

¾ cup grated Jarlsberg or other Swiss-type cheese

1 tablespoon chopped fresh dill or 1½ teaspoons dried dill

PREHEAT THE OVEN to 375°F. Butter two 1-cup ramekins or other baking dishes. Line each with the smoked salmon and set aside.

IN A MEDIUM BOWL, whisk together the eggs with ¼ cup of the crème fraîche. Add the grated cheese and stir to mix. Pour this mixture into the baking dishes, folding over any exposed smoked salmon edges.

STIR THE DILL into the remaining ¼ cup crème fraîche, and spread it carefully over the top of the egg mixture to evenly cover. Set the baking dishes on a baking sheet and bake until the custard has set and the top is golden, 25 to 30 minutes. Serve right away.

Inspirational Hash Browns

All Seasons River Inn,
Leavenworth, Washington

Innkeeper Kathy Falconer thought she'd cooked the morning potatoes every way possible until inspiration hit for this dish. "Guests loved it. It was a winner!" she says. The hash browns are accented with cheese, green onions, a little garlic, some tomato, and sour cream. Even plain old fried eggs will seem more special alongside these potatoes (a morning version of a baked potato with the works).

In place of the frozen shredded potatoes, you could use 1 pound of fresh russet potatoes. Peel the potatoes and grate them on the largest holes of a box grater. As you grate, transfer the grated potato to a large bowl of cold water, which will prevent discoloration while washing away excess starch from the potatoes, so the hash browns won't be too heavy. Drain the potatoes and pat dry on paper towels, then continue as for the frozen potatoes.

MAKES 6 SERVINGS

---

1 pound frozen shredded potatoes
1½ cups grated cheddar cheese
¾ cup chopped tomato
3 green onions, chopped
½ cup sour cream
½ cup cottage cheese
½ teaspoon garlic powder or 1 teaspoon minced garlic
Pinch freshly grated or ground nutmeg
Salt and freshly ground black pepper

PREHEAT THE OVEN to 350°F. Generously butter a 2-quart baking dish.

COMBINE THE POTATOES and cheese in a large bowl. Add the tomato, green onion, sour cream, and cottage cheese, and stir to thoroughly mix. Add the garlic and nutmeg and season to taste with salt and pepper, stirring to evenly blend. Transfer the mixture to the baking dish and bake until the potatoes are tender and golden brown on top, about 1 hour.

LET THE POTATOES SIT for a few minutes before scooping out portions to serve.

Poached Eggs with Dungeness Crabmeat and Chipotle Hollandaise

Etta's Seafood, Seattle, Washington

This dish is one of the most popular items on Etta's brunch menu. Striking in presentation, with the orange blush of the chipotle hollandaise draped over poached eggs with spinach and crabmeat, it is quite a tasty take on the eggs Benedict theme. The blender method for making the hollandaise sauce is easy and almost foolproof. You can find canned chipotle chiles in adobo sauce in Mexican specialty stores and well-stocked supermarkets.

MAKES 4 SERVINGS

2 tablespoons unsalted butter

8 ounces spinach leaves, rinsed, dried, and tough stems removed

1 cup crabmeat (about 6 ounces)

2 tablespoons white vinegar

8 eggs

Pinch salt

4 English muffins, split and toasted

Chipotle Hollandaise

1 cup unsalted butter

2 egg yolks

2 tablespoons very hot water

2 tablespoons freshly squeezed lime juice

1 teaspoon seeded and minced canned *chipotle en adobo* or to taste

Salt

FOR THE HOLLANDAISE, melt the butter in a small saucepan over medium heat. Put the yolks in a blender and blend for a few seconds. Add the hot water to the yolks and blend for a few seconds more. With the blender blades running, slowly and gradually add the hot butter to the mixture, blending until the sauce is emulsified. (You can pour the hot melted butter from the saucepan into a measuring cup with a spout to make it easier to add it to the blender, but work quickly because the butter must be added while still hot.) Add the lime juice and chipotle and continue blending until very smooth.

Season the hollandaise to taste with salt. Transfer to a heatproof bowl and set the bowl over a pan of hot, not boiling, water while poaching the eggs.

MELT THE BUTTER in a large skillet over medium heat. Add the spinach leaves and cook gently for a few minutes, just until they begin to wilt. Pick over the crabmeat to remove any bits of shell or cartilage. Push the spinach to one side of the skillet and add the crab to heat gently for a minute or so, then remove the skillet from the heat.

HALF-FILL A DEEP SKILLET or sauté pan with water and add the vinegar with a pinch of salt. Bring the water just to a boil, then lower the heat to medium. Add the eggs to the water and poach until the white is set and the yolk is still runny, 3 to 4 minutes.

PUT THE TOASTED ENGLISH MUFFINS on 4 warmed plates. Divide the spinach among the 8 muffin halves, then do the same with the crabmeat. Lift the eggs from the water with a slotted spoon and let the excess water drain off, then set a poached egg on top of the crabmeat on each muffin half. Ladle some of the warm hollandaise over each egg and serve immediately.

Oatmeal Spice Pancakes

Lefty's, Qualicum Beach, British Columbia

Oats add a subtle nuttiness and texture to these pancakes, which also get a boost of flavor from warm spices and tangy buttermilk. At Lefty's, they serve the pancakes with maple syrup and slices of ripe banana.

MAKES 6 TO 8 SERVINGS

---

3 cups all-purpose flour
1 cup quick-cooking oats
¾ cup sugar
4 teaspoons baking powder
1 tablespoon baking soda
1 teaspoon ground ginger
1 teaspoon ground cinnamon
3 cups buttermilk, more if needed
3 eggs, lightly beaten
1 tablespoon vanilla extract
1 tablespoon vegetable oil, plus more for cooking pancakes
Maple syrup, for serving
Sliced bananas, for serving (optional)

IN A LARGE BOWL, combine the flour, oats, sugar, baking powder, baking soda, ginger, and cinnamon. Stir together to evenly mix. Add the buttermilk, eggs, vanilla, and oil and stir just until evenly blended to make a batter that is mostly smooth (a few little lumps won't matter). If the batter's a little thick, add another few tablespoons of buttermilk.

HEAT ABOUT A TABLESPOON OF OIL on a griddle or in a large skillet over medium heat. Add the batter in scant ¼ cupfuls and cook until bubbles dot the surface, 1 to 2 minutes. Flip the pancakes and continue cooking until golden brown on the bottom, 1 to 2 minutes longer. Continue with the remaining batter. Serve the hot pancakes with maple syrup and/or banana slices, if you like.

The Old Farmhouse Bed & Breakfast,
Salt Spring Island, British Columbia

Owner Gerti Fuss notes that these blintzes can be made ahead of time and heated just before serving. Put the filled blintzes on a baking sheet and freeze until firm, about 1 hour, then wrap the blintzes individually and freeze for up to 2 weeks. To serve, Fuss (who makes as many as 100 at a time!) defrosts them on a baking sheet overnight in the refrigerator, covered with a cloth to keep them from drying out, and then reheats them in a 300°F oven until heated through, about 15 minutes.

MAKES 6 SERVINGS

Crêpes
⅔ cup all-purpose flour
2 tablespoons granulated sugar
Grated zest of 1 small orange (about 1 tablespoon)
Pinch salt
3 eggs
1½ cups milk
¼ cup unsalted butter, melted, plus more for cooking crêpes

Filling
8 ounces cream cheese, at room temperature
1 cup cottage cheese or quark
⅓ cup granulated sugar
⅓ cup crème fraîche
1 teaspoon grated lemon or orange zest
Pinch salt

Blueberry Sauce
2 cups fresh or frozen blueberries
¼ cup granulated sugar
2 tablespoons water
1½ teaspoons cornstarch
Powdered sugar, for serving

FOR THE CRÊPES, combine the flour, sugar, orange zest, and salt in a medium bowl and stir with a fork to blend. In another bowl, lightly beat the eggs, then stir in the milk and melted butter. Add the wet ingredients to the dry ingredients and stir just until evenly mixed. Cover the bowl with plastic wrap and let the batter rest in the refrigerator for at least 2 hours before cooking the crêpes. The batter can be made the night before.

FOR THE FILLING, combine the cream cheese, cottage cheese, sugar, crème fraîche, zest, and salt in a food processor and pulse for 15 to 20 seconds. Scrape down the sides with a rubber spatula and blend until smooth, about another 30 seconds. Transfer to a bowl and set aside. (The filling can be made a day in advance; let it come to room temperature before filling the blintzes.)

FOR THE BLUEBERRY SAUCE, combine the blueberries and sugar in a medium saucepan. Cook over medium-high heat, stirring often, until the sugar dissolves and the blueberries give off their juice, 5 to 7 minutes, lightly crushing some of the berries against the side of the pan to make a chunky sauce. In a small dish, combine the water and cornstarch, stirring to mix. Add the cornstarch mixture to the blueberries and stir well. Cook until the sauce thickens, 2 to 3 minutes longer, stirring often; set aside in the saucepan.

TO COOK THE CRÊPES, heat an 8-inch crêpe or omelet pan or medium skillet over medium heat and brush with a little melted butter. Stir the crêpe batter to remix it. Add a scant ¼ cup of the batter to the hot pan and swirl gently so it thinly and evenly covers the bottom of the pan. Cook until the top has turned from shiny to opaque and the edges begin to curl, 1 to 2 minutes, then turn the crêpe and cook a minute or so on the other side. Slide the crêpe onto a plate and continue with the remaining batter, stacking the crêpes directly on top of one another as you go. It's very common for the first crêpe or two to be a total failure, so don't think twice about tossing out early crêpes that don't work. You want a total of 12 good crêpes in the end.

REHEAT THE BLUEBERRY SAUCE over low heat while filling the crêpes. Lay one crêpe on a flat surface and place about 2 tablespoons of the filling in the middle of the crêpe. Fold both sides inward over the filling, then fold the bottom edge upward, and finally fold the top edge down to form a squarish package. Flip the package over so the seams are underneath, and set it on a lightly buttered baking sheet. Continue with the remaining crêpes and filling. Warm the blintzes in a 300°F oven for 10 to 15 minutes before serving.

TO SERVE, SPOON SOME OF THE BLUEBERRY SAUCE onto individual warmed plates, and set 2 blintzes on top of the sauce on each plate. Sprinkle powdered sugar over all and serve right away.

Donna's Baked Pears

The James House,
Port Townsend, Washington

For such a simple recipe, there's quite a lot of flavor in these baked pears. You might even consider serving them for dessert rather than at breakfast, perhaps using vanilla ice cream in place of the vanilla yogurt. The recipe would also work nicely with apples in place of the pears.

MAKES 4 SERVINGS

½ cup packed light or dark brown sugar

2 ripe but firm pears, such as Bartlett or Anjou

½ teaspoon ground cinnamon

¼ teaspoon freshly ground or grated nutmeg

⅛ teaspoon ground cloves

1 tablespoon unsalted butter, cut into 4 pieces

¾ cup orange juice, preferably freshly squeezed

1 cup vanilla yogurt

4 small sprigs mint, for garnish (optional)

PREHEAT THE OVEN to 350°F. Butter a 9-inch baking dish.

SPREAD THE BROWN SUGAR evenly over the bottom of the baking dish. Cut each pear in half and remove the core and stem. Arrange the pears cut sides down on top of the sugar, and dust them with the cinnamon, nutmeg, and cloves. Top each pear half with a nugget of the butter. Pour the orange juice around the pears and bake until the pears are tender when pierced with the tip of a knife, 20 to 30 minutes, depending on the ripeness of the pears.

IF THE COOKING LIQUID is still quite thin, scoop out the pears with a slotted spoon and set them aside on a plate, covered with foil to keep warm. Pour the cooking liquid into a small saucepan and boil over medium-high heat until thickened to the consistency of heavy cream, 2 to 3 minutes.

TO SERVE, cover the middle of each plate with ¼ cup of the yogurt, and set a pear half on top. Spoon some of the warm cooking liquid over each pear, garnish each plate with a sprig of mint, and serve.

Bed-and-breakfast owners perfect the art of efficient breakfast preparation, often devising recipes that can be prepared the night before and slipped into the oven to bake the next morning. This is one such example, though the recipe can be made and baked the same morning as well. When Walla Walla Sweet onions aren't available, you can use regular yellow onions or leeks instead. The strata could also be baked in one large baking dish (about 2-quart capacity) rather than in the individual dishes used here.

MAKES 4 SERVINGS

2 tablespoons unsalted butter
2 cups sliced Walla Walla Sweet onion
1 cup water
½ cup Dungeness crabmeat (about 3 ounces)
4 eggs
1½ cups half-and-half
½ teaspoon Dijon mustard
1¼ cups grated Tillamook pepper Jack cheese
4 cups cubed potato bread (about ½-inch cubes)

MELT THE BUTTER in a large skillet over medium heat. Add the onion and cook, stirring often, until tender and lightly browned, 5 to 7 minutes. Add the water and reduce the heat to medium-low. Continue cooking until the water has evaporated and the onion is very tender, about 15 minutes longer. Pick over the crabmeat to remove any bits of shell or cartilage, stir it into the onion, and set aside to cool.

BUTTER 4 INDIVIDUAL BAKING DISHES, about 2 cups capacity each.

IN A LARGE BOWL, whisk the eggs to blend, then whisk in the half-and-half and mustard. Stir in the crab and onion mixture with 1 cup of the cheese. Add the bread cubes to the bowl, stirring to evenly mix them with the wet ingredients. Spoon the strata mixture into the prepared baking dishes. Cover the dishes with plastic wrap and refrigerate for at least 1 hour or overnight.

SHORTLY BEFORE SERVING, preheat the oven to 350°F.

REMOVE THE PLASTIC from the baking dishes, set them on a baking sheet, and bake for 25 minutes. Top each strata with 1 tablespoon of the remaining cheese and continue to bake until set and the edges are nicely browned, 15 to 20 minutes longer. Take the stratas from the oven and let sit for a few minutes before serving. Serve directly from the dishes, or turn the stratas out onto individual plates and serve right away.

Blackberry Coffee Cake

First Street Haven,
Port Angeles, Washington

A hidden layer of fresh blackberries makes for a tasty surprise in this simple coffee cake. Other berries in season can be used as well, either solo or mixed in a jumbleberry version. This cake is at home both on the breakfast table and as an afternoon snack with a steaming cup of tea.

MAKES 12 SERVINGS

2 cups all-purpose flour
1 cup sugar
1½ teaspoons baking powder
½ teaspoon baking soda
2 cups sour cream
½ cup unsalted butter, melted and cooled
2 eggs, lightly beaten
2 cups blackberries

Topping
½ cup sugar
½ cup finely chopped walnuts
½ teaspoon ground cinnamon

FOR THE TOPPING, stir together the sugar, walnuts, and cinnamon in a small bowl until evenly mixed. Set aside.

PREHEAT THE OVEN to 350°F. Butter a 9- by 13-inch baking dish.

IN A LARGE BOWL, combine the flour, sugar, baking powder, and baking soda and stir to evenly mix. Add the sour cream, melted butter, and eggs, stirring gently until the batter is just evenly blended. Avoid overmixing or the cake will lose some of its lightness.

POUR A GENEROUS half of the batter into the prepared baking dish, spreading it out evenly. Scatter the berries on the batter and pour the remaining batter over them, spreading it evenly (some of the berries may seem too close to the surface, but they'll settle during baking). Sprinkle the topping evenly over the batter and bake until nicely browned and a toothpick inserted in the center comes out clean, 40 to 45 minutes.

LET THE COFFEE CAKE cool slightly before cutting it into squares to serve.

Ham and Apple Frittata

Greystone Manor,
Courtenay, British Columbia

This frittata adds a surprise apple element to the traditional ham-onion-green pepper combination. A tart apple, such as Granny Smith, will be preferable to a sweeter variety for this recipe. Owner Maureen Shipton, garnishes the frittata with herbs and edible flowers from her garden. "I like to use chives, chive flowers, mint, nasturtiums, Johnny-jump-ups, and any other herbs that look colorful and appealing to the eye."

As an optional finish for the frittata, you could pop it under the broiler for a minute or two to lightly brown the top before serving; if you do, be sure you're using an ovenproof skillet (no wooden or plastic handles).

MAKES 6 TO 8 SERVINGS

---

2 tablespoons unsalted butter
1 medium apple (about 1 cup), cored, peeled, and diced
½ cup finely diced onion
½ cup finely diced ham
½ cup finely diced green bell pepper
2 teaspoons minced garlic
8 eggs
2 tablespoons water
½ teaspoon salt
Pinch freshly ground black pepper
1 cup grated cheddar cheese

MELT THE BUTTER in a medium nonstick skillet over medium heat. Add the apple, onion, ham, green pepper, and garlic and cook until tender and aromatic, 3 to 5 minutes, stirring often.

BEAT THE EGGS in a medium bowl with a fork until well blended, then beat in the water with the salt and pepper. Spread the sautéed mixture evenly over the bottom of the skillet, and pour the egg mixture over it slowly. Sprinkle the cheese evenly over the eggs, cover with the pan lid or a piece of foil, and reduce the heat to medium-low. Cook the frittata until the eggs are fully set, 12 to 15 minutes. Carefully slide the frittata onto a warmed serving platter and cut it into wedges to serve.

Orange Pancakes

Chestnut Cottage,
Port Angeles, Washington

The Grand Marnier butter used to top these aromatic pancakes is a luxurious flourish; this is certainly not your average pancake breakfast. The texture of these pancakes, which have ricotta and cottage cheeses in the batter, is a bit more delicate than you might be used to. At Chestnut Cottage, they also serve maple syrup on the side.

MAKES 4 TO 6 SERVINGS

½ cup ricotta cheese
¼ cup cottage cheese
¼ cup unsalted butter, melted, plus more for cooking pancakes
3 eggs, separated
¼ cup all-purpose flour
¼ cup granulated sugar
1 tablespoon grated orange zest
Powdered sugar, for serving

Grand Marnier Butter
½ cup unsalted butter, at room temperature
2 tablespoons powdered sugar
1½ teaspoons freshly squeezed orange juice
1½ teaspoons freshly squeezed lemon juice
1 teaspoon Grand Marnier or other orange liqueur

FOR THE GRAND MARNIER BUTTER, combine the butter, powdered sugar, orange juice, lemon juice, and Grand Marnier in a food processor and pulse to blend evenly, scraping down the sides as needed. Transfer the butter to a bowl and set aside (or refrigerate if made in advance, allowing the butter to come to room temperature before serving).

FOR THE PANCAKES, in a medium bowl, whisk together the ricotta cheese, cottage cheese, melted butter, and egg yolks until well blended, then whisk in the flour, granulated sugar, and orange zest and continue whisking to make a smooth batter. In a large bowl or in the bowl of a mixer, whip the egg whites until they hold stiff peaks. Fold about one-quarter of the egg whites into the batter, then use a rubber spatula to gently fold in the remaining egg whites in two batches.

HEAT A LITTLE MELTED BUTTER in a large skillet (preferably nonstick) over medium heat. When hot, form a few pancakes, using a scant ¼ cup of batter for each. Cook until bubbles form evenly over the top, 3 to 4 minutes, then flip the pancakes and cook until browned on the bottom, 1 to 2 minutes longer. Repeat with the remaining batter, keeping the pancakes warm in a low-heat oven until ready to serve.

ARRANGE THE PANCAKES on warmed plates, spoon a dollop of the Grand Marnier butter on top, and serve with a final sprinkling of powdered sugar.

Salmon Kedgeree

Toad Hall, Sequim, Washington

Kedgeree is an old-time but still popular English breakfast dish, traditionally made using smoked haddock and curried rice, which hints of colonial days in India. This tasty Northwest version uses richly flavored salmon, both fresh and smoked, in place of the haddock. The recipe would also be good with leftover poached or baked salmon in place of the fresh salmon.

MAKES 6 SERVINGS

4 eggs
3 cups water
Salt and freshly ground black pepper
1½ cups white basmati or other long-grain rice
¼ cup unsalted butter
2 shallots, finely chopped
1 teaspoon mild curry powder
8 ounces salmon fillet, skin and pin bones removed, cut into ½-inch cubes
8 ounces hot-smoked (kippered) salmon, skin and pin bones removed, flaked
¼ cup minced flat-leaf (Italian) parsley

PUT THE EGGS in a pan with enough cold water to cover by about 1 inch. Put the pan over high heat and bring to a boil, then reduce the heat to medium-high and simmer the eggs for 10 minutes, counting from the time that the water comes to a full boil. Drain the eggs and run cold water over them for a few minutes to stop the cooking and help cool the eggs quickly (which helps make them easier to peel). Peel the eggs and cut them into eighths, setting aside 6 pieces for garnish.

COMBINE THE WATER with a good pinch of salt in a small saucepan and bring just to a boil over high heat. Stir in the rice, cover the pan, and cook over low heat until the rice is tender and all the water has been absorbed, 18 to 20 minutes. Take the pan from the heat, fluff the rice with a fork, and set aside.

MELT THE BUTTER in a large skillet over medium heat. Add the shallot and curry powder and cook, stirring, until the shallot is tender and the curry powder is toasted and aromatic, 2 to 3 minutes. Add the fresh salmon cubes and cook, stirring often, until the salmon pieces are evenly cooked, 3 to 5 minutes. Set aside ¼ cup of the flaked smoked salmon for garnish and add the rest to the skillet, along with the rice and hard-cooked eggs. Cook, stirring gently, until heated through, 2 to 3 minutes. Stir in the parsley and season to taste with salt and pepper.

SPOON THE KEDGEREE into a warmed serving bowl, arrange the reserved egg wedges and smoked salmon on top, and serve right away.

Savory Torte with Spinach and Mushrooms

Turtleback Farm Inn,
Eastsound, Washington

This spinach and mushroom variation is a newer addition to the breakfast repertoire at Turtleback Farm Inn. Owner Susan Fletcher notes that they also make a layered torte with smoked salmon, using buckwheat crêpes. "For a more substantial meal, you could add chopped and sautéed ham to the filling," Fletcher suggests. "I usually serve meat on the side, as not all of our guests eat meat."

MAKES 4 TO 6 SERVINGS

Sour cream, for serving
Minced chives or green onion tops, for serving

Filling
2 tablespoons unsalted butter
1 large bunch spinach (about 1 pound), rinsed, dried, and tough
    stems removed, or 10 ounces frozen chopped spinach, thawed and
    squeezed dry
8 ounces mushrooms, wiped clean, trimmed, and finely chopped
8 ounces cream cheese, cut into cubes, at room temperature
¼ teaspoon freshly grated or ground nutmeg
Salt and freshly ground black pepper

Crêpes
1 cup milk
1 cup all-purpose flour
4 eggs
2 tablespoons unsalted butter, melted, plus more for cooking crêpes
Pinch salt

FOR THE CRÊPES, combine the milk, flour, eggs, butter, and salt in a blender and mix until well blended, about 30 seconds. Transfer the batter to a bowl and refrigerate, covered, for at least 1 hour and up to 4 hours. (The batter should have the texture of heavy cream; add a bit more milk if needed.)

HEAT A 10-INCH CRÊPE PAN or nonstick skillet over medium heat and brush with a little melted butter. Stir the crêpe batter to remix. Add a scant ¼ cup of the batter to the hot pan and swirl quickly so it thinly and evenly covers the bottom of the pan. Cook until the bottom is lightly browned and the edges begin to curl, 1 to 2 minutes, then turn the crêpe and cook until browned on the second side. Slide the crêpe onto a plate and continue with the remaining batter, stacking the crêpes directly on top of one another as you go. It's very common for the first crêpe or two to be a total failure, so don't think twice about tossing out early crêpes that don't work. You want a total of 6 good crêpes in the end.

MELT THE BUTTER in a large skillet over medium heat. If using fresh spinach, add it in handfuls, allowing each handful to wilt before adding the next, then add the mushrooms and cook, stirring often, until tender and the liquid given off during cooking has evaporated, 8 to 10 minutes. If using frozen spinach, first sauté the mushrooms for a few minutes, then add the spinach and continue cooking until the liquid has evaporated. Take the skillet from the heat and stir in the cream cheese and nutmeg, adding salt and pepper to taste, and stir until the filling is evenly mixed. Keep the filling warm over low heat.

PREHEAT THE OVEN to 350°F.

CUT A RECTANGLE OF FOIL about 3 times as long as the crêpes, and lay it on the work surface. Set 1 crêpe in the center of the foil, spread one-fifth of the filling (about ⅓ cup) over it, and top with a second crêpe. Repeat the layering of crêpes and filling, ending with the sixth and final crêpe. Fold the foil over the torte, set it on a baking sheet, and bake until it is fully heated through, 10 to 12 minutes. Unwrap the torte, cut it into 8 wedges, and serve, adding a dollop of sour cream and a sprinkle of chives on top.

Apricot-Cranberry
Bread Pudding

Portland's White House, Portland, Oregon

A rich and decadent way to start the day, this bread pudding is prettily speckled with orange and red from the apricots and cranberries. Innkeeper Lanning Blanks notes that you can transform the bread pudding into a doubly decadent French toast by frying it in thick slices on a buttered griddle until golden. The gingered whipped cream offers a bright, peppery finish.

MAKES 8 TO 10 SERVINGS

5 cups cubed day-old bread
½ cup finely chopped dried apricots (about 12 whole dried apricots)
¼ cup dried cranberries or other dried berries
1 cup whipping cream
1 cup milk
⅛ teaspoon salt
3 whole eggs
1 egg yolk
¼ cup plus 2 tablespoons granulated sugar
1 teaspoon vanilla extract
2 tablespoons unsalted butter, melted

Gingered Whipped Cream
1 cup whipping cream, well chilled
2 tablespoons powdered sugar
1 teaspoon grated fresh ginger or ½ teaspoon ground ginger

PREHEAT THE OVEN to 350°F. Generously butter a 9½- by 4-inch loaf pan. Cut a strip of parchment paper 3½ inches wide and 16 inches long, and use it to line the bottom and ends of the pan.

PUT THE CUBED BREAD into the prepared loaf pan, scattering ¼ cup of the apricots and the cranberries over the bread as you go so the fruit will be distributed more or less evenly throughout. Set aside.

COMBINE THE CREAM, milk, and salt in a large saucepan over medium-high heat and bring just barely to a boil, then immediately remove from the heat. In a large bowl, combine the eggs, egg yolk, ¼ cup of the sugar, and the vanilla and whisk until smooth. Whisking the egg mixture constantly, slowly drizzle in about half of the cream mixture. Add the remaining hot cream in 2 batches, whisking well after each addition. Pour the custard mixture over the bread and fruit. Leave it to soak so that the bread absorbs some of the liquid, about 15 minutes, gently pressing on the bread occasionally to help the top evenly absorb the custard as well. Sprinkle the remaining 2 tablespoons of sugar over the top, and drizzle with the melted butter.

PUT THE LOAF PAN in a larger baking dish and fill the dish with about 1 inch of hot water. Bake until the pudding is set and slightly puffed, about 1 hour. Carefully remove the pan from the oven and transfer the bread pudding to a wire rack to cool.

FOR THE GINGERED WHIPPED CREAM, whip the cream with an electric mixer at medium-high speed until soft peaks begin to form, then add the powdered sugar and ginger and continue beating to medium peaks. Refrigerate until ready to serve.

TO SERVE, RUN A KNIFE AROUND THE EDGE OF THE LOAF pan and turn the bread pudding out onto a cutting board. Peel off and discard the parchment paper and cut the bread pudding into slices about 1 inch thick. Serve with a dollop of the whipped cream, sprinkling some of the remaining chopped apricots over all.

Appetizers

Steamed Littleneck Clams with Black Beans *The 42nd Street Cafe*

Trio of Seafood Tartare with Soy and Wasabi Sauce

The Cannery Seafood House

Roasted Oysters with Hazelnut Butter *The Place Bar and Grill*

Potato and Goat Cheese Stuffed Peppers with Spicy Tomato Sauce

Matt's in the Market

Peter Canlis Shrimp *Canlis*

Grilled Tamarind-Glazed Quail *CinCin Restaurant & Bar*

Smoked Salmon Cakes with Celery Root Rémoulade *Marché*

Chile Con Queso *Santiago's Gourmet Mexican Cooking*

Mussels in Lavender-Garlic Broth *The Robin Hood*

Oregon Blue Cheesecake *The Vintner's Inn at Hinzerling Winery*

Ebi Shinjo (Shrimp Dumplings) *Tojo's*

Blackened Pan-Fried Oysters *The Shoalwater*

Artichokes Stuffed with Herbed Cream Cheese and Bay Shrimp

Ray's Boathouse

Grilled Scallops with White Asparagus and Mâche Salad

The Aerie Resort

Penn Cove Mussels with Hard Cider, Bacon, and Apple Chutney

Whitehouse-Crawford

Pico de Gallo *Hacienda del Mar*

Vegetable and Cheese Terrine *Abigail's Hotel*

Steamed Littleneck Clams with Black Beans

The 42nd Street Cafe, Seaview, Washington

The Northwest's native clams get an Asian treatment here, steamed with sake, soy sauce, rice wine vinegar, ginger, and other aromatic ingredients. "Being on the Long Beach Peninsula," says chef/owner Cheri Walker, "we love to make a beach fire, set the broth to boil over the fire, and steam open the clams." If only we could all indulge in the same treat so easily! This stovetop version is more realistic for most of us, however. You could double the recipe to serve as a main course, if you like. Other hardshell clams, such as Manilas, can be used in place of the littlenecks from nearby Willapa Bay that Walker uses.

MAKES 4 APPETIZER SERVINGS

½ cup sake
¼ cup dry sherry
¼ cup soy sauce
¼ cup fermented Chinese black beans, rinsed several times under
    running water
2 tablespoons freshly squeezed lemon juice
2 tablespoons rice wine vinegar
1 teaspoon grated ginger
1 teaspoon Asian sesame oil
1 teaspoon packed light brown sugar
1 teaspoon sesame seeds
2 pounds littleneck clams, shells scrubbed

COMBINE THE SAKE, sherry, soy sauce, black beans, lemon juice, vinegar, ginger, sesame oil, brown sugar, and sesame seeds in a medium stockpot and whisk together. Bring the liquid to a boil over high heat.

ADD THE CLAMS and stir to coat with the cooking liquid, then reduce the heat to medium-high, cover the pot, and cook until the clams have opened, shaking the pan gently a few times, 5 to 7 minutes.

TO SERVE, scoop the clams into individual bowls, discarding any that did not open, and ladle some of the cooking liquid over them. Serve immediately.

Trio of Seafood Tartare with Soy and Wasabi Sauce

The Cannery Seafood House,
Vancouver, British Columbia

Lobster oil is a signature recipe of executive chef Frédéric Couton, and is sold at The Cannery. (Information about the oil and recipes that use it are available at www.canneryseafood.com.) He wouldn't divulge the secret to the recipe, and rightfully so, but in its place you can simply use an extra drizzle of extra virgin olive oil. The chef serves the tartare topped with some nori "chips" made by cutting a sheet of nori (the dry seaweed sheets also used to wrap sushi) into quarters and lightly frying it in shallow vegetable oil until crisp. You could also serve the tartare with good crackers or thin slices of toasted baguette.

Since tartare, by nature, is a dish of raw seafood or meat, the quality of the product you start with is paramount—get the freshest and best you can find. Asian markets are a good source for top-quality seafood, as they sell to a clientele that demands absolute freshness, and they typically offer sushi-grade fish, the perfect choice.

MAKES 4 APPETIZER SERVINGS

4 ounces salmon fillet, skin and pin bones removed
4 ounces sushi-grade tuna
4 ounces sea scallops
¼ cup extra virgin olive oil
2 tablespoons freshly squeezed lime juice
2 tablespoons lobster oil (optional)
2 tablespoons minced chives
4 teaspoons minced shallot
Salt and freshly ground black pepper
Whole chives, for garnish

Soy and Wasabi Sauce
¼ cup soy sauce
2 tablespoons wasabi powder
1 teaspoon honey

FOR THE SAUCE, whisk together the soy sauce and wasabi powder in a small bowl. Add the honey and mix well. Set aside.

FILL A LARGE BOWL with ice and a cup or two of cold water to make an ice bath, which will keep the seafood chilled while you prepare the tartare. Set a medium bowl in the larger bowl, nestling it down about halfway into the ice bath. Cut the salmon, tuna, and scallops into ⅛-inch dice, and put them in the medium bowl. Add the olive oil, lime juice, lobster oil (if using), chives, and shallot, and stir gently to evenly mix. Season to taste with salt and pepper. Let the fish sit over the ice for about 5 minutes, to allow the flavors to blend gently.

TO SERVE, spoon the tartare into the center of individual plates, pressing it gently into a round disk about 1 inch thick. Whisk the sauce one last time to mix, then drizzle it around the seafood tartare. Garnish with whole chives, laying them directly across the tartare, and serve right away.

Roasted Oysters with Hazelnut Butter

The Place Bar and Grill,
Friday Harbor, Washington

One of our most requested recipes is this simple one for roasted oysters," says chef/owner Steven Anderson, noting that the Westcott Bay petite oysters they use are raised on the opposite side of San Juan Island from them. "To our mind, they may be the best oysters in the world." You can use any small Northwest oyster—such as Kumamotos—and the results will be equally dazzling.

Oysters in the shell are typically sold by the dozen; the extra four can be a special half-shell treat raw before dinner starts, or just roast them up with the others to share among your guests. In place of the rock salt for lining the baking sheet, you can use foil: cut a piece about twice as long as the baking sheet and loosely crumple it up to fit in the baking sheet, then press the oyster shells down into the crumpled foil to sit securely.

MAKES 8 APPETIZER SERVINGS OR 4 MAIN-COURSE SERVINGS

¼ cup hazelnuts
Rock salt, for a serving bed
½ cup unsalted butter, at room temperature
¼ cup grated Parmesan cheese, or any other hard Italian cheese
1½ teaspoons chopped basil
1 teaspoon freshly squeezed lemon juice
½ teaspoon chopped garlic
½ teaspoon anise liqueur such as Pernod or Sambuca (optional)
32 petite oysters, preferably Westcott Bay

PREHEAT THE OVEN to 350°F. Scatter the hazelnuts in a baking pan and toast in the oven until lightly browned and aromatic, 8 to 10 minutes, gently shaking the pan once or twice to help the nuts toast evenly. Transfer the nuts to a lightly dampened dish towel and wrap it around the nuts. Let sit until partly cooled, then rub the nuts in the towel to help remove the papery skin. Let the hazelnuts cool completely before continuing.

INCREASE THE OVEN temperature to 475°F. Cover a rimmed baking sheet with a layer of rock salt about ½ inch deep.

PUT THE COOLED HAZELNUTS in a food processor and pulse to chop them finely. Add the butter and process until well blended. Add the Parmesan, basil, lemon juice, garlic, and anise liqueur. Process well to blend thoroughly, scraping down the sides of the bowl once or twice to assure a smooth mixture.

SHUCK THE OYSTERS (see page 43) and discard the top shells, being careful to remove any bits of shell from the oyster. Be sure to cut each oyster loose from the bottom shell. Set the oyster shells on the prepared pan, nestling them gently into the salt so the shell edge is even and butter won't ooze out during roasting.

TOP EACH OYSTER with a teaspoon of the hazelnut butter and roast the oysters until the butter is golden brown and bubbling, 8 to 10 minutes. Carefully arrange the oysters on individual plates, either perched on more rock salt or on enough greens to hold the oysters upright to keep the juices in, and serve right away

OYSTERS

A bold soul was he, Jonathan Swift surmised, who first ventured to eat an oyster. Whoever that fearless pioneer was, the experiment unleashed a culinary star with which some of the greatest gustatory passion is associated. Oyster lovers devour the bivalve by the dozens in their purest form—on the half shell, shucked just moments before eating, the only "garnish" the bit of briny liquor in which the oyster rests in its shell. Beyond this simple showcase, recipes abound for the prized Northwest oyster, though most connoisseurs prefer simpler preparations so that the character of the oyster comes through.

The only oyster native to the Northwest is the tiny Olympia oyster. All others here are the result of immigration, primarily from Japan. Very much a product of where they are grown, different specimens of the same species take on a distinctive flavor and texture based on the conditions in which they are raised. Voracious filter-feeders, oysters can pass 100 gallons or more of water through their shells each day, so the water they live in has a significant impact on the overall quality of the oyster.

The Pacific species of oyster represents by far the bulk of the oysters grown in the region, though they are most often sold by the name of the specific place they come from—Judd Cove, Totten Inlet, Hama Hama, Sunset Beach, Fanny Bay, Sund Creek, and so on. Three other species make up the remainder of the oysters grown in the Northwest. Kumamotos are smaller than most Pacifics, with deeply cupped shells and a clean, crisp, briny flavor, among the most popular half-shell oysters in the region. European Flat oysters are the newest arrival and are in limited production, though half-shell fans relish their more pronounced briny-metallic flavor. Last but not least is the native Olympia oyster, which may be small in size—the shells are rarely larger than a half-dollar—but are big in flavor and prestige.

How to Shuck an Oyster

Shucking oysters is an acquired skill, not complicated but requiring a steady, firm hand and an eye for the "sweet spot." A blunt, short-bladed oyster knife is an important tool for the job; using a regular table or kitchen knife could prove harmful for both the knife and for your hands. Even with a good oyster knife, you need to protect your hands from the rough, hard shells and the not-infrequent slips of the knife. A heavy kitchen towel folded over several times can do the job, though some shucking knives are sold with a heavy rubber glove with which to hold the oyster.

1. Securely hold the oyster with its deeper cupped shell downward on a sturdy work surface.

2. Find the hinge at the back edge of the shell and carefully but firmly insert the tip of the knife between the shells (you may need to try this in a few different spots before you find one that "gives").

3. Insert the blade just an inch or so and twist the handle of the knife to begin prying apart the shells.

4. Hold the knife blade flat against the top shell and slide the blade across the shell to cut the top adductor muscle. Lift off and discard the top shell.

5. Carefully slide the blade underneath the oyster to sever the muscle holding it to the lower shell. Remove any bits of shell or other debris that may have landed on the oyster.

The oyster is now ready for slurping raw, cooking in the shell, or removing from the shell to pan-fry or serve in a simple oyster stew. The shucking itself, and being able to do so without puncturing the oyster meat, takes practice, so don't be dismayed if early attempts go awry.

Potato and Goat Cheese Stuffed Peppers with Spicy Tomato Sauce

Matt's in the Market, Seattle, Washington

A hidden gem in the Pike Place Market, this tiny restaurant serves up big flavors like this appetizer of stuffed peppers atop a heady tomato sauce. For a slightly spicier variation, you can use poblano chiles in place of the bell peppers. The peppers can be stuffed a day or two ahead of time and heated just before serving. You could also serve these as a vegetarian main course, offering two peppers per person.

MAKES 6 APPETIZER SERVINGS OR 3 MAIN-COURSE SERVINGS

6 red bell peppers
2 russet potatoes (about 10 ounces each)
5 ounces goat cheese
¼ cup chopped cilantro
¼ cup chopped flat-leaf (Italian) parsley
Salt and freshly ground black pepper
3 to 4 tablespoons vegetable stock, preferably homemade (page 61), or water

Spicy Tomato Sauce
2 cans (14½ ounces each) whole tomatoes, drained
1 onion, coarsely chopped
¾ cup chopped cilantro
2 or 3 dried pasilla chiles, stemmed and seeded
2 canned *chipotles en adobo*
Juice of 3 limes
1 tablespoon chopped garlic
1 tablespoon dried oregano
Salt and freshly ground black pepper

ROAST THE RED BELL PEPPERS over a gas flame or under the broiler until the skins blacken, turning occasionally to roast them evenly, about 10 minutes total. Put the peppers in a plastic bag, seal the bag securely, and set aside to cool.

PREHEAT THE OVEN to 400°F.

PIERCE THE POTATOES a few times with the tines of a fork and set them on the rack in the oven. Bake until the potatoes give when you squeeze them, about 45 minutes. Take the potatoes from the oven and set aside to cool. When cool enough to handle but still warm, halve the potatoes and scoop out the flesh, discarding the skin. Mash the potato and goat cheese together. Add the cilantro and parsley and season to taste with salt and pepper. Soften the mixture a bit with vegetable stock, stirring in 1 tablespoon at a time just until the mixture is not heavy but is still firm enough to hold its shape.

FOR THE TOMATO SAUCE, combine the tomatoes, onion, cilantro, pasilla chiles, chipotle chiles, lime juice, garlic, and oregano in a large bowl and stir to mix. Working in batches, purée the mixture in a blender or food processor until smooth. Pour the mixture into a medium saucepan and simmer over medium heat for 15 to 20 minutes, until the sauce is slightly thickened and the flavors are well blended. Season to taste with salt and pepper, adding some vegetable stock or water if the sauce is too thick. Keep warm over low heat.

PREHEAT THE OVEN to 350°F. Lightly oil a baking dish just large enough to hold the peppers.

WHEN THE PEPPERS are cool enough to handle, carefully peel away and discard the skin, core, and seeds. Try not to tear the peppers. Using a small spoon, fill each of the roasted peppers with the potato mixture. Set them in the baking dish and bake until heated through, about 15 minutes.

TO SERVE, SPOON THE SPICY TOMATO SAUCE onto individual warmed plates, top with one of the potato-filled peppers, and serve right away.

Peter Canlis Shrimp

Canlis, Seattle, Washington

Peter Canlis was one of the most influential restaurateurs in Seattle's early years of fine dining. A testament to his impact is the fact that Canlis is still open more than fifty years later, the tradition now continued by his son, Chris, and daughter-in-law, Alice.

For the complete depth of shrimp flavor in this recipe, use the optional shrimp butter to finish the dish. It is made by cooking the shrimp shells with butter, which draws a surprising amount of flavor into the butter.

MAKES 2 APPETIZER SERVINGS

2 tablespoons olive oil
12 large shrimp (about ¾ pound), peeled and deveined (shells reserved for shrimp butter, if using)
1 to 2 teaspoons dried red pepper flakes
2 teaspoons chopped garlic
2 teaspoons freshly squeezed lime juice
¼ cup dry vermouth
¼ cup shrimp butter (see Note) or cold unsalted butter, cut into pieces
Mesclun (mixed young salad greens), for garnish

HEAT THE OLIVE OIL in a large skillet over medium-high heat until hot and just beginning to smoke. Add the shrimp and cook until lightly browned, about 2 minutes on each side, and then pour off any oil remaining in the pan. Add, in this order, the red pepper flakes, garlic, lime juice, and vermouth, and then simmer to reduce the liquid by half, 1 to 2 minutes, shaking the pan gently. Add the butter, take the pan from the heat, and swirl the pan to gently melt the butter and incorporate it into the pan juices.

SPOON THE SHRIMP and the butter sauce onto individual plates, garnish with a small mound of mesclun, and serve immediately.

NOTE: To make shrimp butter, melt ½ cup unsalted butter in a medium saucepan over medium heat, then add the shells from the shrimp and cook until the shrimp shells are deep red and the butter is quite aromatic, about 10 minutes. Strain the butter to remove the shells, and then chill. Keep the butter cold until just before adding it to the cooked shrimp.

Grilled Tamarind-Glazed Quail

CinCin Restaurant & Bar,
Vancouver, British Columbia

Marinating with honey gives quail a lightly charred and crisp exterior," says executive chef Romesh Prasad, "which contrasts wonderfully with the sweet quail meat." He also notes that you could use brown sugar or maple syrup in place of the honey. An elegant first course when served atop bright, crisp mesclun greens, the quail could instead be served with oven-roasted potatoes and vegetables for a main course.

Tamarind is a unique pod fruit that yields a dark brown sour-sweet pulp used in everything from sauces to refreshing cold drinks in Asia, the Middle East, and other warm climes. Look for tamarind paste in ethnic markets or on well-stocked grocery shelves.

MAKES 8 APPETIZER SERVINGS OR 4 MAIN-COURSE SERVINGS

1 cup water
½ cup minced shallot or onion
½ cup soy sauce
¼ cup cider vinegar
2 tablespoons honey
2 tablespoons five-spice powder
1 tablespoon tamarind paste
1 tablespoon minced garlic
1 tablespoon minced ginger
8 quail, cut in half
4 cups mesclun greens (about 4 ounces)
2 tablespoons extra virgin olive oil
Salt and freshly ground black pepper

IN A SMALL SAUCEPAN, combine the water, shallot, soy sauce, vinegar, honey, five-spice powder, tamarind paste, garlic, and ginger. Bring to a boil over medium-high heat and simmer for 2 minutes, stirring occasionally. Take the pan from the heat, let cool completely, and then strain into a large bowl. Add the quail, turn to evenly coat in the marinade, then cover the bowl and marinate in the refrigerator for at least 3 hours or up to 12 hours.

(Alternatively, you can combine the cooled marinade and quail in a large, resealable bag to marinate.)

PREHEAT AN OUTDOOR GRILL. Lightly brush the grill rack with oil. Take the quail from the marinade, allowing the excess to drip off, and grill the quail until well browned on the outside but still juicy inside, 2 to 3 minutes per side. Baste with additional marinade while cooking.

PUT THE MESCLUN GREENS in a large bowl and drizzle the olive oil over them. Season to taste with salt and pepper and toss to evenly mix. Divide the salad among individual plates and top each with a grilled quail. Serve right away.

Smoked Salmon Cakes with Celery Root Rémoulade

Marché, Eugene, Oregon

Smoked salmon really stars in these easy cakes from chef/owner Stephanie Pearl Kimmel. A flavorful start to any meal, the cakes will be only as good as the smoked salmon you start with, so seek out tender, moist fish that has a well-balanced flavor. Hot-smoked (kippered) salmon, firmer and flakier than cold-smoked salmon, is the type to use here. Nutty-crisp celery root *rémoulade*—a simple salad of thinly shredded celery root—is an ideal partner alongside. Chef Kimmel serves the cakes with an herb aïoli.

MAKES 4 APPETIZER SERVINGS

1 pound moist hot-smoked salmon, skin removed
1 cup dried bread crumbs, more if needed
½ cup good-quality mayonnaise, preferably homemade (page 61)
2 eggs, lightly beaten
1 teaspoon chopped chives
1 teaspoon chopped dill
1 teaspoon chopped flat-leaf (Italian) parsley
½ teaspoon chopped thyme
1 teaspoon freshly squeezed lemon juice
Hot pepper sauce
3 to 4 tablespoons unsalted butter or olive oil

Celery Root Rémoulade
1 large celery root (about 1 pound)
Juice of 1 lemon
Salt
½ cup good-quality mayonnaise, preferably homemade (page 61)
2 tablespoons Dijon mustard
2 tablespoons whipping cream
Freshly ground black pepper
2 tablespoons chopped parsley

FOR THE RÉMOULADE, peel the celery root and cut it with a sharp knife into julienne strips about ⅛ inch thick, or coarsely grate it in the food processor.

Put the lemon juice in a large bowl, add a good pinch of salt, and let sit until the salt dissolves. Stir in the mayonnaise, mustard, and cream with a few grindings of pepper. Add the celery root and toss to evenly coat it with the dressing. Taste the *rémoulade* for seasoning, adding more salt or pepper to taste. Sprinkle with the parsley, cover, and refrigerate for at least 15 minutes or until ready to serve (the *rémoulade* can be made up to a day in advance).

CRUMBLE THE SMOKED SALMON into a medium bowl, being careful to remove any bones as you go. Add the bread crumbs, mayonnaise, eggs, chives, dill, parsley, and thyme and stir to evenly blend. Stir in the lemon juice, adding hot pepper sauce to taste. Form the salmon mixture into 8 cakes about 3 inches across and ½ inch thick.

HEAT THE BUTTER or olive oil in a large skillet (preferably nonstick) over medium heat. Add the salmon cakes and sauté until nicely browned and heated through, 3 to 5 minutes on each side.

ARRANGE 2 SALMON CAKES on each plate and add a generous spoonful of the celery *rémoulade* alongside. Serve right away.

SMOKED SALMON

Necessity is the source of many gastronomic legacies, and smoked salmon is one prime example. The smoking process originally was a means of preserving salmon, but the technique is now used more for the extraordinary embellishment of flavor it brings to the fish than for its preserving aspects.

In other regions and cultures, salmon is typically cold-smoked, the brined fish infused with smoke but without the application of heat, leaving the flesh soft, supple, and quite rich. The tradition in the Northwest, however, is one of hot-smoked, also called kippered, salmon, which dates back to the native custom of slowly cooking full "sides" (fillets) of salmon perched over low embers of alder or cedar wood. The fish is first brined with salt and typically a sweet element, whether brown sugar, honey, or another sweetener. Seasonings are often added at this point as well–spices, herbs, garlic, and other flavorings, though in judicious portions to avoid overpowering the salmon. Brines can be dry and simply rubbed over the fish or blended with water for a wet bath in which the fish soaks.

Once brined, the fish is briefly rinsed, then it is air-dried (preferably with the aid of a fan) until a thin skin has formed over the surface of the flesh. A low fire is prepared in an outdoor smoker or grill, and a generous handful of smoking chips are soaked in water to increase the production of smoke. Slow cooking of the fish over this combination of heat and smoke may take up to an hour or more, producing deeply flavored, moist, and tender flesh. We're lucky in the Northwest to have access to a large supply of smoked salmon, from widely available brands sold in grocery stores to specialty "house-smoked" varieties available in area seafood markets. The recipe for Smoked Salmon Cakes with Celery Root *Rémoulade* (page 49) is a wonderful showcase for this regional hallmark.

Chile Con Queso

Santiago's Gourmet Mexican Cooking,
Yakima, Washington

If you don't have a fondue pot, heat a ceramic dish in a 200°F oven while making the *chile con queso* in a saucepan, and then pour the mixture into the warm dish just before serving. This will keep the *chile con queso* warm and maintain its creamy texture. It becomes harder to dip as it cools. The type of salsa you use is your choice—green or red, hot or mild. Instead of the jalapeño, you could add a small can of drained, diced Anaheim chiles for a milder flavor.

MAKES 6 TO 8 APPETIZER SERVINGS

---

2 tablespoons unsalted butter
6 green onions, thinly sliced
1 jalapeño chile, cored, seeded, and minced
1 tablespoon all-purpose flour
1½ cups salsa
2 cups grated cheddar and/or pepper Jack cheese
2 tablespoons minced cilantro
Tortilla chips, for serving

MELT THE BUTTER in a fondue pot over medium heat. Add the green onion and jalapeño and sauté, stirring occasionally, until the onion is tender, 2 to 3 minutes. Stir in the flour and continue to cook for 2 to 3 minutes, stirring constantly. Stir in the salsa and bring just to a boil. Add the cheese and cook, stirring constantly, to obtain a smooth, creamy texture.

TO SERVE, sprinkle the cilantro over the cheesy mixture and set it on the fondue stand, over a lit can of Sterno to keep the *chile con queso* warm. Serve with a bowl of tortilla chips alongside for dipping.

Mussels in Lavender-Garlic Broth

The Robin Hood (formerly Victoria's),
Union, Washington

The subtle floral element of lavender is a tasty surprise in this garlicky steamed mussel recipe from chef/owner Blake Caldwell. The flourish of tempura leeks on top adds a crunchy, rich contrast to the plump mussels. Cake flour is used for the tempura batter because its low gluten content helps keep the tempura coating light and crisp; you can use 1 cup of all-purpose flour in its place.

MAKES 4 APPETIZER SERVINGS

2 tablespoons olive oil
2 pounds mussels, scrubbed and debearded
2 teaspoons fresh lavender flowers or 1½ teaspoons dried lavender
¼ cup minced garlic
1 cup dry white wine
¼ cup unsalted butter, cut into pieces
Salt and freshly ground black pepper

Tempura Leeks
Vegetable oil, for frying
1 large leek or 2 small leeks, trimmed and cleaned
1¼ cups cake flour
1 teaspoon salt, plus more for sprinkling
2 egg whites, beaten until frothy
1 cup ice water

FOR THE TEMPURA LEEKS, heat about 3 inches of oil in a large, heavy saucepan (the oil should not come more than halfway up the sides of the pan) over medium-high heat to about 350°F.

WHILE THE OIL is heating, cut the leek into fine julienne strips about 3 inches long. For the tempura batter, whisk together the flour and salt, then add the egg whites and ice water. Whisk together just until evenly blended.

WHEN THE OIL is heated, add the julienned leek to the batter and stir to evenly coat. Use your fingers to lift out about one-quarter of the batter-coated leeks, then gently (and carefully) drop them into the oil in a bundle. Repeat with another one-quarter of the leeks, and fry until the leeks are lightly browned and crisp, 2 to 3 minutes. Using a large slotted spoon, transfer the tempura leeks to a paper towel–lined baking sheet and sprinkle with salt. Repeat with the remaining leeks, allowing the oil to reheat between the batches if needed. Keep the leeks warm in a low oven while cooking the mussels.

HEAT THE OLIVE OIL in a large sauté pan or deep skillet over medium-high heat, then add the mussels, lavender, and garlic, in that order. Sauté just until the garlic and lavender become aromatic, about 15 seconds, then pour the wine into the pan. Cover and cook until the mussels have opened, shaking the pan gently once or twice, 3 to 5 minutes. Add the butter with salt and pepper to taste and cook, uncovered, gently shaking the pan until the butter is melted and the cooking liquid has reduced a bit, 2 to 3 minutes.

TO SERVE, scoop the mussels into individual shallow bowls, discarding any that did not open, and pour the lavender-garlic broth over them. Top each serving with a bundle of tempura leeks and serve right away.

CLAMS AND MUSSELS

Like oysters, the bulk of the clams and mussels that we purchase in Northwest markets have been farm-raised, though the farming operations take place in the natural habitat of deep-cold, nutrient-rich Northwest waters, which makes for a very high-quality product enjoyed by chefs and diners near and far.

Even the odd-looking, oversized geoduck has taken to cultivation, though it's a patient farmer who's willing to wait the six years or so until the giant clam reaches market size of about 2 pounds. Most other clams are harvested at about two to three years of age. One exception is razor clams, which are available only wild from surf-swept ocean beaches. Named for its long, slender, razorlike shells, the razor clam has a sweet-nutty flavor that is accentuated by a simple bread crumb coating and a quick sauté in butter. There's a huge recreational fishery of razor clams by dedicated diggers and some commercial and native harvest as well. Much of the catch stays in the region, making razor clams a key treat to enjoy in the Northwest.

The quintessential Northwest clam is the Manila. When Pacific oysters were introduced to the region from Japan, some Manila clams inadvertently came along for the ride and, like the oysters, took well to the growing conditions in the Northwest. The beautifully patterned hard shells protect a plump, sweet clam that is relished for simple, classic steaming. Littleneck clams are the region's native clam, about the same size as Manila clams but a bit more flavorful, though not as commonly available now as the Manila. Razors and Manilas show up together in the chowder on page 84, and littlenecks are steamed with Asian influence on page 38. Mussels, though indigenous and prolific in the region, were long overlooked as a culinary item. The thin-shelled but determined creatures cling adamantly to piers, docks, and rocky outcrops near tidal level throughout the Northwest. Mussels began gaining favor a few decades ago and are now fully integrated into Northwest cuisine. As with clams, simple steaming—often with white wine, herbs, and maybe a touch of garlic—is a preferred cooking method. In these pages, you'll find two variations on this theme, one with an unexpected floral element from lavender (page 53), the other a hearty cold-weather recipe, in which the mussels are cooked in cider with bacon, apple chutney, and celery root (page 66). Both clams and mussels show up in the Northwest Seafood Pepper Pot (page 77), with fish too, in a redolent broth.

Oregon Blue Cheesecake

The Vintner's Inn at Hinzerling Winery,
Prosser, Washington

This savory take on cheesecake makes a great addition to a holiday buffet or cocktail party spread. "We have used it with great success at many port tastings, and as a final cheese course at the inn," notes chef Mike Wallace. For a dinner party, you could serve the cheesecake in thin wedges on individual plates, with greens alongside, tossed with a vinaigrette dressing accented with walnut oil. Any way you serve it, you'll have enough for a crowd.

MAKES 20 TO 24 APPETIZER SERVINGS

½ cup finely crushed cheese crackers
1 pound cream cheese, at room temperature
8 ounces Oregon blue cheese or other blue cheese, crumbled
1 cup sour cream
3 eggs
¼ cup medium salsa
¼ cup all-purpose flour
¼ teaspoon salt
½ cup finely chopped green onions
½ cup finely chopped walnuts
Crackers and/or thin slices of baguette, for serving

PREHEAT THE OVEN to 325°F. Butter a 9- or 10-inch springform pan. Sprinkle the cracker crumbs on the bottom of the pan, then turn and tilt the pan so the crumbs coat the sides as well; set aside.

IN A LARGE BOWL, beat together the cream cheese, blue cheese, sour cream, eggs, salsa, flour, and salt, using an electric mixer on medium speed until evenly blended, scraping down the sides as needed. Using a wooden spoon or spatula, fold the green onion into the batter, then pour it into the springform pan, smoothing the top. Scatter the walnuts evenly and bake until set, about 45 minutes. Take the pan from the oven and let cool completely on a wire rack, then cover and refrigerate for at least 8 hours or overnight.

TO SERVE, let the cheesecake come to room temperature. Remove the sides of the springform pan and set the cheesecake on a serving platter, with crackers and/or thin slices of baguette alongside.

Ebi Shinjo
(Shrimp Dumplings)

Tojo's, Vancouver, British Columbia

Chef/owner Hidekazu Tojo is one of the superstars in Vancouver's culinary constellation, his creative contemporary Japanese offerings complemented by more traditional classics such as these shrimp dumplings. In true Japanese style, freshness is key here, so use the best-quality fresh shrimp you can find to get the most out of this simple, delicious recipe. The bright, fresh greens—mizuna and watercress are good choices—are an ideal foil for the rich shrimp. You could toss the greens with a simple ginger-enhanced vinaigrette if you like.

MAKES 6 APPETIZER SERVINGS

½ cup coarsely chopped onion
1 small carrot, coarsely chopped
4 fresh shiitake mushrooms, stemmed and chopped
1 pound shrimp, peeled, deveined, and coarsely chopped
1 egg
2 teaspoons cornstarch
2 teaspoons sugar
1 teaspoon soy sauce
1 teaspoon dry hot mustard
½ teaspoon sake
¼ teaspoon salt
Vegetable oil, for frying
Greens, for serving

COMBINE THE ONION, carrot, and mushrooms in a food processor and pulse to chop them finely. Add the shrimp and pulse a few times to finely chop and evenly blend the mixture (avoid overprocessing; the purée should still have a fine, chunky texture rather than becoming a smooth paste). Transfer the mixture to a bowl, and add the egg, cornstarch, sugar, soy sauce, mustard, sake, and salt. Stir well until evenly blended and somewhat sticky. Cover the bowl with plastic wrap and refrigerate for 1 hour.

HEAT ABOUT 3 INCHES OF OIL in a large, heavy saucepan (the oil should come no more than halfway up the sides of the pan) over medium-high heat to about 350°F. When the oil is hot, form the shrimp mixture into 12 cakes of about 2 tablespoons each and gently add them directly to the oil. Fry until the cakes are nicely browned on all sides and cooked through, 2 to 3 minutes. Using a large slotted spoon, transfer the cakes to paper towels to drain while frying the remaining shrimp cakes, allowing the oil to reheat between batches as needed.

ARRANGE THE GREENS to one side of each plate, set the hot shrimp cakes alongside, and serve right away.

Blackened Pan-Fried Oysters

The Shoalwater, Seaview, Washington

The secret to these oysters is to keep it simple!" advises co-owner Ann Kischner, who echoes the way many Northwesterners feel about enjoying oysters: the simpler the better. Here the classic pan-fried oyster is embellished with a touch of heat from Cajun seasoning. The plump golden oysters are served with a simple homemade tartar sauce, some of which also gets a bit of heat, Cajun-style.

Don't be shy about using plenty of oil, notes Kischner. "The oysters are pan-fried," she says, "not sautéed. This way the oysters cook quickly, stay crispy on the outside, plump and juicy on the inside." They use extra-small oysters at Shoalwater, but you could use slightly larger oysters if you prefer; you just may need a bit more flour to coat them.

MAKES 4 APPETIZER SERVINGS

¾ cup all-purpose flour
2 to 3 tablespoons Cajun seasoning
48 extra-small oysters, shucked and drained
Vegetable oil, for frying

Tartar Sauce
    1½ cups mayonnaise, preferably homemade (recipe follows)
    ¼ cup minced dill pickle
    2 tablespoons minced shallot or onion
    2 teaspoons minced lat-leaf (Italian) parsley
    1 teaspoon Dijon mustard
    Salt and freshly ground black pepper
    1 teaspoon Cajun seasoning

FOR THE TARTAR SAUCE, combine the mayonnaise, pickle, shallot, parsley, and Dijon mustard in a small bowl and stir to mix. Season to taste with salt and pepper. Spoon half of the tartar sauce into another bowl and stir in the Cajun seasoning for a spicy complement to the regular tartar sauce. Refrigerate the sauces until ready to serve.

IN A SHALLOW DISH, combine the flour and Cajun seasoning and stir well to blend. Add the oysters, a few at a time, and toss to thoroughly coat them with the seasoned flour, then shake off the excess and set them aside on a floured tray while coating the remaining oysters.

HEAT ABOUT ½ INCH OF OIL in a large, heavy skillet (such as cast iron) over medium-high heat. Gently add about a dozen oysters to the skillet, allowing plenty of room between them. Pan-fry the oysters until they are nicely browned on the bottom and the edges begin to curl, about 1 minute. Turn the oysters over and brown the other side, about 1 minute longer. Use a slotted spoon to lift the oysters onto a paper towel–lined baking sheet, and keep them warm in a low oven while frying the remaining oysters.

TO SERVE, arrange the oysters on individual plates, spoon some of each tartar sauce alongside, and serve right away.

Homemade Mayonnaise

1 egg yolk
2 teaspoons white wine vinegar
¾ cup olive oil (not extra virgin)
Salt and freshly ground white pepper

IN A MEDIUM BOWL, combine the egg yolk with the vinegar and whisk to blend. Begin adding the olive oil, a few drops at a time, whisking constantly, until the yolk begins to turn pale and thickens slightly, showing that an emulsion has begun to form. Continue adding the rest of the oil in a thin, steady stream, whisking constantly. Season to taste with salt and white pepper.

ALTERNATELY, COMBINE THE EGG YOLK and vinegar in a food processor and pulse to blend. With the motor running, begin adding the oil a few drops at a time until an emulsion begins to form, then continue adding the rest in a thin, steady stream. Add the salt and pepper to taste and pulse to blend.

REFRIGERATE THE MAYONNAISE, covered, until ready to serve; it can be made a day or two in advance.

MAKES A GENEROUS ¾ CUP

Artichokes Stuffed with Herbed Cream Cheese and Bay Shrimp

Ray's Boathouse, Seattle, Washington

Chef Charles Ramseyer uses a pastry bag to pipe the herbed cream cheese into the steamed artichokes, which you can do as well if you want a fancier finish to the filling, though a plain old spoon works well too. The artichokes can be stuffed up to 2 hours in advance and refrigerated until ready to serve. To eat, use the leaves to scoop up some of the cream cheese filling, scraping the tender flesh from the base of the leaf as you draw it between your teeth.

MAKES 4 APPETIZER SERVINGS

4 artichokes
2 lemons, cut in half
4 ounces cooked bay shrimp

Herbed Cream Cheese

8 ounces cream cheese, at room temperature
¾ cup good-quality mayonnaise, preferably homemade (page 61)
½ cup grated Parmesan cheese
1 shallot, minced
¼ cup minced celery leaves
1 tablespoon freshly squeezed lemon juice
1 tablespoon minced tarragon
2 teaspoons minced basil
1 teaspoon Worcestershire sauce
1 teaspoon celery salt

FOR THE HERBED CREAM CHEESE, beat the cream cheese with a mixer at medium speed until soft. Add the mayonnaise, Parmesan, shallot, celery leaves, lemon juice, tarragon, basil, Worcestershire sauce, and celery salt. Continue blending until the mixture is smooth and evenly mixed; refrigerate until ready to serve.

CUT THE TOP INCH FROM THE ARTICHOKES and use kitchen shears to cut off the sharp tips from the leaves. Cut off the stem where it meets the bottom of the artichoke and score an **X** on the bottom of each artichoke. Rub all cut surfaces with one of the lemon halves. Put the artichokes in a large pot of cold water and squeeze in the juice from the remaining 3 lemon halves, dropping the lemons in as well. Set a heatproof plate on top of the artichokes to keep them thoroughly submerged in the water. Bring the water just to a boil over medium-high heat, then lower the heat to medium and simmer until the bottoms of the artichokes are tender and the outer leaves pull off easily, about 30 minutes. Drain the artichokes and set them upside down on paper towels to drain and cool.

WHEN THE ARTICHOKES ARE COOL, lift out the small center leaves and scoop out the fuzzy choke with a small spoon, being careful to leave the tender artichoke bottom intact. Spoon the herbed cream cheese into the artichokes, smoothing the top. Top each artichoke with some of the shrimp and serve right away.

Grilled Scallops with White Asparagus and Mâche Salad

The Aerie Resort,
Malahat, British Columbia

At The Aerie Resort, chef Christophe Letard uses oversized sea scallops from Qualicum Beach on the eastern shore of Vancouver Island, and the white asparagus comes from a nearby grower in the island's Cowichan Valley, emphasizing this kitchen's commitment to using local products. When white asparagus isn't available, green asparagus is a fine substitute, though the lemon juice will fade the bright green color slightly. Mâche is a tender, bright green that has a wonderful, slightly nutty flavor; other tender salad greens could be used in its place.

MAKES 4 APPETIZER SERVINGS

12 white or green asparagus spears, trimmed and tough skin peeled
Juice of 1 lemon
8 very large sea scallops
2 tablespoons finely chopped chives
2 tablespoons finely chopped chervil or flat-leaf (Italian) parsley
1 bunch mâche (about 4 ounces)

Rhubarb Relish
½ cup grapeseed or olive oil
2 stalks rhubarb, peeled and finely diced
2 shallots, finely chopped
Salt and freshly ground black pepper
½ cup raspberry vinegar
2 tablespoons honey

FOR THE RHUBARB RELISH, heat 2 tablespoons of the oil in a medium skillet over medium heat. Add the rhubarb and shallot and cook, stirring often, until tender, 3 to 5 minutes. Season to taste with salt and pepper, then add the raspberry vinegar and honey. Increase the heat to medium-high and boil to

reduce the mixture by half, 5 to 7 minutes. Whisk the remaining oil into the rhubarb relish and set aside to cool.

PREHEAT AN OUTDOOR GRILL.

BRING A MEDIUM SAUCEPAN OF SALTED WATER TO A BOIL. Add the asparagus to the boiling water and blanch until just nearly tender, 2 to 3 minutes. Drain the asparagus well and dry quickly on paper towels. Cut any thick asparagus spears in half lengthwise. In a large bowl, toss the asparagus with the lemon juice and season with salt and pepper.

SEASON THE SCALLOPS WITH SALT AND PEPPER. Lightly rub the grill rack with oil, and grill the scallops until well browned on the outside but still slightly translucent in the center, 1 to 2 minutes per side. (Alternatively, the scallops can be pan-seared in a skillet over medium-high heat, using 2 tablespoons of olive oil.)

TO SERVE, DIVIDE THE ASPARAGUS SPEARS among 4 individual plates, placing them in a single layer. Set 2 scallops on top of the asparagus on each plate, arranging them side by side in the center. Stir the chives and chervil into the rhubarb relish and spoon it around the scallops. Top the scallops with the mâche and serve right away.

Penn Cove Mussels with Hard Cider, Bacon, and Apple Chutney

Whitehouse-Crawford,
Walla Walla, Washington

This elaborate steamed mussel recipe from chef Jamie Guerin serves up a wonderful complement of autumn flavors—smoky bacon, apples, spices, nutty celery root—nearly a meal in itself. In fact, if you doubled the amount of mussels, you could serve them as a main course with salad and bread alongside.

Although you can omit it to save time, the chunky apple chutney is a distinctive addition to this dish. Choose apples that will hold their shape in cooking, such as Fujis. Any extra chutney will be delicious alongside roasted pork or chicken, or even on a roast beef sandwich.

MAKES 4 APPETIZER SERVINGS

2 tablespoons unsalted butter
1½ cups finely julienned celery root (about ½ medium celery root)
2 teaspoons minced garlic
2 pounds Penn Cove mussels, scrubbed and debearded
4 slices thick-cut smoked bacon, cut into ½-inch pieces
1½ cups hard cider
¼ cup chopped flat-leaf (Italian) parsley

Apple Chutney

3 tablespoons unsalted butter
¾ cup diced onion
2 teaspoons minced garlic
2 teaspoons minced or grated ginger
2 teaspoons ground coriander
2 teaspoons mustard seeds
½ teaspoon curry powder
½ teaspoon five-spice powder
½ teaspoon cayenne pepper
¼ cinnamon stick

3 tart apples, peeled, cored, and cut into ½-inch dice
¼ cup apple cider vinegar
1 tablespoon honey
1 tablespoon molasses

PREHEAT THE OVEN to 350°F.

FOR THE APPLE CHUTNEY, melt 2 tablespoons of the butter in a medium saucepan over medium heat. Add the onion, garlic, and ginger and cook, stirring occasionally, until the onion is translucent, 3 to 5 minutes. Add the coriander, mustard seeds, curry powder, five-spice powder, cayenne, and cinnamon stick and cook, stirring, until they are aromatic and evenly coat the onion, 2 to 3 minutes. Add the apples and stir to combine with the onion. In a small bowl, stir together the vinegar, honey, and molasses, then stir this into the apple mixture.

TRANSFER THE CHUTNEY to a shallow baking dish and spread it out evenly. Roast the chutney until the apples are just tender, 30 to 40 minutes, gently stirring once or twice. Take the dish from the oven, add the remaining tablespoon of butter, and stir to evenly mix with the chutney. Set aside, stirring occasionally as the chutney cools; the liquid will thicken and coat the apples. (The chutney can be made up to 1 week in advance and refrigerated in an airtight container.)

HEAT 1 TABLESPOON OF THE BUTTER in a large, deep skillet or sauté pan over medium heat. Add the celery root and garlic and cook, stirring constantly, until the garlic is aromatic and the celery root begins to soften, 3 to 5 minutes. Add the mussels, ½ cup of the apple chutney, and the bacon, and toss to combine. Pour the cider into the skillet, cover, increase the heat to medium-high, and cook until the mussels are open, gently shaking the skillet occasionally, about 5 minutes.

WHEN THE MUSSELS OPEN, add the parsley and remaining tablespoon of butter to finish, gently shaking the pan to incorporate. Spoon the mussels and sauce into individual shallow bowls, discarding any mussels that did not open, and serve right away.

Pico de Gallo

Hacienda del Mar,
Port Angeles, Washington

Pico de gallo, "rooster's beak" in Spanish, is a fresh salsa that offers bright, bold flavors. Delicious simply as a dip for crisp, salty tortilla chips, it would also be tasty over quesadillas, as a topping for huevos rancheros for a morning eye-opener, or served with grilled flank steak.

MAKES ABOUT 5 CUPS

3 large tomatoes, finely chopped
½ onion, finely chopped
2 green onions, finely chopped
1 jalapeño chile, cored, seeded, and minced
2 tablespoons finely chopped cilantro
Juice of ½ lime
Salt and freshly ground black pepper
Tortilla chips, for serving

IN A LARGE BOWL, combine the tomatoes, onion, green onion, jalapeño, and cilantro. Stir to evenly mix, then drizzle the lime juice over the mixture and season to taste with salt and pepper.

SERVE RIGHT AWAY, with a big bowl of tortilla chips alongside for dipping, or refrigerate until ready to serve. The flavor will be best if served within an hour or two of making.

Vegetable and Cheese Terrine

Abigail's Hotel, Victoria, British Columbia

At Abigail's, this elaborate terrine is served as a breakfast dish, but the fresh, bright flavors and colors make the terrine a compelling way to start an evening meal as well. Or serve it as a light lunch dish, with a piece of poached chicken or pan-seared salmon alongside. The preparation is time consuming, but the end result is both delicious and very appealing to the eye, with crêpes delineating the different layers. Five different cheeses are used, with contrasting flavors and textures, though you could streamline it by using just a couple of cheeses.

MAKES 10 TO 12 APPETIZER SERVINGS

---

1 small zucchini, cut lengthwise into ¼-inch strips

4 to 5 tablespoons olive oil

2 teaspoons minced fresh oregano or 1 teaspoon dried oregano

Salt and freshly ground black pepper

3 red bell peppers

1 large leek, white and pale green parts only, split, cleaned, and chopped

8 ounces mushrooms, wiped clean, trimmed, and chopped

2 teaspoons minced fresh thyme or 1 teaspoon dried thyme

1 carrot, cut into matchsticks about 2 inches long and ¼ inch thick

2 small bunches (about 1 pound) spinach, well rinsed, tough stems removed

2 eggs, lightly beaten

¾ cup crumbled feta cheese

2 teaspoons minced fresh dill or 1 teaspoon dried dill

8 crêpes (page 33)

½ cup grated Asiago cheese

½ cup grated Monterey Jack cheese

½ cup grated fontina cheese

¼ cup grated Havarti cheese

LINE A 9½- BY 4-INCH LOAF PAN with parchment paper and spray with a nonstick vegetable spray or rub lightly with oil.

PREHEAT AN OUTDOOR GRILL or preheat the broiler. Lightly brush the zucchini strips with 2 to 3 tablespoons of the olive oil, sprinkle with the oregano, and season to taste with salt and pepper. Grill or broil the strips just to mark and lightly brown them (they should remain a bit firm), 2 to 4 minutes. Set aside.

ROAST THE RED PEPPERS over a gas flame or under the broiler (or on the grill, if used for the zucchini) until the skins blacken, turning occasionally to roast evenly, about 10 minutes total. Put the peppers in a plastic bag, securely seal the bag, and set aside to cool. When the peppers are cool enough to handle, peel away and discard the skins. Remove the core and seeds and cut the peppers into strips. Set aside.

HEAT 2 TABLESPOONS OF THE OIL in a medium skillet over medium heat. Add the leek, mushrooms, thyme, and salt and pepper to taste and sauté until the mushrooms are tender and the liquid they give off has evaporated, 7 to 10 minutes. Set aside.

BRING A MEDIUM SAUCEPAN OF SALTED WATER TO A BOIL, and fill a small bowl with ice water. Add the carrot matchsticks to the boiling water and cook until just tender, 3 to 5 minutes. The carrots should still have a bit of bite to their texture. With a slotted spoon, transfer the carrots to the ice water until cool, then drain well, season with salt and pepper, and set aside.

REFILL THE SAUCEPAN WITH SALTED WATER and bring to a boil. Add the spinach and cook, stirring, just until the leaves are fully wilted but remain bright green, 30 to 60 seconds. Drain and rinse with cold water to cool the spinach quickly, then pat dry on paper towels and let cool. Coarsely chop the spinach, put it in a medium bowl, and add the eggs, feta cheese, and dill, with salt and pepper to taste, stirring to evenly mix. Set aside.

PREHEAT THE OVEN to 350°F.

TO ASSEMBLE, TRIM A CRÊPE to fit the bottom of the loaf pan, and set it in the pan. Cover the crêpe completely with all the zucchini strips in an even layer, trimming them to fit, if necessary, and sprinkle with ¼ cup of the Asiago cheese. Trim another crêpe and lay it on top of the zucchini, pressing gently to even the layer. Lay all the red pepper strips in a layer to cover, sprinkle with the Monterey Jack cheese, and cover with another trimmed crêpe. Spoon the leek and mushroom mixture into the loaf pan (first discarding any accumulated liquid from the bowl), smoothing it lightly to keep the layers neat, sprinkle with the remaining ¼ cup Asiago cheese, and cover with another trimmed crêpe. Lay all the carrots over the crêpe in an even layer, sprinkle with the fontina cheese, and cover with a trimmed crêpe. Spread the spinach mixture evenly on top, sprinkle with the Havarti cheese, and cover with a final trimmed crêpe.

BAKE UNTIL THE TERRINE IS SET and heated through and the center has risen a bit, about 1 hour. If the top of the terrine is browning too quickly, cover it loosely with a piece of lightly oiled foil.

TAKE THE TERRINE FROM THE OVEN and set it on a wire rack to cool. Refrigerate overnight in order to let it set completely. To unmold, run a small knife around the edge of the loaf pan to loosen the terrine. Place a small chopping board on top of the terrine, and carefully turn them over together. Gently lift off the loaf pan and peel away the parchment lining. To slice, fill a pitcher with hot water and have ready a clean dish towel. Using a sharp knife, cut the terrine into ¾-inch-thick slices, dipping the knife into the hot water and drying it quickly with the towel between slices.

Soups and Stews

Forest Mushroom Bisque *Canlis*

Northwest Seafood Pepper Pot *Christina's*

Spinach Soup with Cilantro *Whitehouse-Crawford*

Sunchoke Soup with Skillet Roasted Scallops *West*

Beet Soup *Point No Point Resort*

Razor Clam Chowder with Turnip, Truffle, and Thyme
   Earth and Ocean

Green Chile and Mushroom Soup with Basil Oil *Duck Soup Inn*

Garlic Soup *Durlacher Hof Alpine Country Inn*

Yukon Gold Potato and Goat Cheese Soup with
   Sheep's Sorrel and Garlic Croutons *Wildwood*

Hot and Sour Shrimp Soup *Yarrow Bay Beach Café*

Cold Curried Asparagus Soup *The Vintner's Inn at
   Hinzerling Winery*

Forest Mushroom Bisque

Canlis, Seattle, Washington

Bisques are creamy, rich soups based on a flavorful purée. The foundation of this one is a generous amount of fall's wild mushrooms, one of the more prized culinary treats each year in the Northwest. At Canlis, the chefs often use chanterelles, hedgehog mushrooms, or morels when they're in season, though the bisque is also delicious made with cultivated varieties such as shiitake mushrooms. The flavor and texture of the bisque will vary with the type (or types) you choose to use. It's made extra-rich with heavy cream at the restaurant, but you could lighten the bisque a touch by using half-and-half instead.

MAKES 6 SERVINGS

6 tablespoons unsalted butter
1 onion, thinly sliced
1½ pounds mixed wild mushrooms, brushed clean, trimmed,
    and coarsely chopped
3 cups chicken stock, preferably homemade (page 105)
1 cup whipping cream or half-and-half
Salt and freshly ground black pepper
½ cup dry sherry
¼ teaspoon freshly grated or ground nutmeg, or to taste
Black or white truffle oil, to taste (optional, for drizzling)

MELT 5 TABLESPOONS OF THE BUTTER in a medium saucepan over medium heat. Add the onion and sauté until tender and translucent, about 5 minutes. Add all but 1 cup of the mushrooms and cook until tender, stirring occasionally, about 5 minutes. Add the stock, cover, and cook just until the liquid comes to a slow boil, 8 to 10 minutes. Transfer the mixture in small batches to a blender or food processor and blend until smooth; set aside.

FINELY CHOP THE REMAINING 1 CUP MUSHROOMS. Melt the remaining tablespoon of butter in a small skillet over medium-high heat, add the mushrooms, and cook, stirring often, until the mushrooms are tender, 3 to 5 minutes. Season to taste with salt and pepper; keep warm over low heat.

COMBINE THE CREAM AND SHERRY in a large saucepan, bring to a boil over medium-high heat, and cook until the alcohol has evaporated and the mixture has thickened slightly, about 2 minutes. Stir in the puréed mushroom mixture, and season to taste with nutmeg, salt, and pepper. Cook for a few minutes to allow the mushroom bisque to fully reheat.

LADLE THE HOT BISQUE into individual soup bowls, spoon some of the sautéed mushrooms in the center, and add a small drizzle of truffle oil (if using). Serve right away.

Wild mushrooms are among the most prized foods in the Northwest, where each fall the damp but relatively mild conditions prove ideal for chanterelles, porcini, oyster mushrooms, lobster mushrooms, cauliflower mushrooms, matsutakes . . . the list of delicious edibles is a delightfully long one. Colder winter temperatures reduce the number of mushrooms available, though unless the season is severely cold, you will still be able to find hardier winter (yellow foot) chanterelles and black trumpet mushrooms, among others. Before long, with the spring showers and warming temperatures, it'll be time for those most prized of local fungi: morel mushrooms. Distinctive with their rich brown, deeply pitted caps, the first morels of the season add lightness to the steps of mycologists and inspire plenty of culinary enthusiasm in chefs and home cooks alike. The season of the similarly prized *Boletus edulis* (also known as cèpe or porcini) may overlap with that of morels, but its peak season is summer at higher elevations, continuing into the fall and winter closer to sea level.

Regional mycological societies are a great way to learn about the bounty of wild mushrooms in the Northwest, complete with foraging trips on which you can study the habitat of the delicious fungi and how the pros track them down. Most Northwest cooks, however, do their "foraging" at area farmers markets and well-stocked grocery stores, where the picking is easier and someone else has done the important work of identifying the mushrooms, which should be left to those experienced folks who know what they're doing.

Wild mushrooms are at home in a wide range of dishes. In these pages, you'll find wild mushrooms in an interesting vegetarian entrée, Wild Mushroom, Leek, and Wild Rice Cakes (page 163), and in a silky Forest Mushroom Bisque (page 74).

Keep in mind that mushrooms shouldn't be washed in water; they'll absorb liquid that will later seep out during cooking and dilute the mushroom's flavor. It is best to simply brush away any dirt or other debris from mushrooms with a soft brush (such as a pastry brush) or a paper towel. Some mushrooms have deep indentations or other crevasses that may hide dirt; if you cut the mushroom in half, you should be able to easily and fully clean it. Another important consideration is that wild mushrooms must always be fully cooked before you eat them. Some toxins in wild mushrooms are eliminated by cooking but can cause illness if consumed raw.

Northwest Seafood Pepper Pot

Christina's, Eastsound, Washington

Chef/owner Christina Orchid notes that you can use "other seafood at will" in this full-flavored stew. Whatever you choose, be sure to layer the chunkier and longer-cooking items on the bottom, with lighter shellfish on top. Christina uses tomato water rather than tomato juice, made by draining freshly chopped ripe tomatoes in a fine sieve over a bowl in a refrigerator overnight.

Poblano chiles—sometimes labeled "pasilla"—are dark green and quite tame in heat.

MAKES 6 TO 8 FIRST-COURSE SERVINGS OR 4 MAIN-COURSE SERVINGS

2 poblano chiles
2 tablespoons peanut or olive oil
1 medium red onion, chopped
1 tablespoon chopped garlic
1 tablespoon finely diced ginger
1 piece (3 inches) lemongrass, split lengthwise and smashed
1 to 2 tablespoons curry powder
2 fresh kaffir lime leaves (optional)
4 cups fish stock (recipe follows) or chicken stock (page 105),
  preferably homemade
2 cups tomato juice
8 ounces ling cod, skin and pin bones removed, cut into 2-inch cubes
8 ounces salmon fillet, skin and pin bones removed, cut into 2-inch cubes
12 large shrimp, peeled and deveined
16 Manila clams or other small clams (about 1 pound), scrubbed
20 mussels (about 1½ pounds), scrubbed and debearded
2 cups peeled, seeded, and diced, tomatoes
Basil sprigs, for garnish
Cilantro sprigs, for garnish

ROAST THE POBLANO CHILES over a gas flame or under the broiler until the skin blackens, turning occasionally to roast evenly, about 10 minutes total. Put the chiles in a plastic bag, securely seal the bag, and set aside to cool. When cool enough to handle, peel away and discard the skins. Remove the core and seeds and cut the chiles into ½-inch dice; set aside.

HEAT THE OIL in a medium saucepan over medium heat. Add the onion and garlic and cook, stirring, until tender and aromatic, 5 to 7 minutes. Add the ginger, lemongrass, curry powder, and lime leaves (if using). Increase the heat to high and cook, stirring, until the mixture is quite fragrant and the curry is evenly coating the onion, about 1 minute. Slowly pour in the stock followed by the tomato juice and cook for 5 minutes, stirring often.

IN A LARGE POT, layer the pieces of fish followed by the shrimp, clams, and mussels. Gently pour the broth over the seafood, then top with the chopped tomatoes and poblano chiles. Cover the pot and bring just to a boil over high heat, then lower the heat to medium-high and cook until the mussels and clams have opened, about 5 minutes.

TO SERVE, SPOON THE STEW into individual shallow bowls, being careful to distribute the different seafoods evenly. Top each with a small sprig of basil and cilantro and serve right away.

Basic Fish Stock

Fish stock is one of the quickest stocks to make at home, simmering for only 20 minutes. Longer cooking can bring on a bitter flavor from the fish bones. Avoid using salmon, Chilean sea bass, and other rich fish.

2 pounds white fish bones, cut into pieces and rinsed well
1 onion, sliced
1 large carrot, sliced
2 stalks celery, sliced
Bouquet garni of 3 parsley stems, 2 sprigs thyme, and 1 bay leaf, tied
    together with string
½ teaspoon black peppercorns
2½ quarts (10 cups) water, more if needed

PUT THE FISH BONES IN A LARGE STOCKPOT with the onion, carrot, celery, bouquet garni, and peppercorns. Add the water (it should cover the contents of the pot; if it doesn't, add more) and bring just to a boil over medium-high heat. Use a large spoon to skim away any scum that rises to the surface. Reduce the heat to medium-low and simmer, uncovered, until the stock is well flavored, about 20 minutes. Take the pot from the heat and let cool slightly, then strain through a cheesecloth-lined sieve into a large bowl; discard the solids. Refrigerate for up to 3 days before using, or freeze for up to 3 months.

MAKES ABOUT 2 QUARTS (8 CUPS)

Spinach Soup with Cilantro

Whitehouse-Crawford,
Walla Walla, Washington

This is a simple soup to make," notes chef Jamie Guerin. "The key is to cook the spinach quickly so the soup has a fresh spinach flavor and beautiful color. Garnish with toasted pine nuts or a fresh salsa if you'd like." If making the soup in advance, cool it quickly in a bowl set in a sink of ice water to help preserve the color, then gently reheat the soup just before serving.

Note that when you use a blender to purée a hot mixture, as is done here, the heat creates extra pressure in the container, which can force the lid off unexpectedly. Be sure to purée the soup in small batches and hold the lid on quite firmly while blending.

MAKES 4 TO 6 SERVINGS

---

2 tablespoons unsalted butter

1 medium russet potato, peeled and cut into chunks

1 small onion, sliced

1 leek, white and pale green parts only, split, cleaned, and sliced

2 cloves garlic, chopped

6 cups chicken stock (page 105) or vegetable stock (page 141), preferably homemade

1 pound fresh spinach, rinsed, dried, and tough stems removed

½ cup lightly packed cilantro leaves

Salt and freshly ground black pepper

MELT THE BUTTER in a large saucepan over medium heat. Add the potato, onion, leek, and garlic and cook, stirring often, until the onion and leek are tender and aromatic, 3 to 5 minutes. Add the stock and bring the liquid to a boil over medium-high heat, then reduce the heat to medium and simmer until the potatoes are very tender and the flavors are well blended, about 30 minutes. Add the spinach and cilantro and cook just until the spinach is tender but still bright green, 1 to 2 minutes.

WORKING IN SMALL BATCHES, purée the soup in a blender until smooth, then return the soup to the pan and reheat. Season to taste with salt and pepper and serve right away.

Sunchoke Soup with Skillet-Roasted Scallops

West (formerly Ouest),
Vancouver, British Columbia

The sunchoke (also known as Jerusalem artichoke) is a little-known but delicious tuber with a nutty-earthy-sweet flavor reminiscent of an artichoke heart, hence that part of its name. The plant is a member of the sunflower family, which contributes the other half of the nomenclature: sun + choke. Jerusalem is said to be a corruption of the Spanish *(girasol)* or Italian *(girasole)* word for sunflower.

Executive chef David Hawksworth strains the puréed soup before serving, with ultra-silken results, but even unstrained it is smooth and luxurious, and you'll have a lot less cleanup. A blender will produce the smoothest texture; if you use a food processor the result will be slightly coarser. Although the scallops add a lavish touch, the soup is equally delightful without them.

MAKES 4 TO 6 SERVINGS

1½ pounds sunchokes
6 tablespoons unsalted butter
1 small white onion, coarsely chopped
1 large leek, white part only, sliced
1 stalk celery, coarsely chopped
1 small carrot, coarsely chopped
1 clove garlic, crushed
1 sprig thyme
1 bay leaf
4 cups chicken stock, preferably homemade (page 105)
1 cup milk
½ cup whipping cream
1 teaspoon freshly squeezed lemon juice, plus more to taste
Salt and freshly ground black pepper
4 teaspoons olive oil
12 sea scallops
4 sprigs chervil or flat-leaf (Italian) parsley

USE THE EDGE OF A SPOON or a vegetable peeler to scrape away the thin skin from the sunchokes, dropping them into a bowl of water as you finish to help minimize discoloration. When all the sunchokes have been peeled, drain them well and coarsely chop them.

MELT THE BUTTER in a large saucepan over medium heat. Add the sunchokes, onion, leek, celery, carrot, garlic, thyme, and bay leaf. Cook, stirring often, until the vegetables begin to soften, 8 to 10 minutes (the vegetables shouldn't brown; reduce the heat if needed). Add the chicken stock, milk, and cream, bring the liquid just to a boil over high heat, then reduce the heat to medium-low and simmer until the vegetables are very tender, 30 to 40 minutes.

REMOVE AND DISCARD THE THYME SPRIG and bay leaf from the soup, then purée the soup in batches in a blender or food processor and return it to the pan. Season the soup to taste with lemon juice, salt, and pepper and keep warm over medium-low heat.

IN A LARGE SKILLET (preferably nonstick) heat the olive oil over medium-high heat until it just begins to smoke. Add the scallops and cook until nicely browned, 1 to 2 minutes on each side (the scallops will remain translucent in the center).

TO SERVE, ARRANGE THE SCALLOPS in the bottom of individual shallow soup bowls and ladle the hot soup around them. Garnish each serving with a sprig of chervil in the center and serve right away.

An "elegant borscht" is how chef Jason Nienaber describes this soup, generous with fresh beets in a light vegetable broth. The soup is topped with sautéed beet greens just before serving, though you could omit that embellishment if you prefer. The soup is especially flavorful when prepared a day or two in advance. Chef Nienaber notes that it's also delicious served cold on a hot summer day.

When it comes to grating the cooked beets, the food processor makes quick and tidy work of the job. Keep in mind that the beets will give off a powerfully red liquid that stains like mad, so be prepared. You may want to wear plastic gloves while handling them.

MAKES 6 TO 8 SERVINGS

---

4 tablespoons olive oil

2 large onions, diced

2 stalks celery, diced

2 carrots, coarsely chopped

2 large leeks, white and pale green parts only, split, cleaned, and sliced

1½ cups dry white wine

2 quarts (8 cups) cold water

1 sprig fennel or ½ teaspoon fennel seeds

2 sprigs thyme

1½ teaspoons black peppercorns

8 beets, with greens attached

Salt and freshly ground black pepper

Crème fraîche or sour cream, for serving

HEAT 2 TABLESPOONS OF THE OLIVE OIL in a medium soup pot over medium heat. Add the onions, celery, carrots, and leeks and sauté until tender and aromatic, 3 to 5 minutes. Increase the heat to medium-high, add the wine, and scrape the bottom of the pot to loosen any browned bits. Add the water and bring just to a boil, then immediately reduce the heat to medium-low to help ensure that the stock remains clear. Add the fennel, thyme, and peppercorns and simmer for 30 to 40 minutes. Strain the sto ough a cheesecloth-lined colander, discarding the solids, and set i e to cool completely. When cool, return the stock to the soup pot.

TRIM THE GREENS FROM THE BEETS, discarding any tough or damaged outer leaves; also cut away and discard the tough stalks. Rinse the greens, drain well, and set aside. Scrub the beets thoroughly, halving larger beets so they will all cook in about the same amount of time. Add the beets to the cooled stock (they should be fully covered with liquid; add a bit more water if needed) and bring to a boil over medium-high heat. Reduce the heat to medium and simmer until the beets are tender when pierced with the tip of a knife, 30 to 40 minutes. Scoop the beets out with a slotted spoon and set aside. Increase the heat to medium-high and boil the stock until reduced by about half, 5 to 10 minutes.

WHEN THE BEETS HAVE COOLED, rub away the skin with your fingers and discard. Finely shred the beets with a cheese grater, a mandoline, or a food processor fitted with a grating disk. Return the beets to the stock, season the soup to taste with salt and pepper, and keep warm over medium heat.

BRING A LARGE SAUCEPAN OF SALTED WATER TO A BOIL and prepare a bowl of ice water. Trim the tough ends from the beet greens, add the beet greens to the boiling water and cook just until wilted and bright green, about 1 minute. Drain, put the greens in the ice water to cool quickly and preserve their vibrant color, then drain again thoroughly. Heat the remaining 2 tablespoons oil in a medium skillet over medium heat, add the drained beet greens, and sauté just until heated through, 2 to 3 minutes. Season lightly with salt and pepper.

TO SERVE, LADLE THE BEET SOUP into individual bowls and top with the sautéed beet greens. Add a dollop of crème fraîche or sour cream and serve right away.

Razor Clam Chowder with Turnip, Truffle, and Thyme

Earth and Ocean, Seattle, Washington

This is a dish I like to serve as autumn transitions into winter," notes chef Johnathan Sundstrom, "when shellfish are at their best, and both razor clams (usually from the Quinault Reservation on the Olympic Peninsula) and Manila clams are plentiful and plump." It's also the time of year when, conditions permitting, fresh Oregon truffles are available, which he likes to shave over the chowder just before serving, "to give the dish a luxurious feel," he says. The chowder is mighty delicious even without the truffles or truffle oil.

MAKES 4 TO 6 SERVINGS

2 tablespoons unsalted butter
½ cup finely diced peeled turnip
½ cup finely diced peeled celery root
½ cup finely diced peeled Yukon Gold potato
2 cups whipping cream
1½ teaspoons chopped thyme
Salt and freshly ground black pepper
8 ounces chopped razor clams
Black truffle oil, for drizzling (optional)
Black truffle shavings, for garnish (optional)

Clam Stock
1 tablespoon unsalted butter
½ cup chopped onion
½ cup sliced leek, white part only
½ cup sliced fennel bulb
2 pounds Manila clams, scrubbed
2 cups dry white wine
3 cups water
1 clove garlic, crushed
3 sprigs thyme
1 bay leaf
10 black peppercorns

FOR THE CLAM STOCK, melt the butter in a large saucepan over medium heat. Add the onion, leek, and fennel and cook, stirring often, until tender and aromatic, 3 to 5 minutes. Add the clams and white wine, bring to a boil over medium-high heat, and simmer until the liquid is reduced by half. Add the water, garlic, thyme, bay leaf, and peppercorns, reduce the heat to medium-low, and simmer gently for 15 minutes. Strain the stock through a fine sieve into a large bowl and set aside. Remove the cooked clam meat from the shells and set aside, discarding the shells.

IN THE SAME SAUCEPAN, melt the butter over medium heat, add the turnip, celery root, and potato, and cook, stirring occasionally, until aromatic and partly tender, about 5 minutes. Add 2 cups of the reserved clam stock (being careful to leave any gritty bits in the bottom of the bowl), the cream, thyme, and salt and pepper to taste. Simmer until the vegetables are tender. Add the razor clams and reserved Manila clams and simmer just until the razor clams are cooked but not tough, about 30 seconds.

CHECK THE SOUP FOR SEASONING, then ladle into warmed bowls. Drizzle with the truffle oil and top with a shaving or two of truffle (if using). Serve immediately.

Duck Soup Inn, Friday Harbor, Washington

There's a little bit of everything in this soup—chiles, spices, potatoes, mushrooms, herbs, even coffee—resulting in a deeply flavorful but delightfully balanced soup. Chef/owner Gretchen Allison notes that the coffee adds another element of roasted earthy taste to echo the earthy mushrooms and the roasted peppers. The drizzle of freshly made basil oil on top adds a welcome touch of brightness just before serving. You can omit the oil, if you like, or cheat by using a top-quality commercial basil oil instead.

MAKES 6 SERVINGS

1 Anaheim chile
1 poblano chile
3 tablespoons unsalted butter
1 large onion, coarsely chopped
1 carrot, chopped
¼ teaspoon fennel seeds
¼ teaspoon cumin seeds
½ cup dry white wine
4 cups chicken stock, preferably homemade (page 105)
½ cup brewed coffee
2 small Yukon Gold potatoes (about 4 ounces), peeled and quartered
8 ounces button mushrooms, wiped cleaned, trimmed, and sliced
1 teaspoon thyme
3 to 4 tablespoons whipping cream, or to taste
Salt and freshly ground black pepper

Basil Oil
½ cup loosely packed basil leaves
¼ cup vegetable oil
Juice of ½ lemon
Pinch salt

FOR THE BASIL OIL, blend the basil, oil, lemon juice, and salt in a blender until finely puréed. Transfer the oil to a bowl and let sit at room temperature for about 30 minutes. Line a sieve with dampened cheesecloth and strain the basil oil through it, letting it naturally seep through for an hour or so, while making the soup.

ROAST THE CHILES over a gas flame or under the broiler until the skin blackens, turning occasionally to roast evenly, about 10 minutes total. Put the chiles in a plastic bag, securely seal the bag, and set aside to cool. When cool enough to handle, peel away and discard the skins. Remove the core and seeds from the chiles and set aside.

MELT THE BUTTER in a large, heavy pot over medium-high heat. Add the onion and carrot and cook until the vegetables are tender and lightly browned, stirring often, 8 to 10 minutes. Add the fennel and cumin seeds and continue to cook, stirring, until the spices are aromatic and lightly toasted, 1 to 2 minutes longer.

ADD THE WINE, bring to a boil, and boil to reduce until most of the liquid has evaporated, 4 to 5 minutes. Add the chicken stock, coffee, potatoes, mushrooms, thyme, and roasted chiles. Bring to a boil over medium-high heat, then reduce the heat to low and simmer, uncovered, for 1 hour. Take the pan from the heat and let the soup cool slightly. Purée the soup in batches in a blender or with an immersion blender until very smooth. Stir in the cream with salt and pepper to taste. Reheat gently if needed.

TO SERVE, LADLE THE HOT SOUP into individual bowls, drizzle each with ½ teaspoon of the basil oil, and serve.

Garlic Soup

Durlacher Hof Alpine Country Inn,
Whistler, British Columbia

August kicks off garlic season in the Northwest, with farms throughout the region selling fat, juicy heads that shoppers snatch up at farmers markets. While garlic is certainly available year-round, super-fresh garlic is a treat worth enjoying while it's in season—and this rustic, full-flavored soup is the perfect way to use it. The garlic used at Durlacher Hof is from Hellmer's Farm in the Pemberton Valley, just north of Whistler.

MAKES 4 SERVINGS

4 ounces lean bacon, finely chopped

10 cloves garlic, preferably fresh, minced

2 large leeks, white and pale green parts only, split, cleaned, and sliced

4 cups water

½ cup sour cream, plus more for serving

1 egg yolk

1 tablespoon all-purpose flour

Salt and freshly ground black pepper

2 tablespoons minced chives, for garnish

Croutons

¼ cup unsalted butter

2 cups finely cubed French bread

COOK THE BACON in a large saucepan over medium heat until it just begins to brown and is quite aromatic, 3 to 5 minutes. Add the garlic and cook for about 1 minute longer (the garlic should not brown). Add the leeks and cook, stirring, until tender, about 5 minutes. Add the water and simmer for 20 minutes.

IN A SMALL BOWL, stir together the sour cream, egg yolk, and flour until well blended. Add this to the soup and cook over medium heat, stirring constantly, until the soup thickens slightly, about 10 minutes. Season the soup to taste with salt and pepper. Keep the soup warm over low heat while making the croutons.

FOR THE CROUTONS, melt the butter in a medium skillet over medium-high heat. Add the bread cubes and sauté, stirring often, until evenly browned, 3 to 5 minutes.

TO SERVE, LADLE THE SOUP into individual bowls and add a small dollop of sour cream to the center. Scatter the croutons and chives around the sour cream and serve right away.

Yukon Gold Potato and Goat Cheese Soup with Sheep's Sorrel and Garlic Croutons

Wildwood, Portland, Oregon

A "combination of all things good in Oregon in the late spring" is how chef/owner Cory Schreiber describes this soup. "Foragers come to the back door of the restaurant with wild sheep's sorrel, which grows near overflowing water springs that keep it bright green and slightly grassy in flavor." If you don't have a source of sheep's sorrel, substitute chives or another flavorful but tender herb. The goat cheese chef Schreiber uses comes from Pierre Kolisch's Juniper Grove Farm in central Oregon.

MAKES 8 SERVINGS

2 tablespoons unsalted butter

2 white onions, chopped

3 stalks celery, chopped

2 leeks, white and light green parts only, split, cleaned, and chopped

1 fennel bulb, trimmed and chopped

2 teaspoons salt

½ teaspoon freshly ground white pepper

2 cups dry white wine

6 cups vegetable stock, preferably homemade (page 141)

1½ pounds Yukon Gold potatoes, peeled and chopped

1 teaspoon chopped thyme

6 ounces fresh farmstead goat cheese, crumbled

2 tablespoons freshly squeezed lemon juice

8 to 10 drops hot pepper sauce

2 ounces fresh sheep's sorrel, trimmed, or ¼ cup minced chives

Garlic Croutons

2 tablespoons olive oil

1 clove garlic, minced

2 cups cubed rustic bread (½-inch cubes)

Salt and freshly ground black pepper

THE NORTHWEST BEST PLACES COOKBOOK

90

IN A LARGE SAUCEPAN, melt the butter over medium heat. Add the onions, celery, leeks, fennel, salt, and pepper. Cover, reduce the heat to low, and cook for 20 minutes, stirring often. Stir in the wine and cook, covered, for 10 minutes longer. Stir in the vegetable stock and bring to a boil over medium-high heat. Add the potatoes and thyme, reduce the heat to medium, and simmer until the potatoes are tender, about 20 minutes. Let cool slightly, 5 to 10 minutes. Add 4 ounces of the goat cheese, the lemon juice, and hot pepper sauce, then purée the soup in batches in a food processor or blender. Keep the soup warm over low heat.

PREHEAT THE OVEN to 350°F.

FOR THE GARLIC CROUTONS, heat the olive oil in a large skillet over medium heat. Add the garlic and cook, stirring, until soft but not browned, 2 to 3 minutes. Add the bread cubes, tossing to coat them evenly in the garlicky oil. Transfer the bread cubes to a baking sheet and season with salt and pepper. Bake until golden brown and crisp, about 10 minutes.

TO SERVE, TASTE THE SOUP for seasoning, adjusting with more salt or pepper if needed. Ladle the soup into bowls, garnish with the remaining 2 ounces goat cheese, the sheep's sorrel, and garlic croutons. Serve right away.

Hot and Sour Shrimp Soup

Yarrow Bay Beach Café,
Kirkland, Washington

Don't be daunted by the length of this ingredient list; many of these items need little preparation time, and the balance and contrast of flavors they provide are paramount in this deeply flavored soup. Galangal, kaffir lime leaves, straw mushrooms, and some of the other distinctive ingredients can be found at Asian markets or well-stocked grocery stores, though most have alternatives. There really is no substitute for the citrus-herbal quality of kaffir lime leaves; simply omit them if you're unable to find them. Note that the longer the soup sits before serving, the more the heat of those red pepper flakes infuses the soup . . . so be prepared!

MAKES 6 SERVINGS

6 dried *chiles de arbol* or other dried hot red chiles
3 stalks lemongrass, trimmed and halved lengthwise
1 piece (1½ inches long) galangal or ginger, thinly sliced, plus
    1 teaspoon minced
1½ pounds medium shrimp
1½ tablespoons vegetable oil
5 cups chicken stock, preferably homemade (page 105)
6 fresh kaffir lime leaves, torn
6 serrano or Thai bird chiles
3 cilantro roots or 10 cilantro stems, thoroughly rinsed and tied together
1 can (14 ounces) unsweetened coconut milk
2 tablespoons Thai fish sauce *(nam pla),* plus more to taste
½ teaspoon salt, plus more to taste
1 can (15 ounces) straw mushrooms, drained and rinsed
1 teaspoon dried red pepper flakes, plus more to taste
2 teaspoons Asian sesame oil
1 tablespoon freshly squeezed lime juice
¼ cup chopped cilantro

PUT THE WHOLE DRIED CHILES in a small bowl, cover with warm water, and set aside for 30 minutes to soften. Set the lemongrass pieces on a chopping board and lightly crush them with the bottom of a small pan or with a mallet. Also crush the galangal slices; set the lemongrass and galangal aside. Cut a piece of cheesecloth about 10 inches square and set it aside. Once the dried chiles have softened, drain and dry them thoroughly.

PEEL THE SHRIMP, reserving the shells from 10 of them. Devein the shrimp, split them in half lengthwise, and refrigerate until ready to use. Rinse the reserved shells and pat them dry.

HEAT THE OIL in a medium saucepan over high heat until it just begins to smoke, then add the shrimp shells and soaked dried chiles and cook, stirring constantly, until the shells turn pink and the chiles blacken, 30 seconds to 1 minute. Use a slotted spoon to transfer the shells and chiles to a small bowl and carefully pour the chicken stock into the saucepan.

WHILE THE STOCK COMES TO A BOIL, put the shrimp shells and chiles into the center of the cheesecloth along with the galangal slices, lime leaves, and serrano chiles. Draw up the sides and tie the cheesecloth securely with kitchen string, trimming away excess cheesecloth; return the bundle to the saucepan. When the stock reaches a boil, add the lemongrass and cilantro roots or stems. Reduce the heat to medium-low, cover, and simmer gently to allow the seasonings to infuse the chicken broth, 25 to 30 minutes. Add the coconut milk, fish sauce, and salt, increase the heat to medium-high, and bring to a boil. Add the mushrooms and simmer for 10 minutes.

REMOVE THE CHEESECLOTH BAG, lemongrass, and cilantro roots/stems. Add the red pepper flakes and keep the soup warm over medium heat. Taste for seasoning, adding more salt or fish sauce to taste.

JUST BEFORE SERVING, heat a large skillet over medium-high heat, add the sesame oil and shrimp, and sauté until they turn pink, 1 to 2 minutes. Add the minced ginger and lime juice, toss to mix, and take the skillet from the heat.

TO SERVE, LADLE THE SOUP into individual bowls, top with the hot shrimp (along with any liquids from cooking the shrimp), and sprinkle the chopped cilantro over the soup.

Cold Curried Asparagus Soup

The Vintner's Inn at Hinzerling Winery,
Prosser, Washington

The vineyard we planted back in 1972 was an asparagus field prior to our converting it to grapes," notes owner Mike Wallace. "Consequently, asparagus grew between the rows of vines and was sort of a nuisance." With the unexpected asparagus, Mike Wallace created a number of new recipes, this chilled soup among them. An interesting twist is the use of macaroni, which, when puréed, helps thicken the soup.

MAKES 4 TO 6 SERVINGS

½ cup macaroni
2 pounds asparagus, trimmed
2 tablespoons unsalted butter
¼ cup finely chopped onion
2 teaspoons curry powder
2 cups chicken stock (page 105) or vegetable stock (page 141), prefereably
    homemade
½ cup whipping cream or half-and-half
Salt and freshly ground black pepper
Sour cream, for serving (optional)

BRING A SMALL SAUCEPAN OF SALTED WATER TO A BOIL and add the macaroni, boiling until tender, 10 to 12 minutes. Drain well and set aside to cool.

BRING A MEDIUM SAUCEPAN OF SALTED WATER TO A BOIL and prepare a small bowl of ice water. Cut the top 1 inch from each of the asparagus spears and blanch the tops in the boiling water for 2 minutes. Scoop the tips out with a slotted spoon and add them to the ice water to cool quickly, then drain well and refrigerate until ready to serve the soup.

RETURN THE WATER TO A BOIL, add the remaining asparagus spears, and cook until just tender, 3 to 4 minutes. Drain well (reserving 1 cup of the blanching water), then purée the asparagus spears in a food processor or blender with the cooked macaroni and reserved blanching water until very smooth.

MELT THE BUTTER in a medium saucepan over medium heat. Add the onion and curry powder and sauté until the onion is tender and the curry is aromatic, 2 to 3 minutes. Add the stock and bring to a boil. Stir in the puréed asparagus mixture and the cream and season the soup to taste with salt and pepper. Set aside to cool, then refrigerate until fully chilled.

BEFORE SERVING, TASTE THE SOUP again for seasoning, as cold can dull the flavors a bit. Ladle the soup into individual bowls, scatter the asparagus tips over the top, and add a small dollop of sour cream in the center, if you like.

Sides, Sandwiches, and Salads

Dungeness Crab and Fuji Apple Salad with Curry Mayonnaise
The Peerless Restaurant

Eggplant Jam *The Willows Inn*

Asperges à la Flamande (Flemish-Style Asparagus) *Campagne*

Shrimp with Togarashi Spice and Asian Pears *Diva at the Met*

Four Onion Risotto *Tulio*

Salmon and Potato Pancakes *Adam's Place*

Swedish Rye Bread *The Shelburne Inn*

Blood Orange Salad with Hazelnuts and Point Reyes Blue
Earth and Ocean

Roasted Red Pepper and Artichoke Sandwich *First Street Haven*

Grilled Romaine Salad with Sun-Dried Tomato Vinaigrette
Elliott's Oyster House

Savory Bread Pudding with Cranberries *The Shoalwater*

Mini Jalapeño Muffins *From the Bayou*

Green Bean Salad with Mint Vinaigrette
The Mahle House

Spicy Eggplant Salad *Typhoon!*

Martha's Rolls *Harrison House Bed and Breakfast*

Dungeness Crab and Fuji Apple Salad with Curry Mayonnaise

The Peerless Restaurant, Ashland, Oregon

Sweet crabmeat and sweet-tart-crisp apples make a surprisingly good partnership. Here the combination is further embellished with aromatic curry mayonnaise. For a shortcut, you could simply stir the curry powder into ¾ cup of top-quality purchased mayonnaise. The recipe would also make a great crab salad sandwich or could be spooned into endive leaves for classy cocktail party fare.

MAKES 4 SERVINGS

1⅓ cups Dungeness crabmeat (about 8 ounces)
½ Fuji apple, peeled and cut into small dice
½ cup finely diced fennel bulb
¼ cup finely diced celery
1 shallot, finely chopped
1 teaspoon finely chopped fennel fronds (tops)
1 teaspoon freshly squeezed lemon juice
Salt and freshly ground black pepper
2 to 3 ounces spicy greens (such as mizuna, arugula, or red mustard greens),
   rinsed and dried

Curry Mayonnaise
1 teaspoon curry powder
1 egg yolk
1 teaspoon freshly squeezed lemon juice
½ cup vegetable oil
Salt and freshly ground white pepper

FOR THE CURRY MAYONNAISE, put the curry powder, egg yolk, and lemon juice in a small bowl. Begin adding the oil a few drops at a time, whisking constantly, until the yolk begins to turn pale and thicken slightly, showing that an emulsion has begun to form. Continue adding the rest of the oil in a thin, steady stream, whisking constantly. Season to taste with salt and white pepper and refrigerate until ready to serve.

PICK OVER THE CRABMEAT to remove any bits of shell or cartilage and gently squeeze to remove excess liquid. In a large bowl, combine the crab, apple, fennel, celery, shallot, and fennel fronds. Add the lemon juice and 2 to 3 tablespoons of the curry mayonnaise and fold until well combined. Season to taste with salt and pepper. Spoon the crab salad onto individual plates with a handful of the greens and a spoonful of the remaining curry mayonnaise alongside.

Eggplant Jam

The Willows Inn,
Lummi Island, Washington

Awesome with roasted chicken, sausages, and all sorts of barbecued things!" says owner Riley Starks of this interesting, almost chutneylike jam. "It should be wet with olive oil, dyed red from the paprika, spicy, vinegary, and sweet." He also says that it "just gets better with age," so you might consider making the eggplant jam a day or two before you plan to serve it. Smoked paprika adds quite a distinctive earthy flavor to this savory jam, but if you're unable to find it you could use more of the regular paprika.

MAKES ABOUT 6 CUPS

¾ cup extra virgin olive oil
2 large eggplants, cut into ½-inch cubes
1½ cups dry white wine
1 cup apple cider vinegar or champagne vinegar
1 cup packed light brown sugar
3 to 5 cloves garlic, chopped
1 teaspoon sweet smoked paprika *(pimenton de la Vera)*
1 teaspoon regular paprika
½ teaspoon *sambal oelek* or other hot chile sauce, plus more to taste
Salt

HEAT THE OLIVE OIL in a large, heavy saucepan over medium heat. When the oil is hot, carefully add the eggplant, gently tossing to coat the cubes with oil. Add the wine, vinegar, brown sugar, garlic, smoked paprika, regular paprika, and *sambal oelek*. Bring the mixture to a simmer, stirring occasionally, then reduce the heat to low and cover the pan. Cook until the eggplant is tender, about 30 minutes, stirring once or twice. Remove the lid and cook until the mixture is thickened slightly, about 15 minutes longer.

TAKE THE PAN FROM THE HEAT, season to taste with salt, and let cool. Store in an airtight container and refrigerate until ready to serve, allowing the eggplant jam to come to room temperature before serving.

Asperges à la Flamande (Flemish-Style Asparagus)

Campagne, Seattle, Washington

This recipe shows off our prime Northwest springtime asparagus to great advantage. Chef Daisley Gordon peels and seeds the tomato used in this recipe, though at home you can simply dice the tomato as is. A great side dish for simple roasted chicken or grilled steak, this recipe could also be served as an appetizer or salad course.

MAKES 4 TO 6 SERVINGS

2 eggs
1½ pounds asparagus, trimmed
3 tablespoons unsalted butter
1 plum (Roma) tomato, peeled, seeded, and diced
Juice of ½ lemon
1 tablespoon chopped flat-leaf (Italian) parsley
A few fresh gratings of nutmeg or a pinch of ground nutmeg
Salt and freshly ground black pepper

PUT THE EGGS IN A PAN with enough cold water to cover them by about 1 inch. Set the pan over high heat and bring to a boil, then reduce the heat to medium-high and simmer the eggs for 10 minutes, counting from the time that the water comes to a full boil. Drain the eggs and run cold water over them for a few minutes to stop the cooking and help cool the eggs quickly. Peel the eggs and finely chop them; set aside.

BRING A LARGE, SHALLOW PAN of salted water to a boil over high heat. Add the asparagus spears and cook just until they turn evenly bright green, 1 to 2 minutes. Drain and then run cold water over the asparagus to cool it quickly and help maintain the vivid green color. Drain well on paper towels.

HEAT THE BUTTER in a large skillet over medium heat until fully melted and beginning to foam. Add the asparagus and toss gently until it is heated through and evenly coated in butter, 2 to 3 minutes. Add the chopped eggs, tomato, lemon juice, parsley, and nutmeg, with salt and pepper to taste. Continue tossing for another minute or two to evenly mix, then transfer the asparagus to a warmed serving platter or individual plates. Serve right away.

Shrimp with Togarashi Spice and Asian Pears

Diva at the Met,
Vancouver, British Columbia

At Diva, they use deepwater shrimp from off the coast of British Columbia, shrimp that have a clean, sweet taste with excellent texture. *Togarashi* is a Japanese spice blend that typically has crushed red pepper flakes, dried nori, sesame seeds, dried orange peel, and other flavorful ingredients—a little goes a long way. *Togarashi* is available in Asian markets and well-stocked grocery stores, as are Japanese mayonnaise, shiso leaves, and Asian pears.

English pea oil adds a splash of vibrant color and flavor to the finished dish, though you can omit it with equally tasty results. If you do make the pea oil, use fresh peas for the best sweet flavor. Any extra oil can be used in vinaigrette dressings or tossed with pasta and sautéed shrimp.

MAKES 4 SERVINGS

2 tablespoons vegetable oil
1 pound medium shrimp, peeled and deveined
1 teaspoon *togarashi* spice

English Pea Oil
½ cup freshly shelled English peas
½ cup grapeseed or vegetable oil

Asian Pear Salad
¼ cup shelled fava beans (optional)
2 Asian pears, cored and thinly sliced
¼ cup Japanese mayonnaise or regular mayonnaise, preferably homemade (page 61)
1 cup lightly packed frisée leaves
1 tablespoon freshly squeezed lemon juice, plus more to taste
1 teaspoon finely shredded shiso leaves or mint
Salt and freshly ground black pepper

FOR THE PEA OIL, bring a small pan of salted water to a boil over high heat and prepare a medium bowl of ice water. Add the peas to the boiling water, reduce the heat to medium, and simmer until the peas are just tender and bright green, 1 to 2 minutes. Drain and add the peas to the ice water to cool completely, then drain again and pat dry on paper towels. Combine the cooled peas and oil in a blender and blend until smooth. Pour the purée into a fine strainer lined with lightly dampened cheesecloth and set over a bowl. Let drain, undisturbed, for 1 hour.

FOR THE PEAR SALAD, if using the fava beans, bring a small pan of salted water to a boil. Add the fava beans, reduce the heat to medium, and simmer until the beans are just tender and bright green, about 2 minutes. Drain well and let cool, then peel away the outer skin from each bean. In a medium bowl, combine the pears, mayonnaise, frisée, lemon juice, shiso, and fava beans. Toss gently to evenly mix, then season to taste with salt and pepper. Cover and refrigerate until ready to serve.

JUST BEFORE SERVING, heat the oil in a large skillet over medium-high heat. Add the shrimp and sprinkle the *togarashi* spice evenly over them. Sauté the shrimp, stirring often, until they are pink and just barely opaque through the thickest part, 2 to 3 minutes. Take the skillet from the heat and let cool slightly (the shrimp are served at room temperature at Diva).

TO SERVE, SPOON THE ASIAN PEAR SALAD onto the center of individual plates, flattening the mound slightly. Arrange the shrimp over the salad and drizzle about 1 tablespoon of the pea oil around the salad. Serve right away.

Four Onion Risotto

Tulio, Seattle, Washington

Rich, delicious, and lovely, this creamy white risotto is embellished with varying shades of green from the onions. Chef Walter Pisano suggests serving it alongside grilled or roasted salmon, and it would be tasty with his Braised Sirloin Tip with Artichoke Gremolata (page 170) or the Braised Lamb Shanks (page 177). To serve the risotto as a vegetarian entrée, just replace the chicken stock with vegetable stock.

MAKES 4 TO 6 SERVINGS

6 tablespoons unsalted butter
6 tablespoons olive oil
2 Walla Walla Sweet onions, finely chopped
2 leeks, white and pale green parts only, split, cleaned, and finely chopped
3 cups chicken stock, preferably homemade (recipe follows)
3 cups water
1½ cups Arborio rice
4 green onions, finely chopped
¼ cup minced chives
¼ cup mascarpone cheese
Salt and freshly ground black pepper

IN A MEDIUM SKILLET, heat 3 tablespoons of the butter with the olive oil over medium-high heat. When hot, add three-quarters of the Walla Walla Sweet onions and cook, stirring, until tender and a light caramel color, 10 to 12 minutes. Add the leeks and cook, stirring, for 2 minutes longer. Take the skillet from the heat and set aside.

COMBINE THE CHICKEN STOCK AND WATER in a small saucepan and warm over medium heat, then reduce the heat to low to keep it warm without simmering.

IN A MEDIUM, HEAVY SAUCEPAN, melt the remaining 3 tablespoons butter over medium heat, add the remaining onion, and cook, stirring, until tender, 2 to 3 minutes. Add the rice and stir until the rice begins to toast slightly, 2 to 3 minutes. Add ½ cup of the warm broth mixture and stir gently until the rice fully absorbs the broth. Add another ½ cup broth and stir until it is fully absorbed. Continue this process, stirring gently all the while, until the rice is just barely tender to the bite and the risotto has a rich, creamy texture, 35 to 40 minutes total.

STIR THE CARAMELIZED ONION and leek into the risotto with the green onion, chives, and mascarpone cheese. Season to taste with salt and pepper and serve right away.

Basic Chicken Stock

A wonderful kitchen staple to have on hand, you might consider doubling or tripling the recipe and freezing extra for later use. You'll be glad you did.

2 to 3 pounds chicken backs, necks, or other portions, rinsed well

1 onion, quartered

2 large carrots, coarsely chopped

2 stalks celery, coarsely chopped

Bouquet garni of 3 parsley stems, 2 sprigs thyme, and 1 bay leaf, tied together with string

1 teaspoon black peppercorns

3 quarts (12 cups) water, more if needed P

PUT THE CHICKEN PIECES IN A LARGE STOCKPOT with the onion, carrots, celery, bouquet garni, and peppercorns. Add the water (it should cover the contents of the pot; if it doesn't, add more) and bring just to a boil over medium-high heat. Use a large spoon to skim away any scum that rises to the surface. Reduce the heat to medium-low and simmer, uncovered, until the stock is well flavored, about 2 hours. If needed during cooking, add more hot water to the pot so that the chicken pieces remain fully covered. Take the pot from the heat and let cool slightly, then strain through a cheesecloth-lined sieve into a large bowl; discard the solids. Refrigerate for up to 3 days before using, or freeze for up to 3 months.

MAKES ABOUT 2 QUARTS (8 CUPS)

WALLA WALLA SWEET ONIONS

Until you've tasted one yourself, it's hard to imagine an onion so sweet you could eat it like an apple—though many do just that with the lauded Walla Walla Sweet onions from the arid fields of eastern Washington. A French soldier is credited with bringing the seeds of an Italian sweet onion to Walla Walla in the late 1800s, where a well-established community of Italian farmers helped spur the production of this distinctive onion. The growing conditions proved ideal, the "sweetness" coming from a reduced level of sulfur in the onion, which is what contributes the hot flavor to other onions. In 1995, the U.S. Department of Agriculture issued a marketing order protecting the Walla Walla name by designating a specific geographic region for the Walla Walla Sweet onion, a small part of which extends across the border into Oregon, and prohibiting the use of the name for onions grown outside the region.

Early spring, Walla Walla Sweet onions, which look like oversized green onions, are ideal eaten fresh, served sliced on a burger, or tossed in a green salad. The same can be said for the mature onions that show up in June through August. Some local burger joints get on the bandwagon, offering Walla Walla Sweet onion rings while they're in season. The onions are also delicious grilled, thick slices brushed lightly with oil and cooked alongside your steak or salmon until nicely browned and just a bit of crunch remains in the center. Among the recipes in this book, you'll find the region's sweet onion adorning the creamy Four Onion Risotto (page 104), combined with Dungeness crab in the breakfast Crab Strata (page 24), and cooked long and slow with a splash of tequila for the "drunken" embellishment to Grilled Flatiron Steak (page 138).

Salmon and Potato Pancakes

Adam's Place, Eugene, Oregon

These flavorful savory cakes would make a great side dish with simple sautéed shrimp or grilled salmon or sturgeon—"really, any fish," notes chef Jack Strong. The cakes can also be served as a first course, with a dollop of good tartar sauce or dilled sour cream alongside. Note that you can get double duty out of the oven, baking the potatoes and salmon at the same time. If you have any leftover baked potatoes or cooked salmon, this recipe is a great use for them.

MAKES 4 SERVINGS

---

2 russet potatoes (about 1½ pounds total), scrubbed

8 ounces salmon fillet

2 tablespoons plus 1 teaspoon vegetable oil

Salt and freshly ground black pepper

½ cup finely chopped red onion

⅓ cup chopped green onion

3 tablespoons stone-ground mustard

2 tablespoons minced garlic

2 tablespoons sour cream

1 tablespoon freshly squeezed lemon juice

1 tablespoon chopped dill

PREHEAT THE OVEN to 400°F. Pierce the skin of the potatoes a few times with the tines of a fork. Set the potatoes directly on the oven rack and bake until they give when you pinch the sides (be sure to use an oven mitt!), about 1 hour. When the potatoes are tender, set aside to cool completely.

RUB THE SALMON FILLET with 1 teaspoon of the oil and season lightly with salt and pepper. Set the salmon on a small oiled baking dish and bake alongside the potatoes just until the fish is opaque through the thickest part, 12 to 15 minutes, depending on the thickness of the fish. Take the salmon from the oven and set aside to cool completely, then discard the skin and flake the salmon, discarding the pin bones as well.

PEEL THE COOLED POTATOES and grate them on a box grater or in a food processor fitted with a grating disk. Put the potatoes in a large bowl and add the flaked salmon, red and green onion, mustard, garlic, sour cream, lemon juice, and dill. Season to taste with salt and pepper and stir gently to evenly blend the ingredients. Form the potato mixture into 8 cakes about ½ inch thick, using a scant ½ cup per cake.

HEAT THE REMAINING 2 TABLESPOONS OIL in a large skillet (preferably nonstick) over medium heat. Add the potato cakes and cook until nicely browned on each side and heated through, about 5 minutes on each side. Serve right away.

Swedish Rye Bread

The Shelburne Inn, Seaview, Washington

This recipe is innkeeper Laurie Anderson's version of the traditional Swedish rye bread called limpa, "a family favorite." The tender bread is fully aromatic with orange zest, molasses, and spices, delicious alone or toasted and topped with orange marmalade. Anderson says they've also served the bread with chef/innkeeper David Campiche's chicken and wild mushroom pâte, or with an assortment of cheeses and fruit on an appetizer plate. The "medium" rye flour used here is lighter in texture than dark rye flour.

MAKES 2 LOAVES

½ medium russet potato (about 4 ounces), scrubbed

⅓ cup dark molasses

⅓ cup packed light or dark brown sugar

Grated zest of 1 orange

1 tablespoon unsalted butter, plus more for brushing on loaves

1 teaspoon salt

1½ tablespoons active dry yeast

½ teaspoon fennel seeds

½ teaspoon cumin seeds

½ teaspoon caraway seeds

2 cups medium rye flour

2½ cups unbleached all-purpose flour

PUT THE POTATO IN A SAUCEPAN of cold water, bring the water just to a boil over high heat, then lower the heat to medium and simmer until the potato is tender when pierced with the tip of a knife, 20 to 25 minutes. Drain the potato (reserving 1 ½ cups of the cooking water) and let cool just until you are able to handle it, then peel away the skin with a small knife. While the potato is still hot, press it through a ricer or finely grate it; set aside to cool slightly.

IN A MEDIUM SAUCEPAN, combine 1 cup of the reserved potato water with the molasses, brown sugar, orange zest, butter, and salt. Bring to a boil over high heat, then reduce the heat to medium-high and boil for 6 minutes. Set aside to cool. Sprinkle the yeast over the remaining ½ cup reserved potato water (the water should be lukewarm; reheat gently if needed). Set aside until the yeast is dissolved and bubbly, about 5 minutes.

PUT THE COOLED MOLASSES MIXTURE in a large bowl and stir in the yeast. Add the potato, followed by the fennel seeds, cumin seeds, and caraway seeds. Stir to mix, then stir in the rye flour, ½ cup at a time, followed by the all-purpose flour. Turn the dough out onto a floured board and knead for 10 minutes. Put the dough in an oiled bowl, cover with a towel, and set aside in a warm place to rise until doubled in bulk, about 1½ hours. Grease a baking sheet. Knock down the dough, then form it into 2 round loaves and set them well apart on the baking sheet. Cover with the towel again and let rise until almost doubled, 45 minutes to 1 hour.

PREHEAT THE OVEN to 300°F.

JUST BEFORE BAKING, make 3 slashes across the top of each loaf, intersecting in the middle to form an asterisk. Bake the bread until the loaves are a deep, rich golden brown, 50 to 60 minutes. Transfer to a wire rack, brushing the tops with butter for a glossy finish, if you like. Let cool at least a bit before cutting into slices to serve.

Blood Orange Salad with Hazelnuts and Point Reyes Blue

Earth and Ocean, Seattle, Washington

Chef Johnathan Sundstrom notes that this salad often shows up on his menu beginning in January, when blood oranges come into season, though it would be tasty with regular navel oranges as well. "I love this Point Reyes Blue," says Sundstrom, "an artisan-produced cheese, similar to Roquefort (though made with cow's milk [rather than sheep's milk]) from Point Reyes, California." Other blue cheese can be used in its place.

MAKES 4 SERVINGS

½ cup hazelnuts

2 blood oranges

8 ounces mixed greens (such as watercress, frisée, and radicchio), rinsed, dried, and torn into pieces

½ red onion, cut into very thin rings

3 ounces Point Reyes Blue cheese, rind trimmed off, finely diced

1 tablespoon minced chives

Sherry Vinaigrette

¼ cup sherry vinegar

1 tablespoon minced shallot

1 clove garlic, minced

½ teaspoon Dijon mustard

½ teaspoon chopped thyme

¼ cup grapeseed oil or more olive oil

¼ cup extra virgin olive oil

Salt and freshly ground black pepper

FOR THE VINAIGRETTE, combine the vinegar, shallot, garlic, mustard, and thyme in a large bowl and whisk to blend. Whisk the grapeseed oil into the vinegar mixture, pouring it in a thin, steady stream, then whisk in the olive oil. Season the vinaigrette to taste with salt and pepper and set aside.

PREHEAT THE OVEN to 350°F. Scatter the hazelnuts in a baking pan and toast in the oven until lightly browned and aromatic, 8 to 10 minutes, gently shaking the pan once or twice to help the nuts toast evenly. Transfer the nuts to a slightly dampened dish towel and wrap the towel around the nuts. Let sit until partly cooled, then rub the nuts in the towel to help remove the papery skin. Let the hazelnuts cool completely before continuing.

CUT BOTH ENDS FROM ONE OF THE ORANGES, just to the flesh. Set the orange upright on a cutting board and use the knife to cut away the peel and pith, following the curve of the fruit. Try not to cut away too much of the flesh with the peel. Repeat with the remaining oranges, then cut each across into ¼-inch slices.

LAY THE BLOOD ORANGE SLICES slightly overlapping in a ring on each plate, leaving the center open. Put the greens in a large bowl, scatter the onion rings, blue cheese, and hazelnuts over them, then drizzle with about half of the sherry vinaigrette. Toss the salad to evenly mix, then arrange it in a pile in the center of each plate. Drizzle the remaining vinaigrette over the oranges, scatter the chives over all, and serve right away.

Roasted Red Pepper and Artichoke Sandwich

First Street Haven,
Port Angeles, Washington

A grown-up twist on the classic grilled cheese, this sandwich combines two different cheeses with roasted peppers and artichokes, bound with a basil- and garlic-enhanced mayonnaise for even more flavor. For a short-cut, you could use bottled roasted red peppers instead of roasting your own.

MAKES 4 SERVINGS

2 small red bell peppers
1½ cups minced water-packed artichoke hearts (about one and a half 14-ounce cans)
8 slices sourdough bread
4 slices cheddar cheese (about 2 ounces)
4 slices provolone cheese (about 2 ounces)
Unsalted butter, at room temperature, for toasting sandwiches

Basil Aïoli
1 cup mayonnaise, preferably homemade (page 61)
¼ cup chopped basil
1 tablespoon minced garlic
1 teaspoon olive oil
Pinch dried red pepper flakes, plus more to taste

FOR THE BASIL AÏOLI, combine the mayonnaise, basil, garlic, olive oil, and red pepper flakes in a food processor or blender and purée until smooth. Taste the mayonnaise for seasoning, adding more pepper flakes to taste.

ROAST THE RED PEPPERS over a gas flame or under the broiler until the skins blacken, turning occasionally to roast evenly, about 10 minutes total. Put the peppers in a plastic bag, securely seal the bag, and set aside to cool. When cool enough to handle, peel away and discard the skins. Remove the core and seeds, finely chop the peppers, and set aside.

IN A MEDIUM BOWL, stir together the peppers, artichokes, and ½ cup of the basil aïoli. (Reserve the leftover aïoli for another use, as a sandwich spread or as a dip for steamed shrimp or fried calamari.) Set 4 of the bread slices on the counter and spread each with one-quarter of the artichoke mixture. Top each with a slice of cheddar and a slice of provolone, and top with another slice of bread.

HEAT A LARGE SKILLET OVER MEDIUM HEAT. Butter the top slice of bread for each sandwich and set the sandwiches buttered side down in the skillet (cook the sandwiches in batches if necessary). Cook until the bottom is nicely browned and the cheese is mostly melted, 2 to 3 minutes; meanwhile, lightly butter the top of each sandwich. Flip the sandwiches over and cook on the second side until the bread is nicely browned and the filling is hot, 2 to 3 minutes longer. Cut each sandwich in half diagonally and serve right away.

Grilled Romaine Salad with Sun-Dried Tomato Vinaigrette

Elliott's Oyster House, Seattle, Washington

This is a great accompaniment for those backyard barbecues—when you've got the grill good and hot for the salmon or steaks, you might as well grill your salad too. Grilling adds surprisingly wonderful flavor to halved romaine hearts, which just char lightly on the outside but remain crisp and bright in the center. At Elliott's, they serve the grilled romaine on a bed of julienned roasted beets.

For the garnish of Parmesan shavings, simply draw a vegetable peeler along one long side of a wedge of cheese, peeling off the cheese in thin, wispy curls. Though not as striking a presentation, you could also simply finish the salad with grated Parmesan cheese.

MAKES 4 SERVINGS

2 heads romaine lettuce
Canola oil, for brushing
½ teaspoon granulated garlic
Salt and freshly ground black pepper
Shaved Parmesan cheese, for topping

Sun-Dried Tomato Vinaigrette
½ cup canola oil
¼ cup white balsamic vinegar or white wine vinegar
2 tablespoons finely minced sun-dried tomatoes
1 shallot, finely minced
1 tablespoon finely shredded basil
½ teaspoon minced garlic
Salt and freshly ground black pepper

PREHEAT AN OUTDOOR GRILL.

FOR THE VINAIGRETTE, combine the oil, vinegar, sun-dried tomatoes, shallot, basil, and garlic in a medium bowl and whisk to evenly blend. Season to taste with salt and pepper; set aside.

DUNK THE WHOLE ROMAINE HEADS in a sink of cold water to remove any grit, and drain very well. Remove a couple outer layers of leaves to expose the compact "heart" of the romaine (the extra leaves can be wrapped in damp paper towels and saved for another use). Cut each of the romaine hearts in half lengthwise, being careful to cut evenly through the core, which will help hold each half together. Pat the romaine with paper towels to remove excess water. Brush each romaine heart lightly on all sides with oil, then season lightly with the granulated garlic, salt, and pepper.

SET THE ROMAINE HEARTS on the hot grill and grill until the outer leaves turn bright green and are just lightly charred around the edges, about 1 minute, then turn and grill for about 1 minute longer on the second side.

TO SERVE, SET THE GRILLED ROMAINE HALVES on individual plates and drizzle the sun-dried tomato vinaigrette over. Shave a few curls of Parmesan cheese onto each salad and serve right away.

Savory Bread Pudding with Cranberries

The Shoalwater, Seaview, Washington

"This is a delightful and decadent variation on your grandma's turkey stuffing," notes co-owner Ann Kischner. It's surely no accident that dried cranberries are used, since this historic Seaview inn is near the region's prolific cranberry bogs. Kischner also notes that the individual bread puddings can be made up to a day ahead, refrigerated once cooled, and reheated in a low oven before serving.

Herbes de Provence is a traditional dried herb blend from France, typically including rosemary, sage, marjoram, lavender, oregano, and thyme. If you're unable to find herbes de Provence, you could instead use your own blend of any or all of those dried herbs.

MAKES 12 SERVINGS

¼ cup unsalted butter

1 cup finely diced onion

½ cup finely diced celery

1 tablespoon herbes de Provence

4 whole eggs

2 egg yolks

2 cups half-and-half

½ cup whipping cream

1 teaspoon salt

8 ounces (about ½ loaf) hearty French bread, cut into ½-inch cubes

1 cup dried cranberries

PREHEAT THE OVEN to 400°F. Generously butter a 12-cup muffin pan.

MELT THE BUTTER in a large skillet over medium-low heat. Add the onion, celery, and herbes de Provence and cook, stirring occasionally, until the onion is translucent, 8 to 10 minutes.

BEAT THE EGGS with the egg yolks in a large bowl just to mix, then beat in the half-and-half, cream, and salt until well blended. Stir in the sautéed vegetables, bread cubes, and cranberries. Set aside to soak until the bread has absorbed most of the custard, 30 to 45 minutes, stirring occasionally (refrigerate the mixture if the kitchen is warm).

SPOON THE BREAD MIXTURE into the prepared muffin cups, filling them to the top, trying to distribute the cranberries evenly among the cups. Bake until the tops are nicely browned and the custard is fully set, about 25 minutes.

TAKE THE MUFFIN PAN FROM THE OVEN and let cool on a wire rack for a few minutes. Run a knife around the edge of each bread pudding and invert onto the rack. Serve right away.

Mini Jalapeño Muffins

From the Bayou, Parkland, Washington

This Cajun refuge in the shadows of Pacific Lutheran University has attracted quite a following for its Bayou-fresh recipes. The owners, natives of Opelousas, Louisiana, shared this amazing fact: they bake about 13,680 of these mini-muffins each week! Wonderful served au naturel or with creamed honey and butter, you can make the muffins even spicier by adding an extra tablespoon or so of the jalapeño liquid, though they have a pretty good kick already. The recipe can also be made in regular-sized muffin tins, but bake them for about 15 minutes.

**MAKES ABOUT 4 DOZEN MINI-MUFFINS OR
2 DOZEN REGULAR MUFFINS**

---

8 whole pickled jalapeño chiles
1 tablespoon jalapeño pickling liquid, plus more to taste
1¼ cups yellow cornmeal
1 cup all-purpose flour
¼ cup sugar
2 teaspoons baking powder
2 teaspoons salt
2 eggs
¾ cup milk
2 tablespoons honey

PREHEAT THE OVEN to 375°F. Butter two 24-cup mini-muffin pans.

CUT THE STEMS FROM THE JALAPEÑOS and pulse them in a food processor to finely chop. Add the pickling liquid and process to make a smooth purée, scraping down the sides as needed. You need ⅓ cup of the purée; save any extra for another use or discard.

IN A LARGE BOWL, combine the cornmeal, flour, sugar, baking powder, and salt and stir to blend. In a separate bowl, beat the eggs with the milk, ⅓ cup jalapeño purée, and honey until well blended. Add the egg mixture to the dry ingredients and stir just to blend.

SPOON THE BATTER into the prepared muffin pans, not quite to the top (about 1 tablespoon per muffin). Bake until a toothpick inserted in the center of a muffin comes out clean, about 12 minutes. Turn out onto a wire rack to cool slightly before serving warm, or cool completely and seal in an airtight container until ready to serve.

Green Bean Salad with Mint Vinaigrette

The Mahle House, Cedar, British Columbia

The vibrant green vinaigrette for this salad has a distinct minty-garlic flavor that dresses up blanched green beans in great style. Assemble and toss the salad just before serving, so the vinegar doesn't have a chance to discolor the beans. The vinaigrette can be made up to a few hours in advance and refrigerated; doing so will also give the flavors a chance to develop. Serve this salad as a bold way to start a meal or as a light main course with broiled chicken or fish alongside.

It's best to use a blender rather than a food processor for making the vinaigrette, as a food processor won't purée the mint finely enough for the desired smooth results.

MAKES 4 SERVINGS

---

1 pound green beans, trimmed
½ cup thinly sliced red onion
½ cup crumbed feta cheese
¼ cup chopped toasted pecans

Mint Vinaigrette
¼ cup lightly packed mint leaves
1 clove garlic
⅓ cup vegetable oil
3 tablespoons cider vinegar, plus more to taste
Salt and freshly ground white pepper

FOR THE VINAIGRETTE, combine the mint and garlic in a blender and blend to finely chop. Add the oil and vinegar and blend to evenly mix, 15 to 20 seconds. Season to taste with salt and white pepper and set aside.

BRING A LARGE POT OF SALTED WATER TO A BOIL over high heat and prepare a large bowl of ice water. Add the green beans to the boiling water and cook until bright green and crisp to the bite, 2 to 3 minutes. Drain well, then plunge the beans into the ice water to stop the cooking and preserve their bright color. When cold, drain well and pat dry on paper towels.

JUST BEFORE SERVING, put the green beans in a large bowl and scatter the onion, feta, and pecans over them. Drizzle the mint vinaigrette over the beans and toss to evenly coat, then arrange the bean salad on individual plates and serve.

Spicy Eggplant Salad

Typhoon!, Portland, Oregon

Chef/owner Bo Kline notes that spicy eggplant salad—a quintessential mainstay of Thai cuisine—is "one of the dishes we like to order when tasting and testing restaurants throughout Thailand. It's also a family favorite during the summer." She favors the darker purple Chinese eggplants, which tend to have a less bitter flavor than Japanese eggplants, both of which are long, slender varieties.

MAKES 4 SERVINGS

8 medium shrimp
4 Chinese eggplants
½ red bell pepper, cored and seeded
1 small head butter lettuce or other green lettuce, rinsed and dried
½ cup thinly sliced red onion or shallot
½ cup chopped cilantro
¼ cup sliced green onion
Mint leaves and cilantro sprigs, for garnish

Spicy Lime Dressing
6 tablespoons freshly squeezed lime juice
5 tablespoons Thai fish sauce *(nam pla)*
3 tablespoons sugar
1 teaspoon minced garlic
1 teaspoon minced Thai chile pepper

BRING A SMALL PAN OF SALTED WATER TO A BOIL. Add the shrimp, reduce the heat to medium, and cook just until they are evenly pink and the meat is opaque, 2 to 3 minutes. Drain and let cool, then peel and devein the shrimp. Cut the shrimp in half lengthwise and set aside.

FOR THE DRESSING, whisk together the lime juice, fish sauce, and sugar in a small bowl. Add the garlic and chile, and mix together well. Set aside.

PREHEAT AN OUTDOOR GRILL or preheat the broiler. Lightly pierce the eggplants a couple of times with the tip of a sharp knife. Grill or broil the whole eggplants until they are tender enough that a skewer can easily pierce them, about 10 minutes. At the same time, grill or broil the bell pepper until tender and lightly charred, about 5 minutes. Let the eggplant and pepper cool, then peel the eggplant and cut it into ½-inch dice; peel the pepper and thinly slice it.

ARRANGE A FEW LETTUCE LEAVES on each plate and place the eggplant on top. Top each salad with some of the shrimp, red onion, cilantro, green onion, and red pepper, and then drizzle with the lime dressing. Garnish with mint leaves and cilantro.

Martha's Rolls

Harrison House Bed and Breakfast,
Corvallis, Oregon

T hese were a special holiday treat when I was growing up," says owner Maria Tomlinson, who now serves the rolls—made light and tender with buttermilk and shortening—at her bed-and-breakfast inn, both at breakfast and with savory dishes at dinner time. Despite the use of yeast, this dough does not need the traditional rising time of many bread doughs. The recipe makes about 3 dozen small rolls, great for a brunch spread or a large family gathering.

MAKES 12 TO 16 SERVINGS

2 cups buttermilk
2 teaspoons (1 envelope) active dry yeast
4 cups all-purpose flour
½ cup granulated sugar
1 teaspoon salt
1 teaspoon baking powder
½ teaspoon baking soda
½ cup shortening
½ cup unsalted butter, melted
½ cup packed light brown sugar

PREHEAT THE OVEN to 375°F.

GENTLY WARM 1/4 CUP OF THE BUTTERMILK to about 105°F in a small saucepan over medium heat. Take the pan from the heat, stir in the yeast, and set aside until frothy.

COMBINE THE FLOUR, sugar, salt, baking powder, and baking soda in a large bowl. Cut in the shortening until the mixture resembles coarse crumbs. Add the yeast mixture and the remaining 1¾ cups buttermilk to the flour mixture. Stir until the dough starts to come together, and then turn it out onto a lightly floured surface and gently knead it into a smooth ball.

POUR HALF OF THE MELTED BUTTER into each of two 8-inch round cake pans, and then sprinkle half of the brown sugar over the butter in each pan.

Break off small pieces of dough and roll into walnut-sized balls, making about 40 total. Fill the 2 pans with the dough balls; they should be just touching. Bake until golden brown, 20 to 25 minutes. Remove the pans from the oven and invert onto 2 serving plates, carefully lifting off the cake pans and allowing the buttery sugar mixture to drip down over the rolls. Let cool for a few minutes before serving, allowing guests to pull off their own rolls.

Mains

Five-Spice Duck *Dahlia Lounge*

Lavender-Crusted Free-Range Chicken Breasts
with Blueberry Habanero Chutney *Duck Soup Inn*

Papardelle with Toasted Walnut Sauce *Fiddlehead Bistro*

Chocolate Braised Bison Short Ribs *Cascadia*

Grilled Salmon with Stone Fruit Compote *Elliott's Oyster House*

Grilled Flatiron Steak with Chile-Honey Butter and
"Drunken" Walla Walla Sweet Onions *Whitehouse-Crawford*

Stuffed Portobello Mushrooms with Hazelnut Sauce *The Arbor Café*

Grilled Beef with Grapes *Typhoon!*

Wasabi and Black Pepper Tuna with
French Lentils and Onion Marmalade *Matt's in the Market*

Grilled Venison Tournedos with Blue Cheese and Basil Ravioli
The Aerie Resor

Pacific Rim Crab Cakes with Sesame-Ginger Aïoli
The Place Bar and Grill

Pasta with Bacon, Blue Cheese, and Tomatoes
Lindaman's Gourmet-to-Go

Stuffed Halibut with Crawfish Cream Sauce *From the Bayou*

Smoked Pork Loin with Apple-Onion Relish *Dolce Skamania Lodge*

Nettle and Almond Stuffed Skate Wing with
Nettle Cream Sauce *Oceanwood Country Inn*

Grilled Salt Spring Island Lamb Burgers *Splitz Grill*

Wild Mushroom, Leek, and Wild Rice Cakes *Silverwater Cafe*

Andalusian Flank Steak *Cafe Langley*

Thai-Style Halibut and Shrimp en Papillote *Kasteel Franssen*

Braised Sirloin Tip with Artichoke Gremolata *Tulio*

Seared Sablefish with Burnt Orange Emulsion *C*

Chicken Breasts with Prosciutto and Cambozola *Edgewater Lodge*

Braised Lamb Shanks *Ruby's on Bainbridge*

Cedar Smoked Salmon *Sazerac*

Mint and Nut–Crusted Rack of Lamb
The Dining Room at The Salish Lodge & Spa

Honey Peppered Salmon with Tomato Ginger Sauce
Rock Springs Guest Ranch

Granchio (Crab Capellini) *Bugatti's Ristorante*

Kuku Paka (Chicken in Coconut Sauce) *Spice Jammer Restaurant*

Five-Spice Duck

Dahlia Lounge, Seattle, Washington

Even commercial five-spice powder—like this homemade five-spice mix—can include more than five spices, though star anise, cinnamon, cloves, fennel, and Szechwan pepper are the common backbone ingredients of the distinctive Chinese blend. This rub mixture makes about twice as much as you'll need; the remainder will keep for up to two weeks in the refrigerator, whether for another duck or to rub on a pork loin or chicken for roasting.

At the Dahlia Lounge, the duck is cooked on a rotisserie over an applewood fire, which renders out much of the fat and makes the skin deliciously crisp. If you have a rotisserie attachment for your outdoor grill, this is a great time to use it. The duck would also be tasty grilled over indirect heat, with a foil pan placed on the coal rack directly under the duck to catch the dripping fat, and the coals mounded on either side to provide a moderate grilling temperature.

MAKES 4 SERVINGS

1 duck (4 to 5 pounds), cavity cleaned, excess fat trimmed,
    rinsed and patted dry

Five-Spice Rub

    4 teaspoons fennel seeds
    1 cinnamon stick, broken into pieces
    6 whole star anise
    1 dried chipotle chile, stem and seeds removed, torn into pieces
    1 teaspoon Szechwan peppercorns
    ½ teaspoon whole cloves
    ½ cup packed light brown sugar
    3 tablespoons kosher salt
    1 tablespoon grated ginger
    1 tablespoon minced garlic
    1 tablespoon freshly ground black pepper

128

FOR THE FIVE-SPICE RUB, put the fennel, cinnamon, star anise, chipotle chile, Szechwan peppercorns, and cloves in a small skillet over medium heat and toast for a few minutes until aromatic, shaking the skillet gently. Let cool, then grind the toasted spices in a spice mill or clean coffee grinder, working in 2 or 3 batches if needed. Transfer the ground spices to a bowl and stir in the brown sugar, salt, ginger, garlic, and pepper, stirring until the spice rub is well blended.

RUB ABOUT HALF OF THE SPICE MIXTURE generously all over the skin of the duck (store the remainder in the refrigerator for another use), and place it on a rack set over a pan to catch drips. Refrigerate the duck, uncovered, for at least 3 hours, or preferably overnight.

WHEN READY TO COOK THE DUCK, preheat an outdoor grill. If you have a rotisserie attachment, thread the duck onto the rotisserie and set a drip pan directly under the duck. If you'll be grilling over indirect heat, move the coals to either side of the grill and set a drip pan between the piles of coals. Set the duck on the grill over the drip pan. Cover the grill and cook the duck until the juices run clear and an instant-read thermometer inserted into the thigh reads 175°F, 1½ to 2 hours (cooking time will vary with your grill and the size of the duck). Add coals as needed to keep the heat consistent. Remove the duck from the grill and carve it into breast and leg-thigh portions. Serve right away.

Lavender-Crusted Free-Range Chicken Breasts with Blueberry Habanero Chutney

Duck Soup Inn,
San Juan Island, Washington

Lavender has a powerful taste and needs to be treated with a light touch," warns chef/owner Gretchen Allison. "Too much and your dinner will remind you of your last bubble bath. I like it most when played against other earthy flavors such as thyme and rosemary." You could also use your favorite fresh herbs, such as basil, mint, cilantro, or tarragon, in place of the lavender for this simple but tasty chicken dish, which Allison suggests serving with buttermilk mashed potatoes or creamy polenta.

Any number of different seasonal fruits—apples, apricots, plums, pears, or huckleberries—can be used in place of the blueberries for the chutney. Allison uses farmstead goat cheeses from Quail Croft on San Juan Island; it pays off in flavor to buy the best fresh goat cheese you can find.

MAKES 4 SERVINGS

---

4 boneless, skinless free-range chicken breasts (about 2 pounds)
½ cup buttermilk
1 cup dry bread crumbs
¼ cup chopped flat-leaf (Italian) parsley
2 tablespoons chopped thyme
1 tablespoon chopped fresh lavender flowers or 2 teaspoons dried lavender
1 teaspoon salt
½ teaspoon ground black pepper
¼ cup unsalted butter
4 to 6 ounces goat cheese

Blueberry Habanero Chutney
½ medium onion, finely chopped
½ cup rice vinegar
¼ cup sugar
½ teaspoon salt, plus more to taste
½ habanero chile, cored, seeded, and minced, plus more to taste
2 cups blueberries, fresh or frozen

THE NORTHWEST BEST PLACES COOKBOOK

FOR THE CHUTNEY, combine the onion, vinegar, sugar, salt, and habanero in a medium saucepan. Bring to a boil over high heat, then reduce the heat to medium and simmer until the liquid is reduced to ¼ cup, about 20 minutes. Add the blueberries and cook over medium heat, until the berries are tender and many of them have burst, 5 to 7 minutes, stirring occasionally. Taste for seasoning, adding more salt or habanero to taste. Set aside to cool.

PUT THE CHICKEN BREASTS in a shallow dish and pour the buttermilk over them, turning the breasts to coat them evenly. Cover and refrigerate for at least 10 minutes and up to 1 hour.

COMBINE THE BREAD CRUMBS, parsley, thyme, lavender, salt, and pepper in another shallow dish and gently stir to mix. Take the chicken breasts from the buttermilk, allowing the excess to drip off, then thoroughly coat them in the crumb mixture. Melt the butter in a large, heavy skillet (preferably cast iron) over medium heat. Add the chicken breasts and cook until they are nicely browned on the bottom, about 5 minutes. Turn the breasts over, being careful to not dislodge the crust, and continue cooking until evenly browned and there is no pink in the flesh, about 5 minutes longer.

ARRANGE THE CHICKEN BREASTS on individual plates and crumble the goat cheese over them. Spoon the blueberry chutney alongside and serve right away.

Papardelle with
Toasted Walnut Sauce

Fiddlehead Bistro, Twisp, Washington

This recipe takes a little time—making the toasted rosemary walnuts (an outstanding cocktail snack on their own, by the way), roasting the garlic, making the walnut sauce—but the final results are undeniably worthwhile. The nutty sauce embellished with earthy rosemary makes for an intriguing and delicious pasta topping. Decidedly rich as a main course, the pasta could also be served in smaller portions as a first course or as a side dish to roasted chicken or grilled vegetables. Papardelle is a long, wide noodle not consistently available among the pastas on most retail shelves. Look for it in specialty stores or Italian markets, or use fettuccine or even farfalle (bowties) in its place.

To roast the garlic, set the head of garlic on a piece of foil and drizzle 1 teaspoon of olive oil over it. Wrap the garlic securely in the foil and roast in a 350°F oven until tender when squeezed, 30 to 40 minutes. Set aside to cool, then peel the individual cloves.

MAKES 4 TO 6 SERVINGS

---

1 head roasted garlic and/or 4 cloves raw garlic, coarsely chopped
¼ cup grated Parmesan cheese
¼ cup coarsely chopped flat-leaf (Italian) parsley
1 tablespoon balsamic vinegar
¼ teaspoon freshly ground black pepper, plus more to taste
Salt
¾ cup extra virgin olive oil
12 ounces dried papardelle noodles or other pasta
¼ cup unsalted butter

Toasted Rosemary Walnuts
2 cups walnut halves or pieces
3 tablespoons unsalted butter, melted
¼ cup packed light brown sugar
1 tablespoon finely minced fresh rosemary or 1 teaspoon finely ground
   dried rosemary

¼ teaspoon cayenne pepper
¼ teaspoon freshly ground black pepper
¼ teaspoon salt

PREHEAT THE OVEN to 350°F. Line a baking sheet with a piece of parchment paper or foil and lightly oil the surface.

FOR THE TOASTED WALNUTS, put the walnuts in a large bowl, drizzle the melted butter over them, and toss to coat. Sprinkle the brown sugar, rosemary, cayenne, black pepper, and salt over the nuts and quickly toss to coat the nuts evenly with the seasonings. Spread the nuts on the prepared baking sheet and bake until the sugar has melted and the nuts are golden brown, about 15 minutes. Set aside to cool.

FOR THE SAUCE, put the toasted walnuts in the work bowl of a food processor. Add the garlic, Parmesan, parsley, vinegar, pepper, and salt to taste. Turn on the machine and slowly add the olive oil. Pulse until the mixture is finely chopped but still has some texture; it should not become a smooth purée. Taste for seasoning, adding more salt or pepper to taste; set aside.

BRING A LARGE POT OF SALTED WATER TO A BOIL. When the water is at a rolling boil, add the pasta and cook until al dente, 8 to 10 minutes. Drain well.

HEAT THE BUTTER in a large skillet (preferably nonstick) over medium heat until it is fully melted and has turned a golden brown. Add the cooked pasta and ½ teaspoon salt and toss to coat the pasta well and reheat it. Take the pan from the heat and drizzle the walnut sauce over, tossing to evenly mix. Divide the pasta among individual plates and serve right away.

Chocolate Braised
Bison Short Ribs

Cascadia, Seattle, Washington

Chef/owner Kerry Sear uses local Seattle Chocolates brand chocolate in his kitchen, for both sweet desserts and surprising savory dishes such as these braised bison short ribs. The deeply flavored, bittersweet chocolate adds significant body to this simple braised recipe. Although exotic meats such as bison have become easier to come by in recent years thanks to farming operations, beef short ribs are an ideal alternative. Chef Sear suggests serving this dish with noodles or mashed Yukon Gold potatoes.

MAKES 4 SERVINGS

2½ pounds bison or beef short ribs
Salt and freshly ground black pepper
½ cup unsweetened cocoa powder
3 tablespoons olive oil
½ cup chopped shallot or onion
¼ cup finely diced slab bacon
3 cloves garlic, chopped
1 cup diced carrot
1 cup diced parsnip
1 cup diced celery
8 sprigs thyme
4 bay leaves
2 cups merlot or other dry red wine
3 cups beef or veal stock, preferably homemade (page 171)
12 white pearl onions, peeled
¼ cup chopped bittersweet chocolate

PREHEAT THE OVEN to 350°F. Season the short ribs with salt and pepper, then coat them in the cocoa powder and shake off any excess.

HEAT THE OLIVE OIL in a heavy pot, such as a Dutch oven, over medium-high heat. When the oil is hot, add the shallot, bacon, and garlic and cook until lightly browned and aromatic, stirring constantly, 2 to 3 minutes. Add the ribs to the pot and sear the meat well on all sides. If the cocoa powder begins to burn, reduce the heat to medium.

ADD THE CARROT, parsnip, celery, thyme, and bay leaves, and pour the wine over all. Stir well. Bring the wine just to a boil over high heat, then add the stock and pearl onions. Return the liquid to a boil, then reduce the heat to low. Using a large spoon, skim away any foam that rises to the surface. Cover the pot and put it in the oven to braise until the meat is very tender, about 1½ hours.

TAKE THE POT FROM THE OVEN and lift out the ribs with tongs, setting them aside on a plate, covered with foil to keep warm. Skim away the excess fat from the surface of the cooking liquid, then put the pot over medium-high heat and reduce the liquid until thickened slightly, about 20 minutes. Whisk in the bittersweet chocolate until it is fully melted, and season the sauce to taste with salt and pepper. Remove and discard the thyme sprigs and bay leaves. Return the ribs to the sauce to reheat for a few minutes.

TO SERVE, ARRANGE THE RIBS on individual plates and spoon the sauce and onions over them. Serve right away.

A t Elliott's, chef Matt Fanning serves this salmon on a bed of rice with steamed asparagus alongside. You can also take advantage of the already-hot grill to grill asparagus and thick slices of crusty bread brushed with olive oil to serve with the rich salmon. Chef Fanning prefers to use granulated garlic rather than fresh for seasoning the salmon, as fresh garlic can easily burn in the high heat of the grill, leaving an unpleasant taste on the fish. Granulated garlic (not garlic salt) will add a toasty garlic flavor without burning. The peach used in the compote is briefly grilled, adding a touch of earthy, outdoorsy flavor.

MAKES 4 SERVINGS

4 salmon fillets (8 ounces each), skin and pin bones removed
1 tablespoon olive oil or vegetable oil
½ teaspoon granulated garlic
Salt and freshly ground black pepper

Stone Fruit Compote
1 ripe but firm nectarine, pitted and diced
2 black plums, pitted and diced
4 ounces Bing cherries or other sweet cherries, pitted and halved
Juice of ½ lime
1 tablespoon honey
2 tablespoons finely shredded mint
⅛ teaspoon cayenne pepper
⅛ teaspoon freshly ground white or black pepper
1 ripe but firm peach, pitted and halved

FOR THE FRUIT COMPOTE, put the nectarine, plums, and cherries in a large bowl. Add the lime juice and honey, stir to mix well, then stir in the mint, cayenne pepper, and white pepper. Refrigerate until ready to serve.

PREHEAT AN OUTDOOR GRILL.

LIGHTLY RUB THE GRILL RACK WITH OIL. Set the peach halves cut side down on the grill and grill until nicely browned and slightly softened, 2 to 3 minutes. Set aside to cool, then dice the fruit and stir it into the fruit compote.

RUB THE SALMON PIECES WITH THE OIL, then season lightly with granulated garlic, salt, and pepper. Cook the salmon on the hot grill until just a bit of translucence remains in the center, 3 to 5 minutes per side, depending on the thickness of the fillets.

TO SERVE, ARRANGE THE SALMON PIECES on individual plates and spoon the stone fruit compote alongside. Serve right away.

Grilled Flatiron Steak with Chile-Honey Butter and "Drunken" Walla Walla Sweet Onions

Whitehouse-Crawford, Walla Walla, Washington

The flatiron is a tender and delicious cut that comes from the blade chuck," explains chef Jamie Guerin. Though this steak comes from one of the "lesser" parts of the cow often relegated to pot roast, the flatiron is surprisingly tasty and tender. The trick is that it's not a common cut; you will likely need to special-order the steaks, a worthwhile effort. There isn't another cut quite like the flatiron, but you could use hanger or skirt steak instead, or even a well-marbled rib-eye.

You'll have some of the redolent chile-honey butter left over. The butter will keep, chilled, for up to a week and will be delicious tossed on steamed green beans, sautéed with shrimp, or as a flavorful spread for cornbread.

MAKES 4 SERVINGS

4 flatiron steaks, ¾ inch thick (about 8 ounces each)
Salt and freshly ground black pepper

Chile-Honey Butter
1 dried ancho chile
1 dried New Mexico chile
2 cloves garlic, unpeeled
2 sun-dried tomatoes (oil-packed or plumped dried)
1 tablespoon tequila
1 tablespoon freshly squeezed lime juice
Pinch dried oregano
Pinch ground cinnamon
1 cup unsalted butter, at room temperature
2 tablespoons honey
Salt

Drunken Walla Walla Onions
3 tablespoons olive oil
2 medium Walla Walla Sweet onions, thinly sliced
1 tablespoon ancho chile powder

1 teaspoon ground cumin
¼ cup tequila
2 tablespoons freshly squeezed lime juice
Salt

FOR THE CHILE-HONEY BUTTER, lightly toast the dried chiles in a medium skillet over medium-high heat until aromatic, about 5 minutes, gently tossing them so they toast evenly. Transfer the chiles to a small bowl, add warm water to cover, and set aside to soak until soft, about 30 minutes. While the chiles are soaking, toast the garlic cloves in the same skillet until the skin has blackened and the garlic is aromatic and beginning to soften, about 10 minutes, tossing so the cloves toast evenly. Let the garlic cool until it is easy to handle, then peel away and discard the skin. Drain the chiles and remove the stems, cores, and seeds.

COMBINE THE CHILES, garlic, sun-dried tomatoes, tequila, lime juice, oregano, and cinnamon in a food processor and pulse to finely chop. (If necessary, add a tablespoon or two of water so the mixture blends smoothly.) Add the butter and honey and continue blending to make a smooth mixture. Season the butter to taste with salt and refrigerate until ready to serve. (The butter can be made up to a week in advance and refrigerated.)

FOR THE DRUNKEN ONIONS, heat the olive oil in a large skillet over medium-high heat, add the onions, and cook, stirring often, until it begins to soften, about 10 minutes. Stir in the ancho chile powder and cumin and sauté until the spices are aromatic, about 5 minutes. Take the pan from the heat and add the tequila and lime juice. Return the pan to the heat, very carefully light the tequila with a long match, and gently shake the pan until the flames subside. Reduce the heat to medium-low and continue cooking the onions, stirring occasionally, until very tender, about 20 minutes longer. Season to taste with salt and keep warm over low heat.

PREHEAT AN OUTDOOR GRILL. Season the steaks with salt and pepper. When the grill is heated, lightly brush the grill rack with oil and grill the steaks, 3 to 5 minutes per side for medium-rare, or longer to suit your taste.

TO SERVE, TOP EACH OF THE HOT STEAKS with a heaping tablespoon of the chile-honey butter and spoon the drunken onions alongside.

Stuffed Portobello Mushrooms with Hazelnut Sauce

The Arbor Café, Salem, Oregon

Chef Rebecca Bolderoff created this recipe as a vegetarian selection for a Valentine's Day dinner, and it proved so popular that the dish is occasionally offered as a dinner special at The Arbor Café.

MAKES 4 SERVINGS

1 cup hazelnuts
4 large portobello mushrooms, wiped clean
4 teaspoons olive oil
¼ cup unsalted butter
1 large onion, finely diced
2 shallots, finely diced
1 teaspoon minced tarragon
½ teaspoon minced thyme
8 ounces frozen spinach, thawed, squeezed dry, and chopped
1 cup vegetable stock, preferably homemade (recipe follows)
4 cups herb-seasoned or plain croutons
¾ cup cream cheese (about 6 ounces), at room temperature
Salt and freshly ground black pepper

Hazelnut Sauce
    ¼ cup unsalted butter
    ½ cup brandy
    2 cups whipping cream
    Salt and freshly ground black pepper

PREHEAT THE OVEN to 350°F. Scatter the hazelnuts in a baking pan and toast in the oven until lightly browned and aromatic, 8 to 10 minutes, gently shaking the pan once or twice to help the nuts toast evenly. Transfer the nuts to a lightly dampened dish towel and wrap it around the nuts. Let sit until partly cooled, then rub the nuts in the towel to help remove the papery skin. Let the hazelnuts cool completely, then finely chop them; set aside. Increase the oven temperature to 375°F.

TRIM THE STEMS FROM THE MUSHROOMS and use a spoon to scrape away the dark gills on the underside of each one. Brush each mushroom with 1 teaspoon of the olive oil, on both the top and the bottom. Set the mushrooms top sides down on a baking sheet and bake until nearly tender, 10 to 12 minutes. Set aside to cool while making the stuffing. Increase the oven temperature to 450°F.

MELT THE BUTTER in a medium skillet over medium heat. Add the onion and shallots and cook, stirring, until tender and aromatic, 3 to 5 minutes. Stir in the tarragon and thyme and cook until the onion is just beginning to brown, 5 to 7 minutes longer. Stir in the chopped spinach and set aside.

HEAT THE VEGETABLE STOCK in a small saucepan over medium heat. Put the croutons and half of the hazelnuts in a large, heatproof bowl, pour the stock over them, and set aside until all the liquid is absorbed by the croutons, about 30 minutes. Stir the onion/spinach mixture and cream cheese into the croutons until evenly blended, then season to taste with salt and pepper. Let cool completely. (The stuffing can be made a day in advance and refrigerated.)

FOR THE HAZELNUT SAUCE, melt the butter in a medium saucepan over medium heat. Add the remaining hazelnuts and cook, stirring, until golden brown and aromatic, 2 to 3 minutes. Add the brandy and boil over medium-high heat until reduced by half, then add the cream and cook, whisking often, until reduced by half and the sauce is thick enough to coat a spoon, 18 to 20 minutes. Season to taste with salt and pepper and keep the sauce warm over low heat.

DIVIDE THE STUFFING among the mushrooms, spreading it out evenly and mounding it slightly in the center. Put the mushrooms in an oiled baking dish and bake until the filling is lightly browned and heated through, 8 to 10 minutes.

TO SERVE, SET EACH STUFFED MUSHROOM on an individual plate, spoon the hazelnut sauce over and around the mushrooms, and serve right away.

Basic Vegetable Stock

Feel free to alter the selection of vegetables included in this stock, depending on the recipe in which you'll be using it. Fennel bulb, for instance, would add a touch of anisey sweetness that may or may not be welcome in the soup or other recipe you'll use the stock for.

2 onions, quartered

2 large leeks, white and pale green parts only, split, cleaned, and sliced

3 large carrots, coarsely chopped

3 stalks celery, coarsely chopped

½ cup coarsely chopped celery leaves

Large bouquet garni with 5 sprigs parsley, 4 sprigs thyme, and 2 bay leaves, tied together with string

1 teaspoon black peppercorns

2½ quarts (10 cups) water, more if needed

COMBINE THE ONIONS, leeks, carrots, celery, celery leaves, bouquet garni, and peppercorns in a large stockpot. Add cold water to cover and bring just to a boil over medium-high heat. Reduce the heat to medium-low and simmer until the stock is well flavored, about 1 hour. Take the pot from the heat and let cool, then strain through a cheesecloth-lined sieve into a large bowl; discard the solids. Refrigerate for up to 3 days before using, or freeze for up to 3 months.

MAKES ABOUT 2 QUARTS (8 CUPS)

Grilled Beef with Grapes

Typhoon!, Portland, Oregon

This is one of chef/owner Bo Kline's more nouvelle Thai dishes, a refreshingly simple composition that packs a bold flavor, thanks to the chile- and garlic-enhanced dressing. The recipe could also be transformed into something of a steak salad, with the sliced beef served over an ample bed of greens rather than just a tuft of mesclun alongside for garnish.

MAKES 2 SERVINGS

2 top sirloin steaks (8 to 10 ounces each)
Salt and freshly ground black pepper
3 cups lightly packed mesclun greens
1 cup halved green and/or red seedless grapes

Dressing
    2 tablespoons Thai fish sauce *(nam pla)*
    2 tablespoons freshly squeezed lime juice
    1 teaspoon sugar
    1 teaspoon minced garlic
    1 teaspoon minced Thai chile or other hot chile

FOR THE DRESSING, whisk together the fish sauce, lime juice, sugar, garlic, and chile in a small bowl. Set aside.

PREHEAT AN OUTDOOR GRILL. Season the steaks with salt and pepper, rub the grill rack lightly with oil, and grill the steaks, 3 to 4 minutes per side for rare, or longer to suit your taste. Put the steaks on a cutting board and let sit, covered with foil, for 5 minutes.

SLICE THE STEAKS thinly against the grain with a sharp knife and arrange on a serving platter or individual plates. Add a mound of the mesclun greens to one side and drizzle the dressing over the greens and the beef. Scatter the grapes over the beef and serve right away.

Wasabi and Black Pepper Tuna with French Lentils and Onion Marmalade

Matt's in the Market, Seattle, Washington

One of the smallest restaurants in Seattle, this cozy perch above the Pike Place Market has a big following for its creative dishes, like this one. All the elements here complement one another beautifully—spicy tuna, earthy lentils, sweet-tangy onions—but you could also amend this recipe to use only one of the accents or even enjoy the wasabi–black pepper tuna solo, with white rice and fresh vegetables. Any leftover onion marmalade will be delicious served with roasted pork or chicken.

MAKES 4 SERVINGS

2 tablespoons wasabi powder

2 tablespoons coarsely ground black pepper

2 teaspoons kosher salt

4 ahi tuna steaks (6 ounces each)

2 to 3 tablespoons vegetable oil

Onion Marmalade

2 tablespoons vegetable oil

1 small red onion, thinly sliced

1 Anaheim chile, cored, seeded, and thinly sliced

¼ cup water

2 tablespoons sherry vinegar

2 tablespoons balsamic vinegar

½ teaspoon sugar

½ teaspoon kosher salt, plus more to taste

Pinch freshly ground black pepper

French Lentils

¼ cup plus 1 tablespoon olive oil

1 carrot, finely diced

½ onion, finely diced

1 stalk celery, finely diced

1½ teaspoons minced ginger

1¼ cups lentils

3 cups chicken stock (page 105), vegetable stock (page 141), preferably homemade, or water

¼ cup rice wine vinegar

Salt and freshly ground black pepper

FOR THE ONION MARMALADE, heat the oil in a medium saucepan over medium heat. Add the onion and chile, and cook, stirring occasionally, until the vegetables begin to soften, 8 to 10 minutes. Add the water, sherry and balsamic vinegars, sugar, salt, and pepper and simmer, stirring occasionally, until the mixture reaches a jamlike consistency, 20 to 30 minutes. Taste for seasoning, adding more salt or pepper to taste; keep warm over low heat.

FOR THE LENTILS, heat 1 tablespoon of the olive oil in a large saucepan over medium heat. Add the carrot, onion, celery, and ginger, and cook, stirring, until tender, 5 to 7 minutes. Add the lentils and stir to coat with oil. Add the stock and simmer, uncovered, until tender and the liquid has been fully absorbed, about 30 minutes. (If the lentils are tender but some liquid remains, carefully drain it off.) Take the pan from the heat and stir in the remaining ¼ cup olive oil and the rice vinegar. Season to taste with salt and pepper; keep warm over low heat.

COMBINE THE WASABI, black pepper, and salt on a plate and stir to mix evenly. Press both sides of each tuna steak in the coating mixture, patting to help it adhere.

HEAT THE OIL in a large skillet (preferably nonstick) over medium-high heat. When the oil is hot, add the tuna steaks and sear them quickly on both sides, just long enough to toast the spices, 30 to 60 seconds per side, at which point the tuna will still be quite rare. Be careful not to burn the wasabi; if you wish to cook the tuna further, transfer it to a baking sheet and bake in a 400°F oven for a few minutes longer, though tuna is best cooked to no more than medium.

TO SERVE, SPOON THE LENTILS onto individual plates and set the tuna steaks on top. Top with a generous spoonful of the onion marmalade and serve right away.

Grilled Venison Tournedos with Blue Cheese and Basil Ravioli

The Aerie Resort, Malahat, British Columbia

The earthy, gamy flavor of venison—now farm-raised in British Columbia and other parts of the Northwest—is perfectly complemented by the rich tang of the blue cheese–filled ravioli and further embellished by a tart-sweet sauce of sour cherries. Northwest sour cherries are grown primarily for commercial products (such as canned cherry pie filling), though they are available seasonally in farmers markets. In place of the fresh cherries, you could use sour cherry preserves (omitting the brown sugar) or frozen sour cherries.

At The Aerie Resort, they use a stovetop grill rack to mark the tournedos before finishing the cooking in the oven. The simplified technique described here cooks the venison fully on an outdoor grill, though you could also broil it. Beef tenderloin or four filet mignon steaks can be used in place of the venison tenderloin.

MAKES 4 SERVINGS

1¼ pounds venison tenderloin, trimmed
4 thin slices bacon
4 basil leaves, for garnish

Blue Cheese and Basil Ravioli

¾ cup all-purpose flour
1 egg
1 tablespoon olive oil
½ teaspoon salt
2 medium Yukon Gold potatoes (about 8 ounces), halved
¾ cup crumbled blue cheese
2 tablespoons minced basil
1 shallot, minced
1 clove garlic, minced
¼ cup whipping cream
4 tablespoons unsalted butter, at room temperature
Salt and freshly ground black pepper

Sour Cherry Sauce

3 tablespoons unsalted butter

2 tablespoons packed light brown sugar

8 ounces sour cherries, pitted

2 shallots, minced

2 sprigs thyme

2 bay leaves

2 cups dry red wine

1 cup veal or beef stock, preferably homemade (page 171)

Salt and freshly ground black pepper

FOR THE RAVIOLI DOUGH, combine the flour, egg, olive oil, and salt in a mixer with the paddle attachment and mix at medium speed until well combined and the dough is smooth. Form the pasta dough into a ball, wrap it in plastic, and refrigerate for 30 minutes to 1 hour before rolling out.

FOR THE RAVIOLI FILLING, put the potatoes in a small pan with cold water to cover. Bring to a boil over high heat, then reduce the heat to medium-high and simmer until the potatoes are tender when pierced with the tip of a knife, 15 to 20 minutes. Drain the potatoes in a colander in the sink and let sit until the steam subsides (this draws off excess moisture so the mashed potatoes won't be too wet). Peel away and discard the skin, then mash the potatoes in a medium bowl with half the blue cheese and the minced basil, shallot, and garlic until well blended and smooth. Stir in the cream, 2 tablespoons of the butter, and the remaining blue cheese, with salt and pepper to taste. Set the filling aside while rolling out the pasta dough.

FLATTEN THE BALL OF PASTA DOUGH with the heel of your hand, lightly dust it with flour, and roll it through the widest roller setting of a pasta machine. Fold the ends inward so that the packet is about 4 inches across, then run the pasta through the rollers again, with the folded edges at either side. Repeat this process 6 to 8 more times through the widest roller setting to further knead the dough and make it very smooth, dusting the dough lightly with flour as needed. Decrease the roller width by one setting and pass the full length of the pasta sheet through the rollers. Continue rolling out the dough at thinner and thinner settings until the dough is about $\frac{1}{16}$ inch thick.

LAY THE SHEET OF PASTA DOUGH horizontally on the work surface, squaring off each of the ends with a sharp knife. Very lightly brush one half of the dough with water and top the moistened dough with 2 rows of the blue cheese filling, using about 1 tablespoon of filling for each and leaving about an inch between the rows. Fold the other half of the dough over, matching up the edges. Use your fingers to press the dough down around all the mounds, to fully enclose the filling and securely seal the pasta dough. With a pasta cutter or sharp knife, cut between the mounds of filling to form the individual ravioli. Set the ravioli aside on a lightly floured baking sheet.

FOR THE SAUCE, melt 1 tablespoon of the butter in a medium saucepan over medium-high heat. Add the brown sugar and cook, stirring constantly, until the sugar is melted and begins to caramelize, 2 to 3 minutes. Stir in the cherries, shallots, thyme sprigs, and bay leaves and cook, stirring constantly, until the cherries begin to soften and give off their juices, 2 to 3 minutes. Slowly pour in the red wine and boil until the liquid is reduced by about two-thirds, 15 to 20 minutes. Add the stock and boil to reduce by half, about 10 minutes longer. Strain the sauce and return it to the saucepan. Whisk in the remaining 2 tablespoons butter and season the sauce to taste with salt and pepper. Set aside over very low heat until ready to serve.

TO COOK THE RAVIOLI, bring a large pot of salted water to a boil. Add the ravioli and, when they float to the top of the pot, cook for about 3 minutes longer for them to be fully cooked. When done, remove them from the water with a slotted spoon and drain well in a colander set in the sink. Discard the pasta water, add the remaining 2 tablespoons butter to the pan, and let it melt before returning the ravioli to the pan. Toss gently to coat the ravioli in butter. Keep warm over very low heat.

PREHEAT AN OUTDOOR GRILL.

CUT THE VENISON TENDERLOIN into 4 equal portions, flattening them slightly with your fist so that the tournedos are no more than 2 inches thick. Wrap a slice of bacon around the outside of each tournedo and secure with a piece of kitchen string; season the meat with salt and pepper. Lightly rub the grill rack with oil and add the tournedos, cooking until medium, 3 to 5 minutes on each side.

TO SERVE, SPOON SOME OF THE SAUCE in the center of individual warmed plates. Set a tournedo on the sauce and top with a few of the ravioli, garnishing each plate with a basil leaf. Serve right away.

Pacific Rim Crab Cakes with Sesame-Ginger Aïoli

The Place Bar and Grill,
Friday Harbor, Washington

Asian themes make a natural contribution to many Northwest recipes, particularly those that take advantage of the region's rich supply of seafood. This crab cake recipe is a prime example, with ingredients like lemongrass and ginger, a welcome complement to the sweet Dungeness crabmeat. "This has become an incredibly popular signature seasonal dish for us, both as an appetizer and as an entrée," says chef/owner Steven Anderson, who notes that the versatile aïoli goes well with chilled shellfish such as shrimp, mussels, and clams, or alongside grilled salmon or tuna.

The ingredient list is on the long side, but don't let that intimidate you. Once the chopping is done (enlist a sous-chef if you can), the recipe is easy to put together. And the results are well worth the effort.

MAKES 4 TO 6 SERVINGS

---

2 tablespoons canola oil, plus more for sautéing
3 tablespoons finely chopped yellow onion
3 tablespoons finely chopped celery
3 tablespoons finely chopped red bell pepper
3 tablespoons finely chopped yellow bell pepper
1 tablespoon minced lemongrass (the tender inner core only)
1 teaspoon finely chopped ginger
1 teaspoon finely chopped garlic
½ teaspoon minced Thai chile or dried red pepper flakes
1¼ pounds Dungeness crabmeat (about 7½ ounces)
¾ cup good-quality mayonnaise, preferably homemade (page 61)
2 tablespoons chopped cilantro
2 tablespoons chopped basil
2 tablespoons chopped flat-leaf (Italian) parsley
1 tablespoon freshly squeezed lemon juice
1 tablespoon freshly squeezed lime juice
Pinch freshly ground white or black pepper

¾ cup plus 6 tablespoons panko bread crumbs or other dried bread crumbs,
 plus more if needed
¾ cup all-purpose flour, plus more if needed
1 egg
⅓ cup milk

Sesame-Ginger Aïoli
1 egg yolk
1½ tablespoons freshly squeezed lemon juice
1½ tablespoons freshly squeezed lime juice
4 teaspoons chopped ginger
1 tablespoon chopped garlic
¾ cup canola oil
½ cup Asian sesame oil
1 tablespoon rice wine vinegar
1 teaspoon soy sauce
¼ teaspoon salt
⅛ teaspoon *sambal oelek* or other hot chile sauce
Pinch sugar

HEAT THE OIL in a large skillet over medium heat. Add the onion, celery, red
and yellow bell peppers, lemongrass, ginger, garlic, and chile and sauté until
tender and aromatic, 3 to 5 minutes. Set the vegetables aside to cool.

FOR THE SESAME-GINGER AÏOLI, put the yolk, lemon juice, lime juice, ginger, and garlic in a food processor and blend until smooth. With the motor
running, begin adding the canola oil a few drops at a time until you see that
an emulsion is beginning to form (the mixture will start to thicken), then continue adding the canola oil in a thin stream, followed by the sesame oil, also
in a thin, steady stream. Finally, add the vinegar, soy sauce, salt, chile sauce,
and sugar, and process to thoroughly blend. Taste the aïoli for seasoning, then
transfer it to a bowl, cover, and refrigerate until ready to serve.

PICK OVER THE CRABMEAT to remove any bits of shell or cartilage, then
gently squeeze to remove excess liquid. When the vegetable mixture has
cooled, pour off any liquid that may have accumulated in the skillet so the
crab cakes won't be too wet. Add the crabmeat, mayonnaise, cilantro, basil,
parsley, lemon juice, lime juice, and white pepper. Mix together well, then add
6 tablespoons of the bread crumbs and stir well to thoroughly combine all the
ingredients.

PUT THE FLOUR ON A PLATE AND SET ASIDE. Whisk together the egg and milk in a small bowl and set it next to the flour. Put the remaining ¾ cup bread crumbs on another plate and set it next to the egg mixture; scatter more bread crumbs on a tray or a baking sheet.

SCOOP UP ABOUT A SCANT ½ CUP OF THE CRABMEAT MIXTURE and form it into a ball. Roll the ball in the flour, patting to remove the excess, then dip it in the egg mixture, and finally roll it in the bread crumbs. Flatten the ball into a patty about 3 inches in diameter and ½ inch thick, and set it on the prepared tray while making the remaining crab cakes; you should have 12 crab cakes in all.

HEAT ABOUT ¼ INCH OF OIL in a large, heavy skillet over medium heat. When the oil is hot, gently add about half of the crab cakes and fry until browned and heated through, about 3 minutes on each side. Keep the cooked crab cakes warm in a low oven while finishing the rest. Serve right away, with a dollop of aïoli alongside each serving, passing the rest separately.

ASIAN INFLUENCES

As the regional cuisine of the Northwest began to gain national attention in the 1980s, one of the predominant themes that emerged was the Asian influence found in the most popular restaurants of the region. "Pacific Rim cuisine" became synonymous with the Northwest style, as local chefs and home cooks borrowed liberally from Japanese, Chinese, Thai, Vietnamese, and other Asian cuisines to create a seemingly new regional cooking style. Much earlier in the twentieth century, Asian populations from a wide variety of countries began to arrive and call the Northwest home, bringing with them their culinary traditions and favorite culinary products. Through the years those gastronomic contributions have increasingly been incorporated into the definition of Northwest cuisine. Ginger and sesame oil, Thai fish sauce and kaffir lime are far more common in our area than saffron, smoked paprika, and other trans-Atlantic contributions to American cuisine.

What makes the Asian influences here so compelling is that most often it is individual ingredients, rather than a traditional dish, that are the source of inspiration. The Pacific Rim Crab Cakes with Sesame-Ginger Aïoli (page 149) are an outstanding example, the sweet crabmeat accentuated by the aromatic flavoring of lemongrass, ginger, Thai chile, and cilantro. Even the aïoli is embellished with sesame oil and ginger. Five-spice powder shows up in a marinade for quail (page 47) and as a rub for duck (page 128). Pungent, flavorful fermented black beans add depth of flavor to clams steamed with sake and soy sauce (page 38), wasabi powder coats tuna steaks before searing (page 144), and *togarashi* spice mix livens up local sweet shrimp in a distinctive salad (page 102).

Today, such Pacific influences are fully woven into the cooking style of the Northwest, and you'll find these flavors—whether a subtle drop of sesame oil or a full array of Asian elements—used in kitchens throughout the region. Chefs and home cooks are no longer simply borrowing from these cuisines; instead they have made the ingredients and techniques very much a part of their own repertoires.

Pasta with Bacon, Blue Cheese, and Tomatoes

Lindaman's Gourmet-to-Go,
Spokane, Washington

This pasta dish has a bit of everything: bacon and blue cheese for rich, savory flavor; tomatoes and greens for fresh, bright contrast; basil and garlic for aromatic embellishment, all tossed with chewy pasta for texture. Merrilee Lindaman uses gemelli pasta, a twisted double strand (*gemelli* is Italian for "twins") cut into short pieces; other pasta shapes, such as bowties or fusilli, could be used instead.

MAKES 4 SERVINGS

---

10 ounces bacon
½ cup olive oil
1 tablespoon minced garlic
8 ounces dried gemelli pasta
2 large tomatoes, cored and coarsely chopped
3 ounces greens (such as mesclun mix), rinsed and large leaves torn
¾ cup crumbled blue cheese
2 tablespoons chopped basil
Salt and freshly ground black pepper

COOK THE BACON in a large skillet over medium-high heat until very crisp, about 5 minutes, turning the pieces a few times so they cook evenly. Remove the bacon from the pan, drain on paper towels, and let cool, then cut the bacon strips into ½-inch pieces; set aside.

BRING A LARGE PAN OF SALTED WATER TO A BOIL for boiling the pasta. While the water is heating, put the olive oil in a small saucepan over medium heat, add the garlic, and cook gently just until the garlic floats to the top, 2 to 3 minutes; take the pan from the heat and set aside.

WHEN THE WATER IS AT A ROLLING BOIL, add the pasta and cook until al dente, about 10 minutes. Drain well and put the pasta in a large bowl. Drizzle the warm garlic oil over the pasta and toss to coat it evenly. Add the bacon, tomatoes, greens, blue cheese, and basil, with salt and pepper to taste. Toss to evenly mix and serve immediately.

MAINS

Although crawfish are gathered in the Northwest, the harvest is so small that generally only specialty fish markets carry them. If you can't find them, shrimp are just as tasty here. For the halibut, choose thicker fillet portions so you'll have an easier time cutting the pocket for the stuffing.

MAKES 4 SERVINGS

¼ cup unsalted butter
1 cup chopped onion
½ cup chopped green bell pepper
1 teaspoon minced garlic
Pinch cayenne pepper, or to taste
Salt and freshly ground black pepper
½ cup Dungeness crabmeat (about 3 ounces)
½ cup grated sharp cheddar cheese
⅓ cup dried bread crumbs
1 egg, lightly beaten
4 halibut fillet pieces (8 ounces each)

Crawfish Cream Sauce
    1 red bell pepper
    2 tablespoons olive oil
    1 cup chopped onion
    ½ cup chopped green bell pepper
    1 teaspoon minced garlic
    Pinch cayenne pepper, or to taste
    Salt and freshly ground black pepper
    8 ounces shelled crawfish tails or peeled and deveined medium shrimp
    2 cups half-and-half
    ½ cup freshly grated Parmesan cheese

FOR THE CRAWFISH CREAM SAUCE, roast the red pepper over a gas flame or under the broiler until the skin blackens, turning occasionally to roast evenly, about 10 minutes total. Put the pepper in a plastic bag, securely seal the bag, and set aside to cool. When the pepper is cool enough to handle, peel away and discard the skin. Remove the core and seeds and finely chop the pepper.

HEAT THE OLIVE OIL in a medium saucepan over medium heat. Add the onion, green pepper, garlic, and roasted red pepper. Sauté, stirring, until the onion begins to soften and the mixture is aromatic, 2 to 3 minutes. Season with the cayenne pepper and salt and pepper to taste and continue to cook, stirring occasionally, until the vegetables are tender, 10 to 12 minutes. If using raw shrimp, add them to the pan and sauté until just opaque through, 2 to 3 minutes, and then add the half-and-half. If using cooked crawfish or shrimp, simply add them to the pan with the half-and-half. Increase the heat to medium-high and simmer until reduced by half, about 10 minutes. Add the Parmesan and cook just until the cheese melts. Taste the sauce for seasoning, adding more cayenne, salt, or pepper to taste. Keep warm over very low heat while cooking the halibut.

PREHEAT THE OVEN to 375°F. Lightly oil a heavy baking dish.

MELT THE BUTTER in a medium saucepan over medium heat. Add the onion, green pepper, and garlic and sauté, stirring, until the onion begins to soften and the mixture is aromatic, 2 to 3 minutes. Season with cayenne, salt, and pepper to taste. Continue cooking, stirring occasionally, until the vegetables are tender, about 10 minutes. Take the pan from the heat and let cool slightly.

PICK OVER THE CRABMEAT to remove any bits of shell or cartilage and squeeze gently to remove excess liquid. In a medium bowl, stir together the crab, cheese, bread crumbs, and egg. Add the onion mixture and stir to evenly blend.

CUT A HORIZONTAL POCKET into the side of each halibut fillet, being careful to keep the other 3 sides intact while making a sizeable pocket to hold the stuffing. Spoon one-quarter of the stuffing into each halibut piece and set the stuffed halibut in the baking dish, seasoning the fish lightly with salt and pepper. Bake until the halibut is opaque through the thickest part and the stuffing is hot, about 20 minutes.

TO SERVE, SET THE HALIBUT FILLETS on individual plates, spoon the crawfish cream sauce over them, and serve right away.

Smoked Pork Loin with Apple-Onion Relish

Dolce Skamania Lodge,
Stevenson, Washington

Smoking can seem daunting, although the technique really isn't complicated and the results are so rewarding. You don't even need a fancy smoker; you can smoke on almost any outdoor grill that has a lid. The other vital element is time, both for the brining (essential to infuse flavor and preserve moisture in the meat) and the slow, low-temperature cooking.

The chefs at Dolce Skamania Lodge use hickory or mesquite chips, but alder or other hardwood could be used as well. At the lodge, this aromatic pork with its chutneylike apple-onion relish is served with mashed potatoes embellished with Boursin herb cheese.

MAKES 6 TO 8 SERVINGS

3 quarts (12 cups) water
½ cup kosher salt
½ cup packed light brown sugar
¼ cup balsamic vinegar
2 cinnamon sticks
1 teaspoon dried red pepper flakes
1 teaspoon black peppercorns
1 teaspoon whole allspice
2 bay leaves
2 sprigs thyme
2 sprigs oregano
5 whole cloves
1 whole boneless pork loin (about 2½ pounds)
2 cups smoking chips
Freshly ground black pepper

Apple-Onion Relish
2 tablespoons olive oil
1 large onion, thinly sliced
¼ cup packed light brown sugar
¼ cup apple cider
2 tablespoons red wine vinegar

2 bay leaves
2 cinnamon sticks
½ teaspoon dried red pepper flakes
Salt and freshly ground black pepper
2 Granny Smith apples, cored and cut into ½-inch dice
½ teaspoon ground allspice

TO BRINE THE PORK, combine the water, salt, brown sugar, vinegar, cinnamon sticks, red pepper flakes, peppercorns, allspice, bay leaves, thyme, oregano, and cloves in a large saucepan. Bring the water just to a boil, stirring occasionally to help the salt dissolve, then set aside to cool completely. Put the pork loin in a large bowl, pour the cooled brine over it, cover, and refrigerate for at least 8 hours or overnight.

THE NEXT DAY, prepare a smoker for low heat (about 250°F). If using a regular grill, prepare it for indirect heat (for a charcoal grill, make 2 small piles of briquettes on either side rather than in the center; for a gas grill, follow the manufacturer's directions). Soak the smoking chips in cold water. Take the pork loin from the brine, rinse briefly under cold water, and pat dry with paper towels. Season the pork well with pepper. Drain the smoking chips well and scatter them over the coals. Set the pork on the rack, cover the smoker or grill with the lid, and smoke until the meat has an internal temperature of 165°F, about 2 hours. (You will probably need to replenish the charcoal, a few briquettes at a time, during the smoking process.)

WHILE THE PORK IS SMOKING, prepare the apple-onion relish. Heat the olive oil in a large skillet over medium heat. Add the onion and cook, stirring often, until it is translucent and tender, 5 to 7 minutes. Add the brown sugar and cook, stirring, until the sugar is melted and evenly coats the onion, about 5 minutes. Stir in the apple cider, vinegar, bay leaves, cinnamon sticks, and red pepper flakes, with a pinch of salt and pepper. Cook until the liquid is reduced by half, stirring occasionally, 3 to 5 minutes. Stir in the apple and allspice and cook until the apple is tender, about 15 minutes. Taste the relish for seasoning, adding more salt or pepper to taste. Remove the bay leaves and cinnamon sticks and set the relish aside. (The relish can be made up to 2 days in advance and refrigerated; let it come to room temperature before serving.)

TO SERVE, CUT THE SMOKED PORK LOIN into ½-inch slices and arrange them on individual plates. Spoon some of the apple relish alongside the pork and serve right away.

Nettle and Almond Stuffed Skate Wing with Nettle Cream Sauce

Oceanwood Country Inn,
Mayne Island, British Columbia

A prized fish in Europe, skate doesn't have much of a following in North America. The fish is found in Northwest waters but tends to make it to local markets only sporadically. Look for skate wings at Asian markets, or ask at upscale seafood markets. You could also use sole fillets or other thin white fish fillets, though the firmer skate flesh has a distinctive, almost shellfishlike flavor. You'll need less of other fish fillets, about 2 pounds, as the yield from skate is lower because the cartilage must be cut away from the flesh.

"Nettles can be found in abundance in British Columbia and throughout the Northwest," notes innkeeper Jonathan Chilvers, who offers a brief lesson: "They have heart-shaped, serrated leaves covered with stiff hairs, which release a dose of stinging formic acid when touched. For relief, rub the sting with vinegar. Better yet, wear long sleeves and gloves when you pick them. Quick cooking completely destroys the stinging properties of the plant; then it becomes a most delicious green vegetable." If you're unable to find nettles, the recipe can be made with spinach instead.

MAKES 4 SERVINGS

½ cup slivered almonds
3 cups lightly packed nettle leaves (about 4 ounces)
2½ pounds skate wing, skin removed, cut into 4 equal pieces
Salt and freshly ground black pepper

Nettle Cream Sauce
2 cups lightly packed nettle leaves (about 2½ ounces)
1 tablespoon vegetable oil
1 large shallot, minced
1 cup fish stock (page 78) or chicken stock (page 105), preferably homemade
½ cup whipping cream

Poaching Liquid

4 cups fish stock (page 78), chicken stock (page 105), preferably
  homemade, or water

1½ cups dry white wine

2 large bay leaves

1 teaspoon whole black peppercorns

2 sprigs thyme

PREHEAT THE OVEN to 350°F. Scatter the slivered almonds in a baking pan
and toast in the oven until lightly browned and aromatic, 5 to 7 minutes, gently shaking the pan once or twice to help the nuts toast evenly. Set aside.

BRING A MEDIUM SAUCEPAN OF SALTED WATER TO A BOIL and prepare a
medium bowl of ice water. When the water is at a rolling boil, add 3 cups of
the nettle leaves and cook just until wilted and bright green, 20 to 30 seconds.
Drain well and plunge the nettles immediately into the ice water to fully chill
and set the vivid green color. When chilled, drain again and dry well on paper
towels.

USE A SHARP KNIFE TO REMOVE THE SKATE flesh from the strip of cartilage that runs through the fish. Season the fish pieces with salt and pepper.
Arrange the nettles evenly over each piece and sprinkle with the slivered
almonds. Roll each piece up pinwheel fashion, beginning at the narrow end,
and secure well with kitchen string, leaving a little extra string to help you
remove the skate roll from the poaching liquid.

FOR THE NETTLE CREAM SAUCE, blanch the nettle leaves as above. Heat
the oil in a small saucepan over medium heat, add the shallot, and sauté, stirring, until tender and aromatic, 2 to 3 minutes. Add the nettles and stock,
with salt and pepper to taste. Bring to a boil over high heat, then return the
heat to medium and simmer for 5 minutes. Whisk the cream into the nettle
mixture, pour into a blender, and blend until very smooth, 2 to 3 minutes.
Return the cream mixture to the saucepan and check the seasoning, adding
more salt or pepper if needed. Keep warm over low heat while poaching the
skate.

FOR THE POACHING LIQUID, combine the stock, wine, bay leaves, peppercorns, and thyme in a large saucepan and bring to a boil over high heat. Add
the skate rolls, return the liquid to a boil, then reduce the heat to medium
and simmer to gently poach until the skate is just opaque through, 10 to 12

minutes. If the rolls are not fully submerged in the liquid, turn them gently once or twice while cooking.

TO SERVE, REMOVE THE SKATE ROLLS from the pan and discard the strings. Set the skate rolls on individual plates and pour the warm nettle cream sauce over and around them. Serve right away.

Grilled Salt Spring Island Lamb Burgers

Splitz Grill, Whistler, British Columbia

Salt Spring Island off the eastern coast of Vancouver Island is the largest and best-known of British Columbia's Gulf Islands. Many herds of sheep are raised on the salt-washed island, producing some of the best lamb in the region, the same lamb used by chefs at Splitz Grill for these delicious burgers. They offer a range of options for burger toppings, including the tzatziki and feta here, as well as baba ghanouj (a flavorful eggplant purée), sliced onion, cucumber, and tomato. The tzatziki will be best if made at least a few hours ahead.

You may need to make a special request of your butcher for the ground lamb; not all stores carry it on a regular basis. For fresh bread crumbs, cut the crust away from 3 slices of white bread. Tear the bread into pieces, put them in a food processor, and pulse to the texture of fine crumbs.

MAKES 4 SERVINGS

1½ pounds ground lean lamb
1 cup fresh bread crumbs
1 egg, lightly beaten
4 cloves garlic, minced
1 tablespoon minced mint
1 teaspoon cumin seeds
1 teaspoon salt
½ teaspoon freshly ground black pepper
4 kaiser rolls
½ cup crumbed feta cheese

Tzatziki
½ English cucumber, peeled and seeded
½ cup plain yogurt
½ cup sour cream
Juice of ½ lemon
2 cloves garlic, minced
Hot pepper sauce
Salt and freshly ground black pepper

FOR THE TZATZIKI, grate the cucumber into a medium bowl, pouring off the liquid that accumulates in the bowl. Add the yogurt, sour cream, lemon juice, and garlic, with pepper sauce, salt, and pepper to taste. Cover and refrigerate until ready to serve.

PREHEAT AN OUTDOOR GRILL.

IN A LARGE BOWL, combine the lamb, bread crumbs, egg, garlic, mint, cumin seeds, salt, and pepper and mix well until all the ingredients are thoroughly combined. Form the lamb mixture into 4 patties about 1 inch thick.

WHEN THE GRILL IS HEATED, lightly brush the grill rack with oil. Add the lamb burgers and grill, covered, until medium to medium-well, 5 to 6 minutes per side, or to your taste. While the burgers are cooking, lightly toast the kaiser rolls around the outer edge of the grill. Just before taking the burgers from the grill, top each with some of the feta cheese, cover the grill, and cook just until the cheese begins to melt, a few seconds longer.

SERVE THE BURGERS on the toasted kaiser rolls, topping each with a spoonful of the tzatziki.

Wild Mushroom, Leek, and Wild Rice Cakes

Silverwater Cafe,
Port Townsend, Washington

This is one of the most popular vegetarian entrées at Silverwater Cafe, though the flavorful cakes could also be served as a hearty appetizer in smaller portions to serve eight. The creamy mustard sauce is a wonderfully aromatic finish.

MAKES 4 SERVINGS

3 cups water
1 cup wild rice
¼ cup unsalted butter
6 ounces chanterelle, oyster, and/or shiitake mushrooms, brushed clean, trimmed, and thinly sliced
2 large leeks, white and pale green parts only, split, cleaned, and thinly sliced
1 tablespoon minced fresh sage or 1 teaspoon dried sage
1 teaspoon salt
¼ teaspoon freshly ground white pepper
¾ cup dried bread crumbs (seasoned or regular)
4 eggs, lightly beaten
1 tablespoon chopped flat-leaf (Italian) parsley
3 to 4 tablespoons olive oil

Dijon Sauce
1 tablespoon olive oil
½ cup thinly sliced onion
2 teaspoons packed light brown sugar
1 cup whipping cream
½ cup Dijon mustard

COMBINE THE WATER and wild rice in a medium saucepan and bring to a boil over high heat. Reduce the heat to medium-low, cover, and cook until the rice is tender, about 1 hour.

WHILE THE RICE IS COOKING, make the Dijon sauce. Heat the olive oil in a saucepan over medium-low heat. Add the onion and cook slowly, stirring occasionally, until soft and lightly caramelized, 15 to 20 minutes. Add the brown sugar and cook, stirring, until dissolved, about 5 minutes. Stir in the cream and mustard, increase the heat to medium, and simmer until slightly thickened and the flavors are nicely blended, about 15 minutes, stirring frequently. Set aside.

WHEN THE RICE IS COOKED, drain off any remaining water from the pan and transfer the rice to a large bowl; set aside to cool.

MELT THE BUTTER in a medium skillet over medium heat. Add the mushrooms and leeks and cook, stirring, until tender, about 15 minutes. Add the sage, salt, and pepper and cook gently for 5 minutes, stirring constantly. Take the skillet from the heat and set aside to cool.

ADD THE COOLED MUSHROOM MIXTURE to the rice and toss to mix, then add the bread crumbs, eggs, and parsley, stirring to evenly mix.

HEAT 2 TABLESPOONS OF THE OIL in a large, heavy skillet over medium heat. Scoop heaping ¼-cupfuls of the rice mixture into the skillet, a few at a time, flattening them slightly to make an even cake. Cook until golden brown and cooked through, 3 to 5 minutes on each side. As each batch is done, transfer the rice cakes to a baking sheet and keep warm in a low oven while cooking the rest, adding more oil to the skillet as needed.

TO SERVE, REHEAT THE DIJON SAUCE over medium heat. Arrange the rice cakes on individual plates, drizzle the Dijon sauce over and around them, and serve right away.

Andalusian Flank Steak

Cafe Langley, Langley, Washington

Flank steak truly shines on the grill, the hot fire giving the lean meat plenty of flavor, enhanced by this spicy marinade. At Cafe Langley, the chef/owner Garibyan brothers prefer to use mesquite charcoal, which burns very hot and adds another element of flavor to the meat. Scotch bonnet chiles are among the hottest around; take care to wash your hands (or use plastic gloves), the knife, and the cutting board immediately after preparing them.

MAKES 4 SERVINGS

1 flank steak (1½ to 2 pounds)

Marinade
1 bunch green onions, finely chopped
¼ cup extra virgin olive oil
¼ cup Worcestershire sauce
3 cloves garlic, minced
1 teaspoon ground cumin
1 teaspoon ground allspice
1 teaspoon thyme
1 teaspoon salt
½ teaspoon freshly grated or ground nutmeg
½ teaspoon seeded and minced Scotch bonnet or habanero chile
½ teaspoon freshly ground black pepper

Steak Sauce
2 red bell peppers
½ cup beef stock, preferably homemade (page 171)
¼ cup diced prosciutto (about 1 ounce)
2 tablespoons packed light or dark brown sugar

SCORE BOTH SIDES OF THE FLANK STEAK in a crisscross pattern with the tip of a sharp knife and put it in a shallow dish just large enough to hold it.

FOR THE MARINADE, combine the green onions, olive oil, Worcestershire sauce, garlic, cumin, allspice, thyme, salt, nutmeg, chile, and black pepper in a small bowl and stir to mix. Pour half of the marinade over the steak, rubbing it well into the scored slits, then turn the steak over and rub the remaining marinade into the other side of the steak. Cover the dish with plastic wrap and refrigerate for at least 8 hours or overnight.

FOR THE STEAK SAUCE, roast the red peppers over a gas flame or under the broiler until the skin blackens, turning occasionally to roast evenly, about 10 minutes total. Put the peppers in a plastic bag, securely seal the bag, and set aside to cool. When the peppers are cool enough to handle, peel away and discard the skins. Remove the core and seeds, then purée the peppers in a food processor. Add the stock, prosciutto, and brown sugar and pulse a few times to evenly blend the ingredients, scraping down the sides as needed. Transfer the mixture to a medium saucepan and bring just to a boil over medium-high heat, then reduce the heat to medium-low and simmer the sauce until slightly thickened, 15 to 20 minutes, stirring occasionally. Keep warm over low heat until ready to serve. (The sauce can be made 1 day in advance and refrigerated.)

JUST BEFORE SERVING, preheat an outdoor grill. When the grill is heated, lightly brush the grill rack with oil. Take the flank steak from the marinade, allowing any excess to drip off. Grill the steak 3 to 4 minutes per side for medium-rare, about 5 minutes per side for medium, or more to suit your taste.

TRANSFER THE STEAK to a cutting board and let it sit for 5 to 10 minutes, covered with foil to keep warm. To serve, cut the flank steak across the grain into ½-inch slices at a slight angle and arrange them on individual plates, spooning the warm sauce alongside.

Thai-Style Halibut and Shrimp en Papillote

Kasteel Franssen, Oak Harbor, Washington

Truly a blend of culinary styles, this recipe uses the classic French papillote technique (cooking foods encased in parchment paper) for Northwest halibut embellished with aromatic Asian accents. Choose thinner halibut fillet portions, which will cook in about the same time as the vegetables and shrimp. Cooking in paper captures all the moisture and aroma during cooking, so the fish has a maximum of flavor when your guests dig in. The sweet chili sauce used in the sauce recipe is a staple of Southeast Asian cuisine; it can be found in Asian markets and on well-stocked grocery shelves.

MAKES 4 SERVINGS

4 cups trimmed and sliced mixed vegetables (such as carrots, zucchini, baby bok choy, snow peas, and napa cabbage)

1 cup bean sprouts

4 halibut fillet pieces (6 ounces each)

4 large shrimp, peeled and deveined

2 green onions, sliced

1 tablespoon slivered lemongrass

1 egg white, lightly beaten (optional)

Sauce

1 tablespoon peanut or vegetable oil

2 teaspoons minced garlic

2 teaspoons minced ginger

½ cup sweet chili sauce

¼ cup rice wine vinegar

2 teaspoons soy sauce

FOR THE SAUCE, heat the oil in a small saucepan over medium heat. Add the garlic and ginger and cook, stirring, until aromatic and tender but not browned, about 1 minute. Add the sweet chili sauce, vinegar, and soy sauce and bring just to a boil over medium-high heat. Take the pan from the heat and set aside to cool.

PREHEAT THE OVEN to 400°F.

CUT 4 PIECES OF PARCHMENT PAPER about 18 inches long, and fold each piece in half lengthwise. Beginning about 3 inches down one of the folded sides, trace an oversized half heart, as if you were making a big valentine, and cut along the traced lines.

OPEN THE HEARTS ON THE COUNTER, or work with one heart at a time if you don't have enough counter space. On one half of each piece of paper, scatter one-quarter of the mixed vegetables and bean sprouts in the center. Top with a piece of halibut and 1 shrimp, then scatter one-quarter of the green onion and lemongrass over the top. Avoid creating a tall pile; instead, spread the vegetables out a bit, or the package will be harder to enclose. Drizzle about 1 tablespoon of the sauce over the fish. If you like, briskly beat the egg white in a small bowl with a fork and lightly brush the edge of the paper with it. This will help seal the packets.

FOLD THE OTHER HALF OF THE PARCHMENT PAPER over the filling, matching up the edges as evenly as possible. Starting at the folded edge at the top of the heart, begin making short folds that overlap slightly, working all around the open cut edges to fully seal them. When you get to the tapered end, gently twist the final fold to hold it securely.

SET THE PARCHMENT PACKAGES on 2 baking sheets and bake until they are well puffed and lightly browned, about 15 minutes. Take the sheets from the oven, carefully transfer the packets to individual plates, and serve right away. Either snip open the tops of the packets with kitchen shears or encourage your guests to simply tear their packets open with their fingers, being careful to avoid the first puff of hot steam that will rise up with wonderful cooking aromas. Pass the extra sauce separately.

HALIBUT AND BLACK COD

While salmon may seem to dominate the culinary scene when it comes to Northwest fish, the region boasts an array of other finned delights. From dozens of types of rockfish (yellow-eye being among the most common) to the ancient and firm-fleshed sturgeon to buttery-rich black cod (sablefish), the region's supply of fish gives our cooking repertoire plenty of variety.

Found primarily in the cold waters of the North Pacific, Pacific halibut, with its mildly flavored, snow-white flesh, is perhaps the second most preferred Northwest fish. The females of the species live longer and grow larger than the males, the record catch weighing nearly 500 pounds. Commercially harvested halibut average about 20 to 40 pounds. A member of the flounder family and cousin to other flatfish such as sole, the halibut is a mottled brown-gray color on top to mimic the ocean floor; the underside of the fish, seldom seen by predators, is pure white. Recipes you'll find here include Thai-Style Halibut and Shrimp en Papillote (page 167) and Stuffed Halibut with Crawfish Cream Sauce (page 154), in which the Northwest fish gets a Cajun touch.

At the other end of the flavor spectrum from halibut is black cod (also commonly known as sablefish), though it is not in the codfish family. The slender fish boasts white flesh that has a distinctly rich and pronounced flavor, with a delicate flaky texture. On page 173, you'll find Seared Sablefish with Burnt Orange Emulsion, a simple preparation served with spring vegetables, the tart-sweet emulsion providing a delicious contrast to the fish.

Braised Sirloin Tip with Artichoke Gremolata

Tulio, Seattle, Washington

Braising has been regaining popularity recently, chefs and diners alike embracing the full-flavored, tender, comforting results that the technique brings to meats of all kinds. Long, slow cooking is the key, so don't be in a rush. Gremolata, a blend of minced garlic, parsley, and lemon zest, is a common Italian garnish for braised meats, especially osso buco. Chef Walter Pisano's variation uses artichokes, a wonderful contrast to the richly flavored beef. Top-quality canned baby artichokes that aren't preserved in a heavy brine can be used in place of the fresh artichokes. Rinse them well under cold water and slice them thinly, omitting the blanching step used for the fresh artichokes.

MAKES 6 TO 8 SERVINGS

½ cup olive oil
4 pounds sirloin tip steak, cut into 2-inch cubes
Salt and freshly ground black pepper
2 onions, finely diced
2 carrots, finely diced
2 stalks celery, finely diced
2 turnips, peeled and finely diced
3 tablespoons diced prosciutto or bacon
3 tablespoons tomato paste
1 bottle (750 ml) dry red wine
3 cups beef stock, preferably homemade (recipe follows)
1 sprig rosemary
2 bay leaves

Artichoke Gremolata
1 small lemon
10 baby artichokes
3 tablespoons minced flat-leaf (Italian) parsley
¼ cup olive oil

HEAT THE OLIVE OIL in a heavy pot, such as a Dutch oven, over medium heat. Season the meat cubes with salt and pepper. Brown the meat, working in

2 or 3 batches, until all the pieces are evenly browned, 8 to 10 minutes. Return all the meat to the pot and add the onions, carrots, celery, turnips, and prosciutto. Continue to cook, stirring, until the vegetables begin to soften, about 5 minutes. Stir in the tomato paste, then pour in the wine. Reduce the heat to medium-low and simmer, covered, for 25 minutes. Add the beef stock, rosemary, and bay leaves. Simmer, partly covered, until the meat is very tender, 2 to 2½ hours longer.

SHORTLY BEFORE SERVING, prepare the artichoke gremolata. Grate the zest from the lemon and set aside. Halve the lemon and squeeze the juice into a large bowl of cold water, dropping the lemon halves in as well. Use your fingers to snap off the few outer layers of tough, darker green leaves from an artichoke. With a vegetable peeler or paring knife, peel away the skin from the artichoke base and stem. Finally, cut away the top of the artichoke to about ½ inch above the artichoke bottom. Thinly slice the artichoke, put it in the bowl of water, and repeat with the remaining artichokes.

BRING A MEDIUM PAN OF SALTED WATER TO A BOIL over high heat. Drain the artichoke slices, discard the lemon halves, and add the artichokes to the boiling water. Cook just until barely tender, 1 to 2 minutes. Drain well and let cool, then combine the artichokes with the parsley, lemon zest, and oil in a medium bowl. Toss to mix and season to taste with salt and pepper.

REMOVE THE ROSEMARY SPRIG and bay leaves from the pot. Spoon the beef and sauce into individual shallow bowls, scatter the artichoke gremolata over it, and serve right away.

Basic Beef or Veal Stock

For a light-colored stock, don't roast the bones and instead simply simmer them as directed. To increase the stock's depth of flavor, boil it after straining until reduced by about a fourth.

4 pounds beef or veal bones

2 onions, quartered

2 large carrots, coarsely chopped

2 stalks celery, coarsely chopped

Bouquet garni of 3 parsley stems, 2 sprigs thyme, and 1 bay leaf, tied together with string

1 teaspoon black peppercorns

3 quarts (12 cups) water, more if needed

PREHEAT THE OVEN to 425°F.

PUT THE BONES IN A LARGE ROASTING PAN and scatter the onions, carrots, and celery around them. Roast until the bones are well browned, about 30 minutes, stirring occasionally so the bones brown evenly.

TRANSFER THE BONES and vegetables to a stockpot. Add the bouquet garni, peppercorns, and enough cold water to cover the bones. Bring just to a boil over medium-high heat. Use a large spoon to skim away any scum that rises to the surface. Reduce the heat to medium-low and simmer, uncovered, until the stock is brown and richly flavored, 3 to 4 hours. If needed during cooking, add more hot water to the pot so that the bones remain fully covered. Take the pot from the heat and let the stock cool slightly, then lift out the bones with tongs and discard them. Strain the stock through a cheesecloth-lined sieve into a large bowl; discard the solids. Refrigerate for up to 3 days before using, or freeze for up to 3 months.

MAKES ABOUT 2 QUARTS (8 CUPS)

Seared Sablefish with Burnt Orange Emulsion

C, Vancouver, British Columbia

Sablefish, also known as black cod, comes from the cold, deep waters of the North Pacific. The delicately flaky flesh has a distinctively rich, sweet flavor, making sablefish a popular fish for smoking, though it's a standout when cooked fresh as well. This recipe has a lovely presentation: brightly colored vegetables serving as a bed for the white fish, a drizzle of rust-orange sauce finishing things off. The acidity of the vinegar-dressed vegetables and the orange juice reduction is a perfect contrast to the richness of the fish.

Chef Robert Clark uses extra virgin olive oil for the vegetables and regular olive oil for the emulsion and cooking the fish; you can do the same if you have both types of oil on hand. If not, use regular olive oil for the whole recipe.

MAKES 4 SERVINGS

¾ pound assorted vegetables, such as snow peas, baby carrots, and green
  beans, trimmed
2 shallots, thinly sliced
2 tablespoons sherry vinegar
6 tablespoons olive oil
4 navel oranges
Salt and freshly ground black pepper
4 sablefish fillet pieces (5 to 6 ounces each)
4 ounces feta cheese, crumbled

BRING A MEDIUM SAUCEPAN OF LIGHTLY SALTED WATER TO A BOIL and fill a medium bowl with ice water. Add the vegetables to the boiling water and blanch until just barely tender, 1 to 2 minutes. With a slotted spoon, transfer the vegetables to the ice water until cool, then drain them well. Put them in a medium bowl with the shallots, vinegar, and 4 tablespoons of the olive oil; toss to mix, and set aside.

PREHEAT THE BROILER.

HALVE 2 OF THE ORANGES and set them cut sides up on a baking sheet. Broil a few inches from the heat until the fruit is soft and the cut sides are lightly caramelized, 5 to 7 minutes. While still warm, juice the oranges and put the juice in a small saucepan; set aside.

CUT BOTH ENDS FROM ONE OF THE REMAINING ORANGES, just to the flesh. Set the orange upright on a cutting board and use the knife to cut away the peel and pith, following the curve of the fruit. Try not to cut away too much of the flesh with the peel. Working over a small bowl to catch the juice, hold the peeled orange in your hand and slide the knife blade down both sides of a section, cutting it from the membrane and letting it fall into the bowl. (Pick out and discard any seeds as you go.) Continue for the remaining sections. Squeeze the juice from the membrane core into the bowl. Repeat with the last orange.

POUR THE JUICE FROM THE BOWL into the saucepan with the other orange juice (the sections will be used for garnish) and cook over medium heat until the orange juice is reduced by about two-thirds, 12 to 15 minutes. Whisk in 1 tablespoon of the oil and season to taste with salt and pepper; keep warm over very low heat.

PREHEAT THE OVEN to 450°F.

GENEROUSLY SEASON THE SABLEFISH fillets with salt and pepper. Heat the remaining tablespoon of oil in a medium skillet (preferably nonstick and ovenproof) over medium-high heat. When the oil is hot, add the fish and sear until nicely browned, 2 to 3 minutes. Turn the fillets over and finish cooking the sablefish in the oven until just opaque through (if the skillet is not ovenproof, transfer the fish to a baking sheet), 4 to 8 minutes, depending on the thickness of the fish.

TO SERVE, PLACE THE VEGETABLES in the center of individual plates and crumble the feta over them. Drizzle the burnt orange juice reduction over and around the vegetables and place the seared sablefish on top. Garnish wih the orange sections and serve right away.

Chicken Breasts with Prosciutto and Cambozola

Edgewater Lodge,
Whistler, British Columbia

An aromatic combination of flavors—herbal basil, rich prosciutto, creamy Cambozola—makes a delicious complement to chicken breasts in this easy recipe from executive chef Thomas Piekarski. You'll have a bit more of the spicy tomato sauce than needed to serve with the chicken, but the extra will be delicious tossed with shrimp or simply served over pasta.

MAKES 4 SERVINGS

4 boneless, skinless chicken breasts (about 6 ounces each)
Salt and freshly ground black pepper
5 tablespoons olive oil
1 tablespoon minced basil
1 tablespoon minced garlic
4 thin slices prosciutto
4 to 6 ounces Cambozola cheese, cut into ¼-inch slices
4 sun-dried tomatoes (oil-packed or plumped dried)

Spicy Tomato Sauce

3 tablespoons olive oil
1 onion, chopped
3 cloves garlic, chopped
1 can (28 ounces) crushed plum (Roma) tomatoes
2 tablespoons minced basil
1 teaspoon minced oregano
1 teaspoon minced thyme
1 teaspoon minced rosemary
2 teaspoons hot pepper sauce, plus more to taste
1 teaspoon sugar
Salt and freshly ground black pepper

FOR THE TOMATO SAUCE, heat the olive oil in a medium saucepan over medium heat. Add the onion and garlic and cook, stirring, until tender and aromatic, 3 to 5 minutes. Add the tomatoes, basil, oregano, thyme, and rosemary and cook, partially covered, stirring occasionally, until the tomatoes are quite soft and the sauce has thickened, about 45 minutes. Stir in the hot pepper sauce and sugar, with salt and pepper to taste. Set the sauce aside until partly cooled, then purée it with an immersion blender or in a food processor (the sauce should still have a bit of texture rather than being silky smooth).

SEASON THE CHICKEN BREASTS with salt and pepper. Stir together 3 tablespoons of the oil with the basil and garlic in a shallow dish and add the chicken breasts, turning to coat them evenly. Cover and refrigerate for at least 1 hour and up to 4 hours.

JUST BEFORE COOKING the chicken, preheat the oven to 375°F.

HEAT THE REMAINING 2 TABLESPOONS OIL in a large skillet over medium-high heat. Add the chicken breasts and brown well, 2 to 3 minutes on each side. Put the chicken breasts in a baking dish and bake until just cooked through (cut into a thick portion to see that there is no more pink), about 15 minutes.

TAKE THE BAKING DISH FROM THE OVEN, leaving the oven set at 375°F. Top each breast with a slice of prosciutto, the Cambozola cheese slices, and a sun-dried tomato. Return the chicken to the oven just until the cheese softens, 1 to 2 minutes.

TO SERVE, SPOON SOME OF THE SPICY TOMATO SAUCE on the bottom of each plate, top with the chicken breasts, and serve.

Braised Lamb Shanks

Ruby's on Bainbridge,
Bainbridge Island, Washington

Lamb shanks are ideal for braising, the inexpensive, otherwise tough meat becoming richly tender and flavorful during the long, slow cooking. Here the shanks are deliciously embellished with herbes de Provence, garlic, and red wine. Polenta or mashed potatoes would be ideal alongside, plus your favorite green vegetable. Large, sturdy resealable plastic bags are another option for marinating the lamb shanks: toss them in a bowl first, then transfer to 2 or 3 bags for storage in the refrigerator.

MAKES 4 TO 6 SERVINGS

¼ cup olive oil
3 tablespoons herbes de Provence
3 tablespoons minced garlic
2 tablespoons balsamic vinegar
2 tablespoons kosher salt
1 bottle (750 ml) full-bodied red wine
4 to 6 lamb shanks (about 1 pound each)
4 cups beef stock, preferably homemade (page 171)

IN A BOWL OR BAKING DISH large enough to hold the lamb shanks, combine the olive oil, herbes de Provence, garlic, vinegar, salt, and 2 tablespoons of the red wine (the rest of the wine will be used for braising the shanks). Stir to mix evenly, then add the shanks and stir them around to coat evenly in the marinade. Cover the bowl and refrigerate for at least 6 hours or up to 24 hours.

WHEN READY TO COOK THE SHANKS, preheat the oven to 350°F.

SET THE MARINATED SHANKS in a baking dish (they should be in a single layer) or on a rimmed baking sheet. Bake the shanks until the narrow end of the meat pulls away from the bone, about 1 hour.

WHILE THE SHANKS ARE ROASTING, put the remaining red wine in a Dutch oven or other large pot. Bring the wine to a boil over high heat, then reduce the heat to medium-high and simmer until the wine is reduced by about half, about 5 minutes. Add the beef stock and set aside.

WHEN THE SHANKS HAVE FINISHED ROASTING, transfer them to the Dutch oven, leaving the oven set at 350°F. Add enough water so that the shanks are just submerged, then cover the Dutch oven and bake until the meat is very tender and falling from the bone, about 2 hours.

TAKE THE SHANKS FROM THE COOKING LIQUID and set aside on a plate, covered with foil to keep warm. Skim the fat from the surface of the cooking liquid, then bring to a boil over high heat and boil until thickened slightly, about 20 minutes. Gently reheat the shanks in the sauce, if needed, then set a shank on each plate, spoon some of the cooking liquid over them, and serve right away.

Cedar Smoked Salmon

Sazerac, Seattle, Washington

S almon truly shines when cooked with wood, whether over smoldering wood chips on a barbecue grill or on a baking plank, as is done here. Cedar baking planks are available in gourmet markets, and there are many online sources for them as well. There are two types of cooking planks: thicker, more durable planks for repeated oven use and thinner planks meant for one-time use on an outdoor grill. This salmon is cooked in the oven, though you could also cook it outdoors.

Chef Jason McClure notes that you can use any kind of honey you prefer; it adds a nice gloss and touch of sweetness, but the flavor won't matter so much against the stronger flavors of citrus zest and chipotle chiles.

MAKES 4 TO 6 SERVINGS

---

1 whole salmon fillet piece (about 2 pounds), skin on, pin bones removed
½ cup kosher salt

Honey-Citrus Glaze
½ cup honey
Grated zest of 1 lemon
Grated zest of 1 orange
Grated zest of 1 lime
1 canned *chipotle en adobo,* finely chopped

SCORE THE FLESH OF THE SALMON fillet lightly with the tip of a sharp knife in a crosshatch pattern. Lay the fillet flesh side up on a rimmed baking sheet or large pan and sprinkle the salt liberally over the fish. Cover with plastic and cure in the refrigerator for 6 to 12 hours. Rinse the fish under cold water and pat dry with paper towels. Clean out the pan the fish cured in and lay the fillet back in the pan, flesh side up.

FOR THE GLAZE, combine the honey, citrus zests, and chipotle in a small bowl and stir well to mix. Brush the glaze evenly over the salmon. Cover the pan and marinate the salmon in the refrigerator for at least 4 hours and up to 24 hours.

WHEN READY TO COOK THE FISH, preheat the oven to 350°F.

TRANSFER THE FISH TO A CEDAR PLANK and set it on a rack in the lower third of the oven. Roast the salmon until just a touch of translucence is left in the center of the thickest part of the flesh, 20 to 25 minutes. Cut the salmon into pieces and serve right away.

SALMON

Celebrated by countless generations of Northwesterners, the distinctive salmon holds an honored place among this region's culinary traditions. Beautiful in its cloak of iridescent silver with varying hues of blue and green, salmon's flavor, aroma, and color are quite unlike those of any other fish. Its compelling and complex character makes salmon one of the foods most closely associated with the Northwest.

Natives revered the salmon, which was among the most reliable and sustaining foods available, eaten fresh in season and smoked, salted, dried, or otherwise preserved for consuming the rest of the year. They valued not only the nutritive aspects of the fish but also the strength, vitality, and grace that the fish represented. These are, indeed, distinguished creatures.

Salmon hatch from eggs that have been deposited on rocky river beds— often a hundred miles or more upstream from the mouth of the river. Juvenile salmon may spend a year or more in fresh water before heading downstream and into the Pacific Ocean, where they spend the bulk of their lives. When mature (from about a year up to seven years, depending on the species), the salmon are mysteriously drawn back to not only the specific river in which they spawned, but to the exact location along the river where the fish first hatched. Once salmon reenter fresh water from the ocean, they cease eating, relying on the stored fat reserves in their flesh for energy. The farther the fish are due to swim, the more fat they must store, which is why fish from the 2,000-plus-mile Yukon River and the nearly 300-mile Copper River are so notably rich and flavorful.

As an ingredient in our kitchens, salmon brings a good deal of flavor and character to any recipe. Simple grilled salmon is a regional classic, the earthy-aromatic elements of outdoor grilling melding beautifully with the richness of the fish. Add a handful of wood chips to the coals and the marriage is even more tasty. In this book, you'll find a Grilled Salmon with Stone Fruit Compote (page 136) and a Honey Peppered Salmon with Tomato Ginger Sauce (page 184). A woody essence can also be achieved by roasting the fish on a baking plank, as you'll find with Cedar Smoked Salmon (page 179). Even on the breakfast table fresh salmon is paired with smoked salmon in a flavorful kedgeree with curry-imbued rice (page 31).

KING SALMON: Also known by the Native name chinook (which is the name of a Native tribe as well), the king salmon is the largest of all Pacific salmon, averaging 15 to 20 pounds, with specimens of more than 40 pounds not uncommon. A 126-pound king dating back to 1949 is the largest on record. The flesh has a moderately pronounced pink-orange hue and a relatively high level of fat, which promotes the distinctive rich flavor. An important commercial species, the king salmon catch is typically smaller than that of other species, but high demand brings top dollar.

SOCKEYE SALMON: Also known as red salmon, sockeye sport the most deeply colored flesh, a near crimson orange. The fat level is a bit lower than that of king salmon, so the fish is flavorful but not quite as rich. The sockeye harvest is significant, both in poundage and in dollar value, making it the most commercially valuable salmon. The average weight of sockeye salmon is about 6 to 8 pounds. The most important market for fresh sockeye is Japan, where its deep red color is particularly revered.

COHO SALMON: Coho or silver salmon are roughly the same size as sockeye, with still lower fat levels, so the flavor is a bit less pronounced but is still well regarded. The color of the flesh is classic "salmon," much like that of the king salmon. The average size of coho salmon is 8 to 10 pounds.

CHUM SALMON: Sometimes called the keta or fall salmon, the latter hints at the fact that this fish's harvest comes in late summer to early fall, while many other salmon peak in early to mid summer. Paler in flesh and lower in fat than most other salmon, the chum is delicately flavored and averages about 8 pounds.

PINK SALMON: The smallest of the Pacific Coast salmon, pinks (sometimes known as "humpies" because of the arched hump that develops on males shortly before spawning) consistently represent the largest catch of Pacific salmon, a significant mainstay for the fishing industry. The softly hued flesh is the leanest of all the salmon. The pink salmon is not as prized for gourmet culinary treatment as other salmon but is a good catch nonetheless and is typically available at bargain prices. The majority of the pink salmon, which average less than 4 pounds, are canned.

Mint and Nut–Crusted Rack of Lamb

The Dining Room at
The Salish Lodge & Spa,
Snoqualmie, Washington

As delicious as this herb- and nut-embellished rack of lamb is (and it is, very), the potato purée alongside it nearly steals the show. Russian Banana fingerling potatoes are recommended for this recipe because the dense, yellowish potatoes hold the cream and butter well while also providing plenty of flavor of their own. Look for this variety at specialty markets or better grocery stores, or substitute Yellow Finn, Yukon Gold, or other fingerling potatoes.

MAKES 4 SERVINGS

¼ cup minced mint
¼ cup panko bread crumbs or other dried bread crumbs
¼ cup pine nuts, lightly toasted
2 tablespoons minced flat-leaf (Italian) parsley
4 lamb racks (6 to 8 ounces each)
Salt and freshly ground black pepper
2 tablespoons olive oil
2 tablespoons Dijon mustard
1 tablespoon minced garlic
1 tablespoon minced shallot
½ cup cabernet sauvignon or other robust red wine
½ cup beef stock, preferably homemade (page 171)
1 tablespoon minced thyme
¼ cup unsalted butter, cut into pieces and chilled

Fingerling Potato Purée
1 pound Russian Banana fingerling potatoes, peeled
½ cup unsalted butter
½ cup whipping cream
Salt and freshly ground black pepper

FOR THE POTATO PURÉE, put the potatoes in a large saucepan and add cold water to cover. Bring the water to a boil, then reduce the heat to medium and simmer until the potatoes are tender when pierced with the tip of a knife, 18 to 20 minutes. Drain the potatoes in a colander and let them sit in the sink to release the steam, which will leave the purée fluffier. In the same saucepan, heat the butter and cream over medium heat until the butter is melted. Add the potatoes and mash with a potato masher or large, sturdy whisk (or press the potatoes through a ricer into the pan), beating well to evenly blend and lighten the potatoes. Season to taste with salt and pepper and keep warm over very low heat while cooking the lamb.

PREHEAT THE OVEN to 375°F.

PUT THE MINT, bread crumbs, pine nuts, and parsley in a food processor and pulse to blend until the mixture has a fine texture. Transfer the crust mixture to a plate and set aside.

SEASON THE LAMB RACKS with salt and pepper. Heat a large, heavy, oven-proof skillet over medium-high heat. Add the olive oil, then add the lamb racks, flesh side down, and sear until the racks are well browned. Turn the racks over in the skillet, then put the skillet in the oven and roast until the lamb is rare (an internal temperature of about 120°F), 5 to 7 minutes, turning the racks once more halfway through the cooking; the lamb will be cooked further after the crust is added.

TAKE THE LAMB RACKS FROM THE OVEN (leaving the oven set) and brush the fleshy top surface of each with the mustard, then press it lightly into the mint crust mixture. Return the lamb to the oven for 5 minutes with mint crust side up, cooking the meat to medium-rare (an internal temperature of about 130°F).

TRANSFER THE LAMB RACKS to a carving board and set aside. Discard from the skillet any burned bits of crust and put the skillet over medium-high heat (be careful to use a hot pad as the handle will be searing hot). Add the garlic and shallot to the skillet and sauté, stirring, until tender and aromatic, about 1 minute. Add the wine and boil until reduced by three-quarters, 2 to 3 minutes. Add the stock with the thyme and reduce again by three-quarters, about 3 minutes longer. Reduce the heat to medium and add the butter, stirring so that it slowly melts into the sauce without becoming oily. Season the sauce to taste with salt and pepper.

TO SERVE, SPOON THE POTATO PURÉE into the center of individual warmed plates. Cut each rack in half and lay the halves over the potato purée. Spoon the sauce around the lamb and serve right away.

Honey Peppered Salmon with Tomato Ginger Sauce

Rock Springs Guest Ranch, Bend, Oregon

The bright, vibrant flavors of the tomato ginger sauce—much like a salsa, really—are an ideal complement to the richly flavored, peppery-sweet salmon. Adding moistened smoking chips to the grill will contribute another level of flavor to this distinctive salmon recipe. The fish could also be baked, at 400°F for 10 to 12 minutes.

MAKES 4 SERVINGS

---

4 salmon fillets (6 to 8 ounces each), skin on, pin bones removed
¼ cup honey
½ teaspoon finely crushed or coarsely ground black pepper

Marinade
1½ cups water
1 cup packed light brown sugar
3 tablespoons minced or grated ginger
1½ teaspoons ground allspice
3 bay leaves
¼ cup kosher salt

Tomato Ginger Sauce
1 cup chopped, seeded tomatoes
2 tablespoons minced or grated ginger
1 tablespoon toasted sesame seeds
Pinch dried red pepper flakes, plus more to taste
2 tablespoons soy sauce
1 tablespoon honey
2 teaspoons Asian sesame oil
¼ cup chopped cilantro

PUT THE SALMON IN A SHALLOW DISH just large enough to hold it. For the marinade, combine the water, brown sugar, ginger, allspice, bay leaves, and salt in a small bowl and stir to mix until the salt is dissolved. Pour the marinade over the salmon, turning to coat both sides evenly, leaving the fish skin side up. Cover the dish with plastic wrap and refrigerate for at least 2 hours or up to 8 hours.

SHORTLY BEFORE SERVING, make the tomato ginger sauce. Combine the tomatoes, ginger, sesame seeds, and red pepper flakes in a medium bowl and stir to mix. Drizzle the soy sauce, honey, and sesame oil over all, and toss to evenly mix. Set aside while grilling the salmon.

PREHEAT AN OUTDOOR GRILL. Take the salmon from the marinade, rinse well, and pat dry, discarding the marinade. Brush the flesh side of each salmon fillet with the honey and dust with the crushed pepper. Cut a piece of foil a bit larger than needed to hold the fillets, and fold up the edges to help hold in the cooking juices during cooking. Lightly oil the foil and set the salmon on top, skin side down. Set the foil packet on the hot grill rack, cover the grill, and cook until the salmon is just nearly opaque through the thickest part, 6 to 10 minutes, depending on the thickness of the fish.

TO SERVE, PUT THE SALMON PIECES on individual plates and drizzle some of the cooking liquid over them. Stir the cilantro into the tomato ginger sauce and spoon it alongside the fish. Serve right away.

Granchio (Crab Capellini)

Bugatti's Ristorante, West Linn, Oregon

A wonderful summertime treat featuring fresh garden basil, vine-ripe tomatoes, and sweet crabmeat, this simple pasta dish makes for quite an elegant summer supper for two. A green salad, some garlic bread, and a crisp white wine would round out the meal perfectly.

MAKES 2 SERVINGS

1 cup Dungeness crabmeat (about 6 ounces)
2 tablespoons olive oil
½ cup chopped shallot
Salt and freshly ground black pepper
2 plum (Roma) tomatoes, finely chopped
16 basil leaves (about ¼ cup), finely shredded
¾ cup dry white wine
6 ounces dried angel hair (capellini) pasta
¼ cup freshly grated Parmesan cheese

BRING A LARGE PAN OF SALTED WATER TO A BOIL. Pick over the crabmeat to remove any bits of shell or cartilage; set aside.

WHILE THE WATER IS HEATING, heat the olive oil in a medium saucepan over medium-high heat. Add the shallot with a pinch of salt and pepper and sauté, stirring constantly, until the shallot is nicely browned but not burned, 2 to 3 minutes. Stir in the tomatoes and basil, then add the white wine. Boil rapidly over high heat until the liquid is reduced by two-thirds, 5 to 7 minutes.

WHEN THE WATER COMES TO A ROLLING BOIL, add the pasta and stir to separate the strands. Boil until just al dente (tender but still with some bite), 3 to 5 minutes. Drain the pasta well, shaking to separate the strands and draw off as much water as possible.

WHEN THE SAUCE HAS REDUCED, it will still be somewhat thin but intensely flavorful. Add the crab to the sauce and cook for another minute or two just to heat it through; season to taste with salt and pepper. Add the drained pasta and the Parmesan to the sauce and toss to coat well. If it seems too thin, continue cooking for another minute or two until the pasta absorbs the extra liquid.

TO SERVE, DIVIDE THE PASTA between 2 warmed plates, arranging some of the crab pieces on top. Serve right away.

DUNGENESS CRAB

Marylanders can rave all they want about their native blue crab, but Northwesterners know the true star among the North American crabs. The iconic Dungeness crab even has a grand Latin name, *Cancer magister*, which seems to make its regal status undeniable.

Named after the Dungeness Spit near Sequim in northwest Washington State, the Dungeness crab is a nearly year-round treat. The commercial harvest kicks off in late fall, often on or around December 1, so shoppers can typically count on a good supply of well-priced crab for holiday feasts and other wintertime celebrations. Come summer, plenty of vacationing sport crabbers set out crab pots from docks near their cabins or in shallow bays with the help of a boat, making Dungeness crab a regular part of Northwest summer dining as well. The low season for fresh crab comes in mid fall, when the mature crabs molt, shedding their too-small hard shell and slowly regenerating a new, larger shell.

Purists insist on eating their Dungeness crab simply steamed or boiled, served with nothing but a smile. Cover the table with newspapers, lay out the still-steaming crab, open some bottles of chilled local beer or crisp white wine, and dig in. Add garlic bread and a green salad—okay, and maybe some melted butter with lemon juice for those who simply *must* dunk—and you've got all the fixings for a classic Northwest crab feed, a most social and delicious gathering.

Others find that delicately sweet crabmeat is a welcome addition to many recipes, from soups to salads to main courses. Here you'll find Crab Cappellini (opposite), crab used in a stuffing for halibut (page 154), and, for breakfast, Poached Eggs with Dungeness Crabmeat and Chipotle Hollandaise (page 17), a twist on eggs Benedict.

Kuku Paka
(Chicken in Coconut Sauce)

Spice Jammer Restaurant,
Victoria, British Columbia

This classic African dish, originally from Zanzibar (now part of Tanzania) on the eastern coast of Africa, is commonly served with fluffy white rice. The chicken pieces are first simmered in a flavorful broth and then coated in the coconut sauce and briefly broiled just before serving. At the Spice Jammer, chef Bilkiz Essa grills the cooked pieces of chicken just before serving, adding a delightfully smoky element to the dish. You can do the same at home, although here the recipe's been modified to broil the chicken instead.

The chicken cooking liquid is flavorful with coconut milk, garlic, ginger, and a soft yellow hint of turmeric. Some is used for the sauce, but the rest would make a good—if slightly exotic—base for a chicken noodle soup, or it could be used in curry dishes.

MAKES 4 SERVINGS

---

2 eggs
3 new potatoes
4 cups water, more if needed
1 cup unsweetened coconut milk
1 tablespoon minced tomato
½ teaspoon minced garlic
½ teaspoon minced ginger
½ teaspoon salt
Dash ground turmeric
1 whole chicken (about 4 pounds), cut into 8 pieces, skinned

Coconut Sauce
1½ cups unsweetened coconut milk
2 tablespoons minced tomato
½ teaspoon minced garlic
1 teaspoon minced green bell pepper (optional)
1 teaspoon chile powder
⅛ teaspoon ground turmeric

1 tablespoon chopped cilantro
Salt

PUT THE EGGS IN A SMALL SAUCEPAN with enough cold water to cover them by about 1 inch. Put the pan over high heat and bring to a boil, then reduce the heat to medium-high and simmer for 10 minutes, counting from the time that the water comes to a full boil. Drain the eggs and run cold water over them for a few minutes to stop the cooking; set aside.

PUT THE POTATOES IN A MEDIUM SAUCEPAN with cold salted water to cover. Bring the water to a boil over high heat, then reduce the heat to medium and simmer until the potatoes are tender when pierced with the tip of a knife, 20 to 30 minutes, depending on their size. Drain and let cool, then cut the potatoes into quarters; set aside.

OIL A BAKING PAN large enough to hold the chicken. Combine the water, coconut milk, tomato, garlic, ginger, salt, and turmeric in a medium pot. Bring the mixture just to a boil over high heat, then reduce the heat to medium and add the chicken pieces. They should be covered in liquid; add more water if needed. Simmer, partly covered, until the chicken is cooked through (cut into a couple of pieces to make sure there's no more pink at the center), about 20 minutes, removing earlier any smaller pieces that may be cooked sooner. Lift the chicken out with tongs and arrange the pieces in the oiled pan; set aside. Reserve 1 cup of the cooking liquid for the sauce (discard the rest or save it for another use).

FOR THE SAUCE, combine the coconut milk, reserved chicken cooking liquid, tomato, garlic, green pepper (if using), chile powder, and turmeric in a small saucepan. Bring to a boil over high heat, then reduce the heat to medium and simmer until the sauce has reduced by about half and is slightly thickened, 10 to 15 minutes. Stir in the cilantro and season the sauce to taste with salt.

PREHEAT THE BROILER. Spoon about half of the sauce evenly over the chicken pieces in the baking pan, keeping the remaining sauce warm over low heat. Broil the chicken 2 to 3 inches from the heat until heated and the tops are lightly browned, 2 to 3 minutes.

TO SERVE, ARRANGE THE CHICKEN PIECES on individual plates with potato and egg wedges alongside. Spoon a little more of the sauce over all, passing the rest separately. Serve right away.

MAINS

Desserts

Rainier Cherry–White Chocolate Crème Brûlée *Dundee Bistro*

Lemon Mousse with Strawberries *Ray's Boathouse*

Plum Kuchen *Durlacher Hof Alpine Country Inn*

Beignets with Chocolate Coffee Ice Cream
The Dining Room at The Salish Lodge & Spa

Ginny's Apple Nut Cake *Mountain Home Lodge*

Stilton Cheesecake with Rhubarb Compote
Diva at the Met, Vancouver

Warm Bread Pudding with Rum Sauce
Woodstone Country Inn, Galiano Island

Raspberry and Almond Tart *Point No Point Resort*

Skagit Mud Brownies *Nell Thorn*

Hand-Formed Sweet Cherry Pies *Palace Kitchen*

Meyer Lemon Cheesecake with Blackberry Sauce *Duck Soup Inn*

Apricot Almond Biscotti *Villa Isola*

Pistachio Gelato *Bugatti's Ristorante*

Warm Chocolate Espresso Pudding Cakes *Turtleback Farm Inn*

Budino *The Arbor Café*

Rhubarb Crisp with Crème Fraîche Ice Cream *Marché*

French Silk Torte *Stephanie Inn*

Poached Anjou Pears with Ricotta and Hazelnut Croustillants and
Red Berry and Rosemary Compote *The Aerie Resort*

Grand Marnier Soufflé *The Old Farmhouse Bed & Breakfast*

Linzertorte *Durlacher Hof Alpine Country Inn*

Rainier Cherry–White Chocolate Crème Brûlée

Dundee Bistro, Dundee, Oregon

Come June and July in the Northwest it's time to get your fill of cherries. The Willamette Valley region surrounding the Dundee Bistro is one of the many places in the region where cherries are grown. "You can find all sorts of perfect cherries along Highway 99 as you tour Oregon's wine country," notes chef Jason Smith. The yellow blush-hued Rainiers are a prize among the sweet cherries available locally, though the season's a fleeting one. In their place, you could use other sweet cherries or summer berries. Even without the fruit, this crème brûlée is a delicious treat. The perfect tool for caramelizing the tops of the crème brûlées is a blow torch, now available in a handy kitchen size. You can also use your broiler to caramelize the dessert tops.

The Ponzi family, owner of the acclaimed Ponzi Winery, owns the bistro as well. The chef suggests that their Ponzi Vino Gelato (a sweet ice wine) would be an ideal complement to this rich dessert.

MAKES 6 SERVINGS

1⅔ cups whipping cream
1 vanilla bean
4 ounces Rainier cherries, pitted and sliced
2 ounces white chocolate, chopped, or white chocolate chips
4 egg yolks
⅔ cup sugar, plus about 2 tablespoons more for caramelizing

PREHEAT THE OVEN to 300°F.

PUT THE CREAM IN A MEDIUM SAUCEPAN. Split the vanilla bean lengthwise and use the back of the knife to scrape out the tiny seeds, and add them, with the bean, to the cream. Bring the cream just to a boil over medium-high heat, then take the pan from the heat. Add the cherries and white chocolate, cover, and let sit for 15 minutes.

IN A MEDIUM BOWL, whisk together the egg yolks with ⅔ cup of the sugar until the yolks turn pale yellow and are slightly frothy. Remove and discard the vanilla bean from the cream, then whisk the cream and cherry mixture into the egg yolks. Ladle the custard into six 6-ounce ramekins, being careful to distribute the cherry pieces evenly.

SET THE RAMEKINS IN A BAKING DISH and add boiling water to the dish so that it comes about halfway up the sides of the ramekins. Bake the custards until set, about 45 minutes. Take the dish from the oven, carefully remove the ramekins, and set them on a wire rack until fully cooled, about 2 hours. (The custard can be baked up to a day in advance and refrigerated. Caramelize the tops just before serving.)

TO SERVE, SPRINKLE THE TOP OF EACH CUSTARD evenly with about 1 teaspoon of sugar. Using a blowtorch, caramelize the tops until deeply browned. Alternatively, put the ramekins on a baking sheet and caramelize the tops a few inches below a preheated broiler. Serve right away.

Lemon Mousse with Strawberries

Ray's Boathouse, Seattle, Washington

This very lemony dessert starts with a delicious homemade lemon curd (which you could also use to fill a lemon tart) and lightens it with whipped cream to make the fluffy mousse. There's a distinct citrus tang, and the sweetness is not overpowering in this refreshing dessert. You could use other seasonal berries in place of, or in addition to, the strawberries for garnishing the mousse. The whipped cream topping could be lightly sweetened, if you prefer, rather than leaving the cream unsweetened.

MAKES 4 TO 6 SERVINGS

¼ cup unsalted butter

3 eggs

¾ cup freshly squeezed lemon juice

½ cup sugar

1¼ cups whipping cream

2 tablespoons grated lemon zest

¾ cup sliced strawberries

MELT THE BUTTER in the top of a double boiler, or in a stainless steel bowl set over a saucepan of simmering water (the bottom of the bowl should not touch the water). In a separate bowl, whisk together the eggs, lemon juice, and sugar until smooth. Add the egg mixture to the melted butter and cook over medium heat, whisking constantly, until it thickens to the consistency of pudding, 8 to 10 minutes. Take the pan from the heat and let the lemon curd cool, then refrigerate until fully chilled.

BEAT 1 CUP OF THE WHIPPING CREAM and the lemon zest with an electric mixer at medium-high speed until soft peaks form. Gently fold the whipped cream into the chilled lemon curd until evenly blended. Spoon the mousse into wine glasses or dessert bowls and chill until set, at least 1 hour.

TO SERVE, WHIP THE REMAINING ¼ cup cream until soft peaks form. Top each mousse with some of the sliced strawberries and a dollop of whipped cream. Serve right away.

Plum Kuchen

Durlacher Hof Alpine Country Inn,
Whistler, British Columbia

Z*wetschgenkuchen* [plum cake] is as basic to German and Austrian cuisine as apple pie is to American cuisine," points out innkeeper Erika Durlacher. This classic recipe is a late summer favorite of her guests. It calls for Italian plums, an oval variety with deep purple skin and amber flesh that is sweeter than other plums, though really any plum could be used with delicious results.

MAKES 8 SERVINGS

2 cups plus 2 tablespoons all-purpose flour
1 cup sugar
1 teaspoon baking powder
¾ cup unsalted butter, cut into pieces and chilled
1 egg
2 tablespoons freshly squeezed lemon juice
1 teaspoon grated lemon zest
2 pounds Italian plums, pitted and quartered
1 teaspoon ground cinnamon
Softly whipped cream, for serving (optional)

PREHEAT THE OVEN to 400°F. Butter a 9- or 10-inch springform pan.

COMBINE 2 CUPS OF THE FLOUR with ¼ cup of the sugar and the baking powder in a medium bowl. Add the butter and cut it into the dry ingredients with a pastry cutter until the mixture has the texture of coarse crumbs. (This can be done in a food processor: pulse to cut the butter into the flour, then transfer the mixture to a medium bowl.)

IN A SMALL BOWL, WHISK TOGETHER THE EGG, lemon juice, and lemon zest until well blended. Add this to the dry ingredients and stir with a wooden spoon to make a smooth dough. Spread the dough out evenly in the spring-form pan, pressing some of it up the sides to form a 1-inch edge on the crust.

ARRANGE THE PLUM WEDGES on the crust in a single layer, skin side up. Sprinkle with ½ cup of the sugar. In a small bowl, combine the remaining

¼ cup sugar with the remaining 2 tablespoons flour and the cinnamon and stir to mix. Sprinkle this over the plums and bake until the crust is browned and the plum juices are bubbling, about 45 minutes.

LET COOL ON A WIRE RACK and serve warm or at room temperature. Remove the sides of the springform pan, cut the kuchen into pieces, and serve, with a dollop of whipped cream alongside if desired.

Beignets with Chocolate
Coffee Ice Cream

The Dining Room at
The Salish Lodge & Spa,
Snoqualmie, Washington

Coffee and doughnuts" will never be seen in the same light again. At The Salish Lodge they use Callebaut chocolate from Belgium, a preferred choice of many pastry chefs. Get the best semisweet chocolate that you can for this luscious ice cream. If you don't have an espresso maker on hand, use instant espresso powder reconstituted per the label's instructions.

When activating dry yeast, it's important to start with water that's warm enough to bring the yeast to life but not so hot that it kills the yeast. The water temperature should be somewhere between 105° and 115°F, warm but not hot to the touch.

MAKES 4 TO 6 SERVINGS

⅓ cup warm water

2 teaspoons (1 envelope) active dry yeast

¼ cup evaporated milk

2 tablespoons granulated sugar

1 egg, lightly beaten

½ teaspoon salt

2 cups all-purpose flour

2 tablespoons shortening or unsalted butter, at room temperature

½ cup whipping cream

¼ cup powdered sugar, plus more for sprinkling

Vegetable oil or shortening, for frying

Chocolate Coffee Ice Cream

4 ounces semisweet chocolate, chopped

6 egg yolks

½ cup granulated sugar

2 cups milk

2 cups whipping cream

¼ cup espresso

1 vanilla bean, split lengthwise, or 1 teaspoon vanilla extract

FOR THE BEIGNETS, place the warm water in a large bowl, sprinkle the yeast evenly over it, and let sit until foamy, about 5 minutes. Whisk in the milk, granulated sugar, egg, and salt, blending well, then stir in 1 cup of the flour and beat until smooth. With a heavy wooden spoon, stir in the shortening, followed by the remaining cup of flour, beating to make a very smooth dough. Cover the bowl and set aside in a warm place until doubled in bulk, about 2 hours. (The dough can also be proofed overnight in the refrigerator.)

FOR THE CHOCOLATE COFFEE ICE CREAM, melt the chocolate in the top of a double boiler and set aside. In a large bowl, whisk together the egg yolks and sugar until well blended and the color begins to lighten. Combine the milk, whipping cream, espresso, and vanilla bean in a large saucepan. Bring just to a boil over medium-high heat. Slowly drizzle about 2 cups of the hot milk into the egg yolks, whisking constantly, then whisk this mixture back into the saucepan with the remaining milk. Return the pan to medium heat and cook, stirring often with a wooden spoon, until the mixture thickens enough to coat the back of the spoon, 5 to 7 minutes. Do not allow the mixture to boil, or the eggs will curdle.

TAKE THE PAN FROM THE HEAT and whisk in the chocolate. Let the mixture cool to room temperature, then refrigerate, covered, until fully chilled. When chilled, pour the mixture into an ice cream maker and freeze according to the manufacturer's instructions. Transfer the ice cream to an airtight container and freeze until set, at least 2 hours.

FOR THE TOPPING, WHIP THE CREAM and ¼ cup of the powdered sugar with an electric mixer at medium-high speed until soft peaks form; refrigerate until ready to serve.

JUST BEFORE SERVING, FRY THE BEIGNETS. Roll the dough out on a lightly floured board to a thickness of ⅛ inch and cut it into roughly 2-inch squares (you should have about 24). Add oil or shortening about 3 inches deep to a large, heavy pot and heat it to 375°F over medium-high heat. Carefully slip 4 or 5 of the dough squares into the hot oil and fry until well puffed and golden brown on both sides, 1 to 2 minutes. Scoop the beignets out with a slotted spoon and drain on paper towels. Continue frying the remaining dough squares, allowing the oil to reheat between batches as needed.

TO SERVE, SCOOP THE ICE CREAM into individual bowls and top with a dollop of whipped cream. Dust the beignets with the powdered sugar. Arrange them alongside the ice cream and serve right away.

Ginny's Apple Nut Cake

Mountain Home Lodge,
Leavenworth, Washington

This cake was developed by my mom [Ginny] in an attempt to use the ever-abundant apples from the old tree in our backyard in California," recalls owner Kathy Schmidt. "We loved it as kids and it's now a hit with all of our guests here in the heart of Washington apple country." Schmidt suggests Granny Smiths as a good option for this recipe; the juicy, tart-sweet apple offers plenty of flavor and texture to the cake.

MAKES 12 SERVINGS

2 eggs, beaten
2 cups granulated sugar
1 teaspoon vanilla extract
½ cup vegetable oil
2 cups all-purpose flour
2 teaspoons baking soda
2 teaspoons ground cinnamon
¾ teaspoon salt
1 cup chopped walnuts
4 cups finely diced apple (about 3 apples)
Apple slices, for garnish (optional)

Lemon Cream Cheese Icing
½ cup cream cheese (about 4 ounces), at room temperature
½ cup unsalted butter, at room temperature
2 tablespoons half-and-half or milk, plus more if needed
2 tablespoons freshly squeezed lemon juice
2 teaspoons grated lemon zest
1 teaspoon vanilla extract
Pinch salt
3 cups sifted powdered sugar, plus more if needed

PREHEAT THE OVEN to 325°F. Butter and flour a 9- by 13-inch baking dish.

WITH A WHISK, BEAT TOGETHER THE EGGS, sugar, and vanilla in a large bowl. Beat in the oil until the mixture is smooth. Sift the flour, baking soda, cinnamon, and salt into a medium bowl. Add the dry ingredients to the egg-sugar mixture and stir with a wooden spoon until blended. Add the walnuts and apple and mix well. Spoon the batter into the prepared baking dish, spreading it out evenly, and bake until the cake is firm and a toothpick inserted in the center comes out clean, about 1 hour. Transfer the cake to a wire rack and cool completely.

FOR THE ICING, BEAT TOGETHER THE CREAM CHEESE, butter, half-and-half, lemon juice, lemon zest, vanilla, and salt with an electric mixer at medium speed until well blended. Beat in the powdered sugar, 1 cup at a time, to form a fluffy frosting. If necessary, add more sugar or more half-and-half to get the frosting to a good spreading consistency.

WHEN THE CAKE IS COMPLETELY COOL, spread the lemon cream cheese icing on top. Garnish with apple slices, if desired, then cut into pieces to serve.

APPLES AND PEARS

If salmon is the main course that comes to mind when people think of the Northwest, surely the dessert most likely to be mentioned would be one with apples. Apples, along with pears, represent a large percentage of the agricultural offerings of the region and have for well over a century. Some of the earliest plantings of apples were made by traders with the Hudson's Bay Company, who passed through these parts in the early 1800s. The only apple native to North America is the crabapple–quite a different specimen from the sweet eating apples we enjoy today thanks to early settlers and more recent immigrants to the region.

For several decades the most valuable agricultural commodity of Washington State has been apples, providing more than half of the apples grown commercially in the United States. Just a few years ago, nearly three-quarters of the Washington apple production was in Red Delicious, the classic–if overwrought–American snacking apple. In recent years, however, interest among consumers and growers alike has led to a shift away from the Red Delicious, and grocery stores now offer a good variety that includes Gala, Fuji, Cameo, and Pink Lady, among others. The selection is even greater if you visit area farmers markets and orchards, where lesser-known varieties such as Criterion, Winesap, Newtown Pippin, and Rome Beauty may be available. Statewide production of the Red Delicious is now about 40 percent and still declining, making room for a welcome variety of other choices.

A versatile ingredient, the apple is delicious in a wide variety of recipes, both savory and sweet. For breakfast, you could serve Baked Apples in Puff Pastry (page 12), Ham and Apple Frittata (page 28), or a light German Apple Pancake (page 9). The fruit provides a crunchy contrast to sweet Dungeness crab in the salad on page 98, and Ginny's Apple Nut Cake (page 199) is a deliciously aromatic, somewhat rustic dessert in which apples shine.

The harvest of Northwest pears is smaller and less valuable than that of apples, but the fruit is equally well loved in the region's kitchens. On page 23, you'll find Donna's Baked Pears, served with yogurt for breakfast. Pears poached in white wine star in a dessert from The Aerie Resort (page 226), served atop a ricotta-filled pastry with a berry compote.

Where there are apples, there's sure to be cider. Many apple growers in the Northwest also turn out flavorful old-fashioned apple cider, including Woodring Orchards in Cashmere, Washington, whose cider is used by Run of the River for their Pure Gold breakfast smoothies (page 239). Some apples and pears also contribute to the production of hard cider, which has a light effervescence and low alcohol content. Spire Mountain in Woodinville, Washington, makes both apple and pear hard ciders, flavorful and refreshing sippers. Chef Jamie Guerin at Whitehouse Crawford in Walla Walla uses the hard apple cider in his aromatic Penn Cove Mussels with Hard Cider, Bacon, and Apple Chutney (page 66).

Stilton Cheesecake with Rhubarb Compote

Diva at the Met,
Vancouver, British Columbia

Not your traditional full-on-sweet finish to a meal, this cheesecake from pastry chef Thomas Haas has a surprisingly delightful balance of savory and sweet flavors, echoed in the rhubarb compote with its mellow tartness and touch of spice from pink peppercorns. Off-season, unsweetened frozen rhubarb makes a good substitute for the fresh used here.

MAKES 12 TO 16 SERVINGS

3 packages (8 ounces each) cream cheese, at room temperature
8 ounces Stilton cheese, rind trimmed, and cheese crumbled (about 1 cup)
1 cup sugar, plus 3 tablespoons for caramelizing (optional)
⅓ cup all-purpose flour
3 eggs
1 container (8 ounces) sour cream
2 teaspoons vanilla extract

Shortbread Crust
1¼ cups all-purpose flour
¼ cup sugar
½ cup unsalted butter, cut into pieces and chilled

Rhubarb Compote
⅔ cup sugar
½ cup port
24 pink peppercorns, coarsely crushed
2 pounds trimmed rhubarb, cut into ½-inch cubes (about 6 cups)

PREHEAT THE OVEN to 350°F. Butter a 10-inch springform pan.

FOR THE SHORTBREAD CRUST, combine the flour and sugar in a food processor and pulse a few times to blend. Add the butter pieces and pulse to finely chop the butter, until the mixture has a sandy texture. Transfer this to the springform pan and press down with your fingers to make a firm, even base. Bake until the crust is set and lightly browned, 15 to 20 minutes. Set aside on a wire rack to cool. Reduce the oven temperature to 300°F.

CREAM TOGETHER THE CREAM CHEESE, Stilton, and 1 cup sugar with an electric mixer at medium speed until well blended and fluffy. Reduce the speed to low and beat in the flour followed by the eggs, adding them one at a time and beating well after each addition, scraping down the sides as needed. Beat in the sour cream and vanilla, then pour the filling onto the cooled crust in the springform pan.

BAKE THE CHEESECAKE until set and golden brown around the edge, about 1½ hours. Transfer the pan to a wire rack and let the cheesecake cool completely, then cover and refrigerate until fully chilled, at least 4 hours or overnight. The cheesecake can be made up to 3 days in advance.

FOR THE RHUBARB COMPOTE, heat the sugar, port, and pink peppercorns in a large skillet (preferably nonstick) over medium-high heat, stirring until the sugar is dissolved. Boil until reduced to about ½ cup, 2 to 3 minutes. Reduce the heat to medium, add the rhubarb, and gently stir to coat with the port reduction. Simmer the rhubarb, stirring just occasionally to avoid breaking up the pieces too much, until it is tender but not mushy, 8 to 10 minutes. Transfer the rhubarb compote to a bowl and let cool, then cover and refrigerate until ready to serve. The compote can be made up to 3 days in advance.

TO SERVE, RUN A KNIFE AROUND THE EDGE of the cheesecake to separate it from the side of the pan. Remove the side of the springform pan and transfer the cheesecake to a serving plate. For the optional caramelized topping, sprinkle the sugar evenly over the cheesecake and heat it with a blowtorch, moving the flame slowly and evenly over the surface just until the sugar melts and turns a rich brown. Cut the cheesecake into wedges and serve, spooning some of the rhubarb compote alongside.

Warm Bread Pudding with Rum Sauce

Woodstone Country Inn,
Galiano Island, British Columbia

In this classic and delicious bread pudding, the bread cubes are speckled with rum-soaked raisins and pecan bits, and a rich rum sauce provides the finishing touch. Rather than baking the bread pudding in individual dishes, you could use a 2-quart baking dish. Increase the baking time to 1 hour if you do.

MAKES 6 SERVINGS

---

6 ounces crustless, day-old French bread (about half a baguette), cut into ½-inch cubes

2 cups milk

¼ cup raisins

⅓ cup dark rum

2 eggs

1 cup granulated sugar

½ teaspoon vanilla extract

¼ cup coarsely chopped pecans or walnuts

Whipped cream, for serving (optional)

Rum Sauce

1 cup packed light or dark brown sugar

½ cup whipping cream

¼ cup light corn syrup

2 tablespoons unsalted butter

2 tablespoons dark rum, or to taste

FOR THE RUM SAUCE, combine the brown sugar, cream, corn syrup, and butter in a medium saucepan. Bring the mixture just to a boil over medium-high heat, stirring often, then reduce the heat to medium and cook until the sugar is fully dissolved and the mixture is smooth, 3 to 5 minutes. Let sit until the sauce has cooled to near room temperature, then stir in the rum to taste. Set aside.

COMBINE THE BREAD AND MILK in a large bowl and set aside for about an hour until the bread is very well soaked, stirring occasionally. Put the raisins in a small bowl with the rum and set aside to plump the raisins.

PREHEAT THE OVEN to 375°F. Generously butter six 8-ounce ramekins and set them in a baking dish.

WHIP THE EGGS WITH A WHISK or with an electric mixer at medium speed until well beaten. Gradually add the sugar and continue beating until the mixture is thick and pale yellow and the sugar is dissolved. Add the vanilla, raisins and their soaking liquid, and nuts to the milk-soaked bread. Fold the beaten eggs into the bread mixture. Spoon the pudding into the ramekins and carefully fill the baking dish with enough hot water to come halfway up the sides of the ramekins. Bake the puddings until they are puffed and well browned, about 45 minutes. Let cool slightly before serving. Reheat the rum sauce over medium heat.

TO SERVE, UNMOLD THE WARM PUDDINGS onto individual plates and drizzle some of the warm rum sauce over them, passing the extra separately. Top with whipped cream, if desired.

Raspberry and Almond Tart

Point No Point Resort,
Sooke, British Columbia

The wonderfully rich almond filling of this tart from chef Jason MacIsaac is brightly contrasted—in color and flavor—by the fresh raspberries that dot the top of the tart. Other seasonal berries could be used in place of the raspberries, or try a mix of different berries for a twist on this indulgent tart.

The addition of sugar and the generous dose of butter make this dough somewhat delicate; it may crack a bit as you roll it out, but you can easily seal up cracks by pinching them together gently with your fingers.

MAKES 8 SERVINGS

1 cup unsalted butter, at room temperature

1 cup granulated sugar

2 cups sliced almonds (about 7 ounces)

3 eggs

2 pints fresh raspberries

Short Crust Pastry

2 cups all-purpose flour

¾ cup unsalted butter, cut into pieces and chilled

⅓ cup powdered sugar

1 tablespoon ice water, plus more if needed

FOR THE PASTRY, combine the flour, butter, and sugar in a food processor and pulse until the mixture has the texture of fine crumbs. Drizzle the water over the mixture and pulse a few more times, just until the dough begins to pull together. If the dough is still quite dry, add another teaspoon or two of water. Turn the dough out onto a work surface and form it into a ball. Wrap the dough in plastic and refrigerate for at least 1 hour (the dough can be made up to a day in advance).

PREHEAT THE OVEN to 375°F.

TAKE THE DOUGH FROM THE REFRIGERATOR and let it sit on a lightly floured work surface for a few minutes. Roll the dough out to a circle about

14 inches across. Line a 12-inch tart pan with a removable base with the pastry, pressing it down well into the pan and laying the excess evenly over the edge. Roll the rolling pin over the top of the pan to cut away the excess dough, then gently crimp the edge of the pastry shell to make a neat finish. Freeze the tart shell until quite firm, about 30 minutes.

JUST BEFORE BAKING THE TART SHELL, prick the bottom of the pastry with the tines of a fork, line with a piece of cheesecloth or foil, and add pie weights or dry beans to generously cover the bottom. Bake the pastry until the edges are lightly browned, about 5 minutes, then carefully remove the cloth and beans and continue baking until the bottom of the crust is lightly browned, about 10 minutes longer. Set the pastry shell on a wire rack and let cool completely. Leave the oven set at 375°F.

COMBINE THE BUTTER, sugar, and almonds in a food processor and process until smooth, scraping down the sides as needed. Add the eggs and process until they are fully incorporated. Pour the filling into the pastry shell and top with the berries, arranging them rounded side up. Bake the tart (with a baking sheet on the rack below to catch any drips) until the filling is uniformly browned and the center no longer jiggles, 40 to 45 minutes.

LET THE TART COOL completely on a wire rack, then remove the sides of the tart pan and cut into wedges to serve.

BERRIES

Nothing says "summer" quite like the variety of berries that are so prolific in the Northwest. Their sweetness, aroma, and jewel-toned colors become an important part of the fabric of summertime cooking in this region. Northwesterners often head to the U-pick berry patches for flats of strawberries, to a neighborhood vacant lot for bushels of blackberries, or to the foothills for a supply of bright red wild huckleberries. It's an embarrassment of riches that comes with the territory.

The family of blackberries alone offers a large selection. Himalayan blackberries are so abundant that many gardeners find themselves battling the hardy vines to make way for other plants. Many Northwest neighborhoods boast a sizable patch or two of these berries, free for the picking for summertime pies and cobblers. The smaller, more fully flavored (and less seedy) evergreen blackberry is even more prized but harder to come by, both in the wild and in area stores. A cross between wild and cultivated blackberries produced the marionberry, named for Marion County in Oregon, where the berry was developed in the 1950s. Boysenberries, loganberries, and tay-berries are among the other blackberry hybrids harvested in the Northwest.

Raspberries come in red, black, and gold varieties, strawberries are boun-tiful and celebrated in local festivals, low bushes packed with plump sweet blueberries grace many home gardens, and the cranberry harvest in southwest Washington State is a time-honored tradition associated with early fall. Berries are strongly represented in this region.

Berries really shouldn't be washed; they'll absorb water and become soggy, watering down a recipe and diluting their wonderful flavor. If your berries seem sandy or otherwise dirty, brush them gently with a paper towel or a pastry brush. Pick over the berries to remove any lingering stems or other debris before using.

The Raspberry and Almond Tart (page 206) serves as a delicious show-case for the sweet, brightly flavored fruit, and blackberries make a simple but flavorful sauce for a tangy Meyer Lemon Cheesecake (page 213). You'll find plump blueberries adorning the Cheese Blintzes (page 20) for breakfast and sweet-tart dried cranberries embellishing a Savory Bread Pudding (page 117) to serve alongside roasted chicken or pork chops.

Although nothing beats the flavor and texture of a freshly picked berry, you can hold onto a bit of summer for later by freezing some of the season's bounty. Simply lay the berries on a baking sheet in a single layer and freeze until solid, at least a couple of hours. Transfer the berries to a resealable freezer bag and freeze for three to four months. While frozen berries won't duplicate fresh ones completely, they are a fine addition to recipes in which the fruit will be cooked, as in the Skagit Berry Oatmeal Muffins (page 11) and the berry compote served with the poached pears on page 226.

Skagit Mud Brownies

Nell Thorn, La Conner, Washington

With their playful moniker, these brownies hint at the muddy nature that the Skagit River delta region—which at one time stretched across much of the now-dry land of the Skagit Valley—can take on at low tide. The rich, chewy brownies cry out for some vanilla ice cream or a dollop of lightly sweetened whipped cream. Around the holidays add 2 cups of dried cherries for a touch of festiveness. Unsweetened cocoa powder rather than flour is used for preparing the baking dish, which helps keep the brownies from sticking but does not coat them in a white, floury dusting—a great baking trick.

MAKES 12 SERVINGS

Unsweetened cocoa powder, for baking dish
2 cups hazelnuts
1 pound top-quality bittersweet chocolate, chopped
1 cup unsalted butter
8 eggs
3 cups sugar
1 tablespoon vanilla extract
2 cups all-purpose flour
½ teaspoon salt

PREHEAT THE OVEN to 350°F. Butter a 9- by 13-inch baking dish and dust it evenly with unsweetened cocoa powder.

SCATTER THE HAZELNUTS in a baking pan and toast them in the oven until lightly browned and aromatic, 8 to 10 minutes, gently shaking the pan once or twice to help the nuts toast evenly. Transfer the nuts to a lightly dampened dish towel, and wrap it around the nuts. Let sit until partly cooled, then rub the nuts in the towel to help remove the papery skins. Let the hazelnuts cool completely, then coarsely chop them; set aside. Leave the oven set at 350°F.

COMBINE THE CHOCOLATE and butter in the top of a double boiler or in a heatproof bowl set over a pan of simmering, not boiling, water (the bottom of the bowl should not touch the water). Cook over medium heat, stirring often, until the chocolate and butter are fully melted. Take the top bowl from the pan and set the chocolate mixture aside to cool.

WHISK TOGETHER THE EGGS in a large bowl, then whisk in the sugar and vanilla to evenly mix. Slowly whisk in the cooled chocolate mixture until smooth and evenly blended. Add the flour, hazelnuts, and salt and stir just until the flour and nuts are evenly incorporated. Pour the batter into the prepared baking pan and bake until set, about 45 minutes.

LET THE BROWNIES COOL slightly in the pan before cutting them into squares to serve.

Hand-Formed
Sweet Cherry Pies

Palace Kitchen, Seattle, Washington

At Palace Kitchen, they serve these rustic cherry pies with a scoop of almond brittle ice cream, but you can serve it with vanilla ice cream or any flavor that will complement the cherries. Use any sweet cherries, such as Bing or Rainier. These free-form pies can also be filled with other fruits; plums, pears, apples, or peaches would be delicious candidates.

MAKES 8 SERVINGS

---

2 pounds sweet cherries, pitted and halved

2 tablespoons plus 2 teaspoons sugar

1 teaspoon cornstarch

1 large egg yolk beaten with 1 tablespoon cold water

Vanilla ice cream, for serving (optional)

Pie Dough
2½ cups all-purpose flour

¼ cup sugar

1 teaspoon salt

1 cup unsalted butter, cut into pieces and chilled

5 to 6 tablespoons ice water

FOR THE PIE DOUGH, combine the flour, sugar, and salt in the bowl of a food processor. Add the butter and pulse a few times, until the butter and flour form crumbs. Transfer the butter-flour mixture to a bowl and add the ice water, a few tablespoons at a time, mixing with a fork or rubber spatula just until the dough is moist enough to hold together. Form the dough into a flattened round, wrap it tightly in plastic wrap, and chill for at least an hour or overnight.

SHORTLY BEFORE BAKING THE PIES, preheat the oven to 425°F. Line 2 baking sheets with parchment paper.

CUT THE DOUGH INTO 8 EQUAL PIECES. On a lightly floured work surface, roll each piece into a circle 7 to 8 inches in diameter and about ⅛ inch thick. Set the pastry circles aside on the prepared baking sheets. If your baking sheets aren't big enough to hold 4 pies at once, bake the pies 4 at a time (2 on each sheet), refrigerating the remaining dough until ready to form and bake the second batch of pies.

TOSS THE CHERRIES IN A BOWL with 2 tablespoons of the sugar and the cornstarch. Divide the filling among the pastry circles, mounding it in the center of each circle and leaving about a 2-inch border of dough around the edge.

BRUSH THE BORDER OF DOUGH on each pie with the egg wash, then fold the dough up around the cherries to partially cover them, pleating the dough as needed. Brush the top of the dough with the egg wash and sprinkle a little of the remaining sugar over the top. When all the pies are formed, bake them until the crusts are crisp and golden and the filling is bubbly, about 20 minutes. Serve the pies warm, with scoops of vanilla ice cream, if desired.

Meyer Lemon Cheesecake
with Blackberry Sauce

Chef/co-owner Gretchen Allison grew up in the Bay Area with a Meyer lemon tree just outside her bedroom window. "I could literally reach my arm out the window and pick a lemon from the tree, with no idea quite how lucky I was," she says, noting that she'd eat the fruit in slices sprinkled with a bit of salt. Meyer lemons are less acidic than other lemons and make a somewhat more balanced addition to recipes such as this. Allison stocks up on Meyer lemons on trips back to the Bay Area, then juices and zests the fruit to freeze and use over the course of a few months.

Winter is the prime season for Meyer lemons, when they show up in a number of markets across the Northwest. Regular lemons can be used in their place, though Allison suggests choosing the smaller, thin-skinned lemons, which give a lot of juice for their size and tend to be not quite as puckery as the larger, thick-skinned lemons.

MAKES 12 SERVINGS

4 packages (8 ounces each) cream cheese, at room temperature
1¼ cups sugar
⅔ cup unsalted butter, at room temperature
⅔ cup freshly squeezed Meyer lemon juice
2 eggs
1 tablespoon finely chopped Meyer lemon zest
Whole fresh blackberries, for serving (optional)
Whipped cream, for serving (optional)

Crust
2 cups fine graham cracker crumbs
2 tablespoons sugar
1 tablespoon finely chopped Meyer lemon zest
⅓ cup unsalted butter, melted

Blackberry Sauce
3 cups blackberries, fresh or thawed frozen
¼ cup sugar, plus more to taste
2 tablespoons Cointreau or other orange liqueur

PREHEAT THE OVEN to 350°F.

FOR THE CRUST, COMBINE the graham cracker crumbs, sugar, and lemon zest in a medium bowl and stir to mix. Drizzle the melted butter over the mixture and stir until the crumbs are evenly coated. Press the crust mixture evenly into the bottom and about 1 inch up the sides of a 9- or 10-inch springform pan. Bake until the crust is lightly browned around the edges, about 10 minutes. Set aside on a wire rack to cool. Reduce the oven temperature to 325°F.

BLEND THE CREAM CHEESE and sugar with a mixer at medium speed until smooth. Add the butter, lemon juice, eggs, and lemon zest and blend gently until the ingredients are thoroughly mixed. Pour the filling into the cooled crust and bake until the cheesecake is just set (the center should jiggle only slightly when the pan is nudged), about 1 hour 15 minutes. Let the cheesecake cool on a wire rack, then refrigerate it until fully chilled, at least 3 hours, before serving. (The cheesecake can be made up to 2 days in advance and refrigerated, covered.)

WHILE THE CHEESECAKE IS COOLING, make the blackberry sauce. Purée the blackberries, sugar, and Cointreau in a blender or food processor until smooth. Strain the sauce through a fine sieve into a medium bowl, pressing on the seeds to extract as much juice as possible. Refrigerate until ready to serve.

TO SERVE, REMOVE THE SIDES FROM THE SPRINGFORM PAN. Use a knife dipped in warm water to cut the cheesecake into wedges, spooning some of the blackberry sauce over and around each slice. Garnish with whole fresh blackberries and top with a dollop of whipped cream, if desired.

Apricot Almond Biscotti

Villa Isola, Langley, Washington

Because our bed and breakfast has an Italian theme," notes owner Dova Thirsk, "I make sure there is always plenty of homemade biscotti on hand." These cookies would be ideal alongside coffee or with an after-dinner bowl of ice cream.

MAKES ABOUT 3 DOZEN BISCOTTI

2½ cups all-purpose flour
1 cup sugar
1½ teaspoons baking powder
4 eggs
1½ teaspoons anise extract
¾ cup finely diced dried apricots
½ cup slivered almonds
1 tablespoon water

PREHEAT THE OVEN to 350°F. Lightly grease a baking sheet.

IN A MEDIUM BOWL, combine the flour, sugar, and baking powder and stir to mix. In a large bowl, whisk together 3 of the eggs. Separate the remaining egg and add the egg yolk to the bowl (reserve the egg white to use as a glaze), then whisk in the anise extract. Add the dry ingredients, apricots, and almonds and stir well to evenly blend.

LIGHTLY FLOUR THE WORK SURFACE and your hands, and knead the dough for about 5 minutes. Divide the dough into 2 equal pieces and shape each into a flattened loaf about 2 inches wide and 14 inches long. Arrange the loaves about 3 inches apart on the prepared baking sheet.

BEAT THE RESERVED EGG WHITE and the water with a fork until well blended. Brush the loaves with the egg white glaze and bake until lightly browned and firm, about 30 minutes. Take the pan from the oven, leaving the oven set at 350°F. Cut each loaf diagonally into slices ½ inch thick, separating the slices slightly so the cut surfaces are exposed. Return the pans to the oven and bake for 10 minutes longer. Turn the oven off and let the biscotti cool in the oven. Once they are cooled, serve the biscotti or store them in an airtight container for up to 1 month.

Pistachio Gelato

Bugatti's Ristorante, West Linn, Oregon

The secret to a light but rich-tasting gelato is using both 2 percent milk and cream," explains chef/owner Lydia Bugatti. "It took me a month and countless batches to get this balance right for that true Italian texture," she adds, noting that this is "the next best thing to being in Italy." There is quite a lot of texture and flavor from the pistachios, thanks to her technique of blending the nuts with some of the custard prior to freezing the gelato.

MAKES ABOUT 1½ QUARTS

6 egg yolks
1¼ cups sugar
2½ cups 2 percent milk
1¾ cups whipping cream
½ vanilla bean
1½ cups shelled pistachios

IN A MEDIUM BOWL, whisk together the egg yolks and sugar until well blended and the yolks lighten slightly in color.

COMBINE THE MILK AND CREAM in a medium saucepan. Split the vanilla bean and scrape out the tiny seeds with the tip of the knife, adding them to the pan. (Discard the bean pod or save it for another use.) Heat the milk mixture just to a boil over medium-high heat.

WHISK ABOUT ⅓ CUP OF THE HOT MILK mixture into the egg yolk/sugar mixture, whisking to thoroughly blend. Slowly whisk in the rest of the milk mixture, then return the custard base to the saucepan. Cook the custard over medium heat, stirring constantly with a wooden spoon, until the mixture thickens enough to coat the back of the spoon, 5 to 7 minutes.

TAKE THE SAUCEPAN FROM THE HEAT. Put the pistachios in a blender with about 2 cups of the custard and blend to very finely chop the nuts, about 30 seconds. Strain the mixture through a fine sieve into a medium bowl, then pour the remaining custard through the sieve as well, pressing on the nuts with a rubber spatula to press out as much of the flavor from the pistachios as possible. Discard the nuts. Let the custard cool, then refrigerate until fully chilled. When chilled, pour the mixture into an ice cream maker and freeze according to the manufacturer's instructions. Transfer the ice cream to an airtight container and freeze until set, at least 2 hours.

Warm Chocolate
Espresso Pudding Cakes

Turtleback Farm Inn,
Eastsound, Washington

Innkeeper Susan Fletcher suggests serving these wonderfully rich, dense chocolate cakes with coffee ice cream; vanilla ice cream or lightly sweetened whipped cream would be great options as well. In place of the fresh espresso, you could use 2 teaspoons of espresso powder dissolved in 2 tablespoons of warm water.

MAKES 8 SERVINGS

¾ cup unsalted butter, cut into pieces
6 ounces bittersweet chocolate, chopped
4½ tablespoons all-purpose flour
2 tablespoons unsweetened cocoa powder
5 eggs, separated
⅓ cup sugar
2 tablespoons hot espresso
1½ tablespoons Kahlúa or other coffee liqueur
½ teaspoon vanilla extract

PREHEAT THE OVEN to 400°F. Butter eight 6-ounce ramekins or custard cups and set them on a baking sheet.

IN A SMALL SAUCEPAN, combine the butter and chocolate and cook over medium-low heat, stirring frequently, until melted and smooth. Take the pan from the heat, add the flour and cocoa powder, and stir until smooth and evenly blended. Set aside to cool until just warm to the touch.

WHIP THE EGG WHITES until they begin to hold soft peaks. Gradually add the sugar and continue beating until the whites are shiny and hold stiff but not dry peaks. In another bowl, whisk together the yolks until well blended, then whisk in the espresso, Kahlúa, vanilla, and reserved chocolate mixture. Continue beating until evenly mixed and smooth.

ADD ABOUT ONE-QUARTER OF THE EGG whites to the chocolate mixture and stir to evenly blend and lighten the batter, then gently fold in the remaining egg whites. Spoon about ½ cup of this batter into each ramekin. Bake the pudding cakes until the edges begin to firm up but the center is still soft when pressed, 8 to 10 minutes.

TO SERVE, LET THE PUDDING CAKES COOL for a few minutes before inverting onto dessert plates.

Budino

The Arbor Café, Salem, Oregon

B*udino* refers to a family of Italian puddings and custards. This rice-based recipe is rich with ricotta and aromatic with citrus zest and rum, with a hidden layer of chocolate in the center. Pearl rice is a type of short-grain rice that has higher starch levels than long-grain rice, contributing to the creamy, rich texture of this dish.

MAKES 12 SERVINGS

7 cups milk

1½ cups pearl white rice

¼ cup unsalted butter

1½ teaspoons grated lemon zest

1½ teaspoons grated orange zest

2 tablespoons cornstarch

1 cup plus 2 tablespoons sugar

2 whole eggs

1 egg yolk

2 teaspoons vanilla extract

1 container (15 ounces) ricotta cheese

2 tablespoons rum

⅓ cup shaved or finely chopped semisweet or bittersweet chocolate

Ground cinnamon, for serving

COMBINE 6 CUPS OF THE MILK with the rice, butter, lemon zest, and orange zest in a medium, heavy saucepan. Cook the rice over medium heat, stirring often to prevent sticking, until it has absorbed most of the milk and the mixture has a silky texture, about 40 minutes. Take the pan from the heat and set aside.

PREHEAT THE OVEN to 300°F. Generously butter a 9- by 13-inch baking dish. In a small bowl, stir together the remaining 1 cup milk with the cornstarch; set aside.

WHISK TOGETHER 1 CUP OF THE SUGAR, the eggs, egg yolk, and vanilla in a medium bowl until evenly blended, then whisk in the milk/cornstarch mixture. Pour this slowly into the rice, stirring constantly. Spoon about half of the rice mixture into the prepared baking dish.

COMBINE THE RICOTTA CHEESE, rum, and remaining 2 tablespoons sugar in a bowl and stir with a wooden spoon to evenly mix and soften the cheese. Drop this in small spoonfuls evenly over the rice in the pan, then sprinkle the chocolate evenly over all. Cover the chocolate with the remaining rice, spreading it out evenly. Bake until the rice is mostly set (it may still jiggle slightly in the center but will firm up as it cools), 45 to 50 minutes. Let cool completely, then cover and refrigerate for several hours or overnight.

TO SERVE, CUT THE BUDINO into pieces and invert each piece onto the serving plate. Top each with a light dusting of cinnamon and serve.

Rhubarb Crisp with Crème Fraîche Ice Cream

Marché, Eugene, Oregon

Chef Stephanie Pearl Kimmel suggests that this crisp would also be great with strawberry ice cream or sweetened whipped cream alongside, perhaps with a drizzle of berry coulis. But the crème fraîche ice cream, with its rich texture and slight tang, is an ideal finish for the sweet-tart rhubarb crisp. Crème fraîche is available in well-stocked grocery stores, though it is also easy to make at home. Chef Kimmel makes it by stirring together 2 cups whipping cream and 2 teaspoons buttermilk and then setting the bowl in a warm place overnight, covered with a dish towel, to thicken.

MAKES 6 TO 8 SERVINGS

½ cup walnuts
1 cup plus 3 tablespoons all-purpose flour
½ cup rolled oats
⅓ cup packed light brown sugar
½ teaspoon ground cinnamon
Pinch salt
⅓ cup unsalted butter, at room temperature
2 pounds rhubarb, washed, trimmed, and cut into ½-inch slices
   (about 6 cups)
¾ cup granulated sugar

Crème Fraîche Ice Cream
½ vanilla bean
2 cups crème fraîche
1 cup half-and-half
⅔ cup granulated sugar
6 egg yolks

FOR THE ICE CREAM, split the vanilla bean in half lengthwise and scrape the fine black seeds into a medium saucepan. Add the vanilla bean pod, crème fraîche, half-and-half, and sugar and warm the mixture over medium heat, stirring occasionally, until the sugar has dissolved, 3 to 5 minutes.

IN A MEDIUM BOWL, whisk the egg yolks just until blended, then whisk in about one-quarter of the warm half-and-half mixture. Return the yolk mixture to the saucepan and cook over medium heat, stirring constantly, until the custard coats the spoon, about 10 minutes. Strain the custard into a medium bowl to remove any lumps, and let it cool to room temperature, then refrigerate until fully chilled. When cold, pour the mixture into an ice cream maker and freeze according to the manufacturer's instructions. Transfer the ice cream to an airtight container and freeze until set, at least 2 hours.

PREHEAT THE OVEN to 375°F.

SCATTER THE WALNUTS IN A BAKING PAN and toast in the oven until lightly browned and aromatic, about 5 minutes, gently shaking the pan once or twice to help the nuts toast evenly. Let cool, then coarsely chop the walnuts. Leave the oven set at 375°F.

COMBINE 1 CUP OF THE FLOUR with the oats, brown sugar, cinnamon, and salt and stir to mix. Working quickly with your hands, mix in the butter until the mixture has a crumbly texture, then stir in the chopped walnuts.

PUT THE RHUBARB IN A LARGE BOWL and sprinkle with the granulated sugar and the remaining 3 tablespoons flour. Toss to evenly mix, and let stand until the rhubarb starts to release its juices, about 5 minutes. Put the rhubarb in a 12-inch oval baking dish, spreading it evenly. Sprinkle the topping over the fruit and bake until the rhubarb is tender and bubbling and the topping is golden brown, about 45 minutes. Serve warm, with scoops of crème fraîche ice cream alongside.

French Silk Torte

Stephanie Inn, Cannon Beach, Oregon

This recipe has become a signature for our dining room," says executive chef John Newman. It is a chocolate lover's delight, a dense mousse-like filling on a hazelnut base, topped with rich chocolate ganache—so decadent, a small slice goes a long way. Start with the best chocolate you can find. Note that the torte contains uncooked eggs, should you have any concern about consuming them.

MAKES 16 SERVINGS

2 cups hazelnuts
1¼ cups granulated sugar
1⅔ cups unsalted butter
½ cup packed light brown sugar
Pinch freshly grated or ground nutmeg
8 eggs
1¼ pounds bittersweet chocolate, melted and cooled
¼ cup half-and-half

Ganache
8 ounces bittersweet chocolate, chopped
1 teaspoon unsalted butter
⅔ cup whipping cream

PREHEAT THE OVEN to 350°F. Scatter the hazelnuts in a baking pan and toast in the oven until lightly browned and aromatic, 8 to 10 minutes, gently shaking the pan once or twice to help the nuts toast evenly. Transfer the nuts to a lightly dampened dish towel and wrap it around the nuts. Let sit until partly cooled, then rub the nuts in the towel to help remove the papery skin. Let the hazelnuts cool completely, then put them in a food processor with ¼ cup of the sugar and pulse to finely grind them, being careful not to over process or the nuts will turn to paste; set aside.

LINE THE BOTTOM OF A 9- OR 10-INCH SPRINGFORM PAN with a round of parchment paper or waxed paper and lightly butter the paper and the pan sides.

MELT ⅔ CUP OF THE BUTTER in a small pan over medium heat and put it in a medium bowl. Add the hazelnuts, brown sugar, and nutmeg. Stir to evenly mix, then put the mixture into the springform pan, pressing with your fingers to form an even, solid layer. Refrigerate until set, 1 to 2 hours.

CREAM TOGETHER THE REMAINING 1 CUP BUTTER and the remaining 1 cup granulated sugar with an electric mixer at medium speed until well blended and fluffy. Beat in the eggs, one at a time, beating well after each addition, then continue beating for another minute or so. With the mixer running, drizzle in the cooled melted chocolate and the half-and-half and mix until the batter is evenly blended and silky. Pour the batter onto the chilled crust and return to the refrigerator to chill until set, at least 2 hours or overnight.

TO MAKE THE GANACHE, put the chopped chocolate and butter in a heat-proof bowl. Bring the whipping cream just to a boil in a small saucepan over medium-high heat and immediately pour it over the chocolate. Let the mixture sit for a minute, then whisk until the chocolate is fully melted and the ganache is smooth. Spread the ganache over the chilled torte.

TO SERVE, RUN A KNIFE AROUND THE EDGE OF THE TORTE to separate it from the pan edge. Remove the side of the springform pan and transfer the torte to a serving plate. Cut the silk torte into wedges, using a knife dipped into warm water, and serve.

Poached Anjou Pears with Ricotta and Hazelnut Croustillants and Red Berry and Rosemary Compote

The Aerie Resort, Malahat, British Columbia

These delightfully simple poached pears could be served alone for a simpler variation on this elegant recipe, but perched atop phyllo packets hiding a ricotta and hazelnut filling, with a vibrant red berry compote around them, they make a dazzling end to any meal.

MAKES 4 SERVINGS

2 cups dry white wine

2 cups water

1 small lemon, halved

¼ cup honey

1 vanilla bean, split lengthwise

1 cinnamon stick

2 whole cloves

2 whole star anise

2 cardamom pods

2 Anjou pears

Red Berry Compote

1 pound (about 3 cups) mixed fresh berries, such as raspberries, blueberries, and blackberries

1 sprig (3 inches) rosemary

2 tablespoons honey, or to taste

Croustillants

½ cup hazelnuts

1 cup part-skim ricotta

¼ cup honey

4 sheets phyllo dough

2 tablespoons grapeseed or vegetable oil, plus more if needed

COMBINE THE WHITE WINE, water, lemon, honey, vanilla bean, cinnamon stick, cloves, star anise, and cardamom in a small saucepan and bring to a boil over medium-high heat. Peel, halve, and core the pears and add them to the poaching liquid. Simmer until tender, 8 to 10 minutes, then use a slotted spoon to remove the pears to a plate. Set aside. Strain the poaching liquid into a bowl and set aside as well.

FOR THE COMPOTE, combine the berries and the rosemary sprig with ½ cup of the reserved poaching liquid in a small saucepan over medium heat. Simmer until the berries are very soft but still hold their shape, stirring gently occasionally. Add honey to taste if the compote is not sweet enough. Discard the rosemary sprig and set the compote aside to cool.

PREHEAT THE OVEN to 350°F. Lightly butter four 4-ounce ramekins.

FOR THE CROUSTILLANTS, scatter the hazelnuts in a baking pan and toast in the oven until lightly browned and aromatic, 8 to 10 minutes, gently shaking the pan once or twice to help the nuts toast evenly. Transfer the nuts to a lightly dampened dish towel and wrap it around the nuts. Let sit until partly cooled, then rub the nuts in the towel to help remove the papery skin. Let the hazelnuts cool completely, then chop them finely. Increase the oven temperature to 400°F.

IN A SMALL BOWL, stir together the ricotta, hazelnuts, and honey. Working with one sheet of phyllo at a time, brush the surface with a thin layer of the oil, then fold the phyllo in half crosswise, brush the top again lightly with oil. Fold in half again 2 more times to make a roughly 4-inch square, lightly brushing the top with more oil as you go. Repeat with the remaining 3 phyllo sheets. Use each phyllo square to line a ramekin, pressing the dough well down into the bottom. Fill each phyllo cup with the ricotta mixture, and fold the phyllo edges down to fully enclose the filling. Bake the *croustillants* until browned and flaky, about 20 minutes. Let them sit for about 5 minutes before carefully taking them from the ramekins.

WHILE THE CROUSTILLANTS ARE BAKING, put 1½ cups of the reserved pear poaching liquid in a heavy saucepan and cook over medium-high heat without stirring until the liquid reduces and reaches a deep caramel color, 8 to 10 minutes. Add the poached pear halves to the caramel and turn a few times to coat them. Reheat them for a minute or two.

TO SERVE, SPOON THE BERRY COMPOTE onto individual plates and top with a *croustillant*. Set a pear half on top of each *croustillant*, drizzle with the caramel sauce, and serve right away.

The Old Farmhouse Bed & Breakfast,
Salt Spring Island, British Columbia

This light soufflé is full of flavor, with both the orange tones of Grand Marnier (you could use a different liqueur in its place, such as nutty Frangelico) and aromatic notes of vanilla bean. It is quite a treat, an ideal finish to a dinner party. For a tasty chocolate soufflé variation, add 3 tablespoons of melted semisweet chocolate in place of the Grand Marnier.

MAKES 4 SERVINGS

¼ cup all-purpose flour
2 tablespoons unsalted butter, cut into pieces
1 vanilla bean
½ cup milk
Pinch salt
2 eggs, separated
3 tablespoons Grand Marnier or other liqueur
2 tablespoons granulated sugar
1½ teaspoons cornstarch
Powdered sugar, for dusting

PREHEAT THE OVEN to 375°F. Butter a 1-quart soufflé dish or four 8-ounce ramekins and coat well with granulated sugar, tapping to remove the excess.

COMBINE THE FLOUR AND BUTTER in a small bowl and use a fork to break up the butter into small bits, blending it well with the flour. Set aside. Split the vanilla bean in half lengthwise and use the tip of the knife to scrape out the fine black seeds. Put the milk and the vanilla bean with its seeds in a small saucepan and bring the milk just to a boil. Take the pan from the heat and add the salt. Let the vanilla bean steep in the milk for 10 minutes, then lift it out and run your fingers down the length of the bean to remove as much of the flavorful essence into the milk as possible.

PUT THE MILK BACK ON THE STOVE over medium heat and slowly whisk in the flour and butter mixture bit by bit. Cook until the flour mixture is very thick, about 5 minutes, whisking constantly, then take the pan from the heat. Whisk in the egg yolks one at a time, whisking well after each addition, then whisk in the Grand Marnier.

BEAT THE EGG WHITES with an electric mixer at high speed until frothy, then add the granulated sugar and cornstarch and continue beating until stiff peaks form. Whisk about 2 tablespoons of the beaten egg whites into the soufflé batter to lighten it. Add the remaining egg whites and gently whisk to fold them into the batter, being careful not to deflate them. Pour the batter into the soufflé dish(es) and bake until well risen and nicely browned, about 12 minutes for individual soufflés, 15 to 17 minutes for one large soufflé. Dust the top(s) with powdered sugar and serve immediately.

The quintessential jam tart, linzertorte hails from the town of Linz in Austria, where, explains innkeeper Erika Durlacher, the recipe would typically be made with red currant jam. The tart will be only as good as the jam you use, so this is a good time to splurge on the best. "Do not cut this when fresh from the oven," Erika warns. "Allow it to mellow at least one day before serving," she suggests, noting that you can keep it for three to four days in the refrigerator, allowing the tart to come to room temperature before serving.

MAKES 10 TO 12 SERVINGS

---

3 eggs
5 ounces whole blanched almonds
1½ cups all-purpose flour
¾ cup sugar
½ cup unsalted butter, cut into pieces, at room temperature
1 tablespoon Stroh rum or other dark rum, preferably spiced
Pinch freshly grated or ground nutmeg
Pinch ground cinnamon
Pinch ground allspice
1 to 2 tablespoons water
1½ cups raspberry, black currant, or red currant jam

PUT 2 OF THE EGGS IN A SMALL SAUCEPAN with enough cold water to cover by about 1 inch. Put the pan over high heat and bring to a boil, then reduce the heat to medium-high, and simmer the eggs for 10 minutes, counting from the time that the water comes to a full boil. Drain the eggs and run cold water over them for a few minutes to stop the cooking and help cool the eggs quickly. When they are completely cold, peel and halve the eggs. Remove the yolks and mash them well with a fork in a large bowl. Discard the egg whites or save them for another use.

PUT THE ALMONDS IN A FOOD PROCESSOR with 2 tablespoons of the flour and process until very finely ground. Add the ground almonds, remaining flour, and sugar to the bowl with the mashed egg yolks and stir to mix well. Add the remaining egg with the butter, rum, nutmeg, cinnamon, and allspice, and stir to make a smooth dough, adding the water if the dough is a bit too dry. Form the dough into a ball, wrap it in plastic, and refrigerate for about 2 hours.

PREHEAT THE OVEN to 350°F.

CUT OFF ONE-THIRD OF THE DOUGH, rewrap it, and return it to the refrigerator. Roll the remaining piece of dough to a circle about 13 inches in diameter and, using the rolling pin, transfer it to a 10-inch tart pan with a removable base. Press the dough gently down the sides of the pan to be sure it is evenly covering the bottom, leaving the dough ½ inch higher than the edge of the pan.

SPREAD THE JAM EVENLY across the bottom of the tart. Roll out the remaining dough to a circle about 11 inches across, and use a fluted pastry wheel or sharp knife to cut it into strips ½ inch wide. Lay the strips across the top of the tart in a crisscross pattern to make a lattice design. Pinch the lattice ends into the pastry edging to seal and flute the tart rim.

PUT THE TART PAN ON A BAKING SHEET and bake the linzertorte until the pastry is golden and firm, 30 to 35 minutes. Let cool on a wire rack, then cover and refrigerate for at least a day before serving. Allow the tart to return to room temperature before removing the tart rim and cutting the linzertorte into wedges to serve.

Beverages

Blue Cowgirl *Christina's*

Kurant Cosmopolitan *Adam's Place*

Bo's Bahia Cooler *Typhoon!*

Avocado Daiquiri *mint*

The 3-Carat Ruby *Ruby's on Bainbridge*

Pure Gold *Run of the River*

Sicilian Martini *Silverwater Cafe*

Nell's Chicory Daiquiri Dock *Nell Thorn*

China Girl *West*

Mango Lassi *Spice Jammer Restaurant*

Blue Cowgirl

Christina's, Eastsound, Washington

The name for this straightforward, colorful cocktail is inspired by the Tom Robbins classic *Even Cowgirls Get the Blues*. The crisp gin with a vibrant splash of blue curaçao makes for a refreshing sipper. A classic martini glass befits this elegant cocktail, though at Christina's they sometimes serve it in a whimsical glass boot.

MAKES 1 SERVING

1½ fluid ounces Bombay Sapphire gin or other gin
¼ fluid ounce blue curaçao
¼ fluid ounce Cointreau
1 lime slice, for garnish

HALF-FILL A COCKTAIL SHAKER with ice and add the gin, blue curaçao, and Cointreau. Cover the shaker and shake vigorously until well chilled.

STRAIN THE COCKTAIL into a martini glass, garnish the rim of the glass with the lime slice, and serve right away.

Kurant Cosmopolitan

Adam's Place, Eugene, Oregon

Cocktails are a big deal at Adam's Place, where the "Eugene Martini Association"—a few hundred loyal customers strong—gathers for the sake of fine cocktail appreciation. This flavorful twist on the now-classic Cosmo brings a hint of currant flavor to the glass.

MAKES 1 SERVING

1½ fluid ounces Absolut Kurant vodka
½ fluid ounce cranberry juice
½ fluid ounce Rose's lime juice
½ fluid ounce Triple Sec
1 lime slice, for garnish

HALF-FILL A COCKTAIL SHAKER WITH ICE and add the vodka, cranberry juice, Rose's lime juice, and Triple Sec. Cover the shaker and shake vigorously until well chilled (a precise 14 shakes at Adam's Place).

STRAIN THE COCKTAIL into a martini glass, garnish the rim with the lime slice, and serve right away.

Bo's Bahia Cooler

Typhoon!, Portland, Oregon

This tropical cocktail—a take on the piña colada—is a refreshing fruity complement to the exotic, zesty fare of Typhoon!'s cuisine. Bartenders there "rim" the glass with finely chopped, toasted coconut, a professional flourish you can duplicate at home if you like. First moisten the rim of the glass with sweet-and-sour mix, lemon juice, or lime juice, then dip the rim into a plate covered with toasted coconut.

MAKES 1 SERVING

1½ fluid ounces Myers's Platinum rum or other light rum

1 fluid ounce Myers's dark rum or other dark rum

3 fluid ounces pineapple juice

2 fluid ounces coconut cream (such as Coco Lopez)

½ cup crushed ice

1 thin orange slice, for garnish

1 maraschino cherry, for garnish

IN A BLENDER, COMBINE THE RUMS, pineapple juice, coconut cream, and ice and blend until smooth. Pour the cocktail into a tall glass.

FOR THE GARNISH, FOLD THE ORANGE slice around the cherry, secure it with a toothpick, and lay it neatly across the rim of the glass. Serve right away.

While making a banana daiquiri, it dawned on owner Lucy Brennan that avocados have much the same texture as bananas, and so the testing began to develop this avocado daiquiri. It took many years to perfect the cocktail, but now the drink has a cult following in Portland. It's novel, certainly—a lovely soft green color—and you really wouldn't guess that it's made with avocado by the flavor.

MAKES 2 SERVINGS

2 cups ice cubes
¼ ripe avocado
4 fluid ounces simple syrup (recipe follows)
2 fluid ounces white rum
2 fluid ounces gold rum
1 teaspoon freshly squeezed lemon or lime juice
1 teaspoon half-and-half
Pomegranate syrup, for garnish (optional)

PUT THE ICE IN A BLENDER and add the avocado, simple syrup, white and gold rums, lemon or lime juice, and half-and-half. Blend until very smooth, 2 to 3 minutes.

POUR THE DAIQUIRI into 2 large, shallow glasses (like those used for margaritas), drizzle with a bit of pomegranate syrup, and serve.

Simple Syrup

1 cup sugar
1 cup water

COMBINE THE SUGAR and water in a small saucepan and warm over medium heat, stirring occasionally, just until the sugar is dissolved, about 5 minutes. Increase the heat to medium-high and bring the syrup just to a boil, then set aside to cool completely. The syrup can be stored in the refrigerator for 1 to 2 months.

MAKES ABOUT 1½ CUPS (12 FLUID OUNCES)

BEVERAGES

The 3-Carat Ruby

Ruby's on Bainbridge,
Bainbridge Island, Washington

This cocktail looks quite a lot like pink lemonade, but it's definitely a grown-up version, with plenty of bright flavor from citrus and a ruby tone from cranberry. Owner Maura Crisp was explaining to a customer that she'd named the restaurant after her grandmother, Ruby, to which the customer exclaimed, "What a wonderful name. You know, I have a 3-carat ruby ring in the bank that I really should get out and wear!" So this is not just a Ruby, but a 3-carat Ruby, tasty enough to deserve the elegant moniker.

MAKES 1 SERVING

½ small lemon, cut into pieces
¼ lime, cut into pieces
2 fluid ounces Ketel One vodka (or your favorite brand)
½ fluid ounce Cointreau or Triple Sec
2 teaspoons superfine sugar
1 fluid ounce club soda
1 fluid ounce cranberry juice

HALF-FILL A COCKTAIL SHAKER WITH ICE and add the lemon and lime pieces, vodka, Cointreau, and sugar. Muddle to blend the ingredients and to extract juice and other essence from the citrus fruits, covering the glass with one hand as much as you can while muddling. (It can be a messy technique, but muddling is a classic bar method that draws out more flavor than simple shaking does.)

STRAIN THE COCKTAIL MIXTURE into a highball glass filled with ice, and top with the soda and cranberry juice. Serve right away.

Pure Gold

Run of the River,
Leavenworth, Washington

They serve up to six different "boat drinks" (named for a Jimmy Buffet song, to go with the breakfast *buffet*) throughout the year at Run of the River, depending on the season and the fresh fruits available. This recipe is a nearly year-round favorite, based on apples that come from the nearby Cashmere/Wenatchee area. The apple cider they use in most of their waker-upper breakfast drinks is from Woodring Orchards in Cashmere, which one Run of the River guest said "tastes like cider my daddy used to drink." Find the best-quality cider you can for the tastiest results.

Other signature morning smoothies include the "Razzmatazz" with fresh raspberries, yogurt, a banana, a tablespoon of wheat bran, and cider; the "Blue Wave" with fresh blueberries, yogurt, a banana, a couple table-spoons of molasses, a tablespoon of flax seeds, and cider; and the "Panama Canal" with peeled orange, pineapple, a banana, shredded coconut, yogurt, and orange juice.

MAKES 4 SERVINGS

---

1 large Golden Delicious apple, cored and diced (skin left on)
1 banana
1 tablespoon chopped almonds
1½ cups nonfat vanilla or plain yogurt
2 cups top-quality cider

PUT THE APPLE, BANANA, AND ALMONDS in a blender and spoon the yogurt over them. Pour in the cider, cover, and blend until very smooth. (If your blender won't accommodate all the ingredients at once, use 1 cup cider to blend, then transfer the mixture to a large bowl and stir in the remaining cider.)

POUR THE MIXTURE into individual glasses and serve right away.

Sicilian Martini

Silverwater Cafe,
Port Townsend, Washington

The complex vanilla-influenced flavor of Tuaca liqueur finds a smooth, balanced partner with vodka in this simple cocktail. For those who like the distinct buzz of coffee, the rim of finely ground coffee beans on this simple martini will be quite a treat, though you could omit that step if you prefer. Tuaca and coffee are regular partners, often appearing in after-dinner drinks together.

MAKES 1 SERVING

Simple syrup (page 237), for coating rim of glass
Finely ground espresso beans, for coating rim of glass
1½ fluid ounces Absolut vodka
¾ fluid ounce Tuaca liqueur
1 whole espresso bean, for garnish

POUR A FEW TABLESPOONS OF SIMPLE SYRUP onto a small plate just a bit larger than the rim of the martini glass you'll be using; put the finely ground coffee on a second plate of the same size. Dip the glass rim in the syrup to coat it about ¼ inch deep evenly around, then dip the rim in the coffee to coat. Set aside.

HALF-FILL A COCKTAIL SHAKER WITH ICE and add the vodka and Tuaca. Cover the shaker and shake vigorously until well chilled.

STRAIN THE MARTINI into the prepared glass. Float the whole espresso bean on top and serve right away.

Nell's Chicory Daiquiri Dock

Nell Thorn, La Conner, Washington

This is an elegant summer cocktail, a refreshing sipper with a subtle bite of sharpness from Campari, a bitter, bright red aperitif from Italy that is often served with soda. "This libation was inspired on a cold December night," say owners Susan and Casey Schanen, "by memories of warm breezes off the Italian Riviera."

MAKES 1 SERVING

---

1 lime wedge
Superfine or regular granulated sugar, for coating rim of glass
1½ fluid ounces Bacardi light rum
1 fluid ounce freshly squeezed lime juice
1 fluid ounce simple syrup (page 237)
½ fluid ounce Campari
Splash of Rose's lime juice

RUB THE LIME WEDGE around the rim of a martini glass to moisten it, then dip the rim into a dish of superfine sugar to lightly coat the rim. Chill the glass while preparing the cocktail.

HALF-FILL A COCKTAIL SHAKER WITH ICE. Add the rum, lime juice, simple syrup, Campari, and Rose's lime juice. Cover the shaker and shake vigorously until well chilled.

STRAIN THE COCKTAIL into the prepared glass. Gently add just a few of the smallest crushed ice pieces to float on top of the daiquiri.

China Girl

This cocktail has a mellow green color from the honeydew melon, belying the exotic flavor that the lychee liqueur adds to the drink. Go ahead and blend up a whole melon's worth of honeydew purée, so you'll be ready to make more cocktails over the course of the evening (or the next couple of days, though the purée is best if freshly made). If the flavor of the melon isn't very sweet, add a dash of simple syrup to help bring out the melon's flavor.

The Soho lychee liqueur is more widely available in Canada than in Washington or Oregon liquor stores; you may need to special-order it.

MAKES 1 SERVING

2½ fluid ounces freshly puréed honeydew melon
1 fluid ounce premium vodka
1 fluid ounce Soho lychee liqueur
1 teaspoon simple syrup (page 237), if needed
½ wedge lemon
1 thin slice star fruit, for garnish

HALF-FILL A COCKTAIL SHAKER WITH ICE and add the puréed melon, vodka, lychee liqueur, and simple syrup (if using). Squeeze in the juice of the lemon wedge and drop the wedge into the shaker as well. Cover the shaker and shake vigorously until well chilled.

STRAIN THE COCKTAIL INTO A MARTINI GLASS. Float the slice of star fruit on top and serve right away.

Mango Lassi

Spice Jammer Restaurant,
Victoria, British Columbia

Lassi is a traditional yogurt drink from India, sometimes as simple as yogurt and water blended with a pinch of cumin and salt, though mango *lassi* is one of the most common and popular variations. The amount of sugar needed will depend on the sweetness of the mango and your personal taste.

To seed and peel a mango, hold the fruit upright on a chopping board. Insert the blade of a large knife across the top of the fruit. Cut downward and at a slight angle outward, so that the blade of the knife follows the curve of the large, somewhat flat central seed, drawing the knife back inward on the bottom half of the fruit. Repeat on the other side of the mango. Use a smaller knife or a vegetable peeler to peel away the tough skin, discarding the seed and the fibrous flesh attached to it. One mango should provide enough flesh for two or three drinks.

MAKES 1 SERVING

¾ cup water
½ cup finely chopped mango
3 tablespoons plain yogurt
1 tablespoon sour cream
1 teaspoon sugar, plus more to taste

COMBINE THE WATER, mango, yogurt, sour cream, and sugar in a blender and purée until thoroughly blended and frothy, about 30 seconds. Put 2 or 3 ice cubes in a tall glass, pour the mango *lassi* over them, and serve right away.

The 42nd Street Cafe
4201 Pacific Highway
Seaview, WA
360-642-2323

Abigail's Hotel
906 McClure Street
Victoria, BC
250-388-5363 / 800-561-6565
www.abigailshotel.com

Adam's Place
30 E Broadway
Eugene, OR
541-344-6948
www.adamsplacerestaurant.com

The Aerie Resort
600 Ebedora Lane
Malahat, BC
250-743-7115 / 800-518-1933
www.aerie.bc.ca

All Seasons River Inn
8751 Icicle Road
Leavenworth, WA
509-548-1425
www.allseasonsriverinn.com

Ann Starrett Mansion
744 Clay Street
Port Townsend, WA
360-385-3205 / 800-321-0644
www.starrettmansion.com

The Arbor Café
380 High Street NE
Salem, OR
503-588-2353

Bugatti's Ristorante
18740 Willamette Drive
West Linn, OR
503-636-9555

C
1600 Howe Street
Vancouver, BC
604-681-1164
www.crestaurant.com

Cafe Langley
113 First Street
Langley, WA
360-221-3090
www.langley-wa.com/cl

Campagne
86 Pine Street
Seattle, WA
206-728-2800

Canlis
2576 Aurora Avenue N
Seattle, WA
206-283-3313
www.canlis.com

The Cannery Seafood House
2205 Commissioner Street
Vancouver, BC
604-254-9606
www.canneryseafood.com

Cascadia
2328 First Avenue
Seattle, WA
206-448-8884
www.cascadiarestaurant.com

Chestnut Cottage
929 E Front Street
Port Angeles, WA
360-452-8344

Christina's
310 Main Street
Eastsound, WA
360-376-4904
www.christinas.net

CinCin Restaurant & Bar
1154 Robson Street
Vancouver, BC
604-688-7338
www.cincin.net

Cliff House Bed and Breakfast
1450 Adahi Road
Waldport, OR
541-563-2506
www.cliffhouseoregon.com

Dahlia Lounge
2001 Fourth Avenue
Seattle, WA
206-682-4142
www.tomdouglas.com

The Dining Room at The Salish Lodge & Spa
6501 Railroad Avenue SE
Snoqualmie, WA
425-888-2556 / 800-272-5474
www.salishlodge.com

Diva at the Met
645 Howe Street
Vancouver, BC
604-602-7788
www.metropolitan.com/diva

Dolce Skamania Lodge
1131 Skamania Lodge Way
Stevenson, WA
509-427-7700 / 800-221-7117
www.dolce.com/skamania/dolce_s
kamania.html

Duck Soup Inn
50 Duck Soup Lane
Friday Harbor, WA
360-378-4878
www.ducksoupinn.com

Dundee Bistro
100-A SW Seventh Street
Dundee, OR
503-554-1650
www.ponziwines.com/touring/
bistro.html

Durlacher Hof Alpine County Inn
7055 Nesters Road
Whistler, BC
604-932-1924 / 877-932-1924
www.dulacherhof.com

Earth and Ocean
W Hotel
1112 Fourth Avenue
Seattle, WA
206-264-6060

Edgewater Lodge
8841 Highway 99
Whistler, BC
604-932-0688 / 888-870-9065
www.edgewater-lodge.com

Elliott's Oyster House
1201 Alaskan Way, Pier 56
Seattle, WA
206-623-4340
www.elliottsoysterhouse.com

Etta's Seafood
2020 Western Avenue
Seattle, WA
206-443-6000
www.tomdouglas.com

Fiddlehead Bistro
201 Glover Street
Twisp, WA
509-997-0343

First Street Haven
107 E First Street
Port Angeles, WA
360-457-0352

From the Bayou
508 Garfield Street
Parkland, WA
253-539-4269
www.fromthebayou.com

Greystone Manor
4014 Haas Road
Courtenay, BC
250-338-1422
www.greystonemanorbb.com

Groveland Cottage
4861 Sequim-Dungeness Way
Sequim, WA
360-683-3565 / 800-879-8859
www.sequimvalley.com

Hacienda del Mar
408 S Lincoln Street
Port Angeles, WA
360-452-5296

Harrison House Bed and Breakfast
2310 NW Harrison Boulevard
Corvallis, OR
541-752-6248 / 800-233-6248
www.corvallis-lodging.com

The James House
1238 Washington Street
Port Townsend, WA
360-385-1238 / 800-385-1238
www.thejameshouse.com

Kasteel Franssen
33575 Highway 20
Oak Harbor, WA
360-675-0724

Lefty's
710 Memorial Avenue
Qualicum Beach, BC
250-752-7530
www.leftys.tv

Lindaman's Gourmet-to-Go
1235 S Grand Boulevard
Spokane, WA
509-838-3000
www.lindamans.com

The Mahle House
2104 Hemer Road
Cedar, BC
250-722-3621
www.mahlehouse.com

Marché
296 E Fifth Avenue
Eugene, OR
541-342-3612
www.marcherestaurant.com

Matt's in the Market
94 Pike Street, Third Floor
Seattle, WA
206-467-7909

mint
816 N Russell Street
Portland, OR
503-284-5518

Mountain Home Lodge
8201 Mountain Home Road
Leavenworth, WA
509-548-7077
www.mthome.com

Nell Thorn
205 N First Street
La Conner, WA
360-466-1500 / 888-466-4113
www.nellthron.com

Oceanwood Country Inn
630 Dinner Bay Road
Mayne Island, BC
250-539-5074
www.oceanwood.com

**The Old Farmhouse
Bed & Breakfast**
1077 N End Road
Salt Spring Island, BC
250-537-4113
www.bbcanada.com/oldfarmhouse

Old Parkdale Inn
4932 Baselind Road
Parkdale, OR
541-352-5551
www.hoodriverlodging.com

Palace Kitchen
2030 Fifth Avenue
Seattle, WA
206-448-2001
www.tomdouglas.com

The Peerless Restaurant
265 Fourth Street
Ashland, OR
541-488-6067 / 800-460-8758
www.peerlessrestaurant.com

The Place Bar and Grill
1 Spring Street
Friday Harbor, WA
360-378-8707

Point No Point Resort
1505 West Coast Road
Sooke, BC
250-646-2020
www.pointnopointresort.com

Portland's White House
1914 NE 22nd Avenue
Portland, OR
503-287-7131
www.portlandswhitehouse.com

Ray's Boathouse
6049 Seaview Avenue NW
Seattle, WA
206-789-3770
www.rays.com

The Robin Hood
(formerly Victoria's)
6790 Highway 106
Union, WA
360-898-4400

Rock Springs Guest Ranch
64201 Tyler Road
Bend, OR
541-382-1957
www.rocksprings.com

Ruby's on Bainbridge
4738 Lynwood Center Road NE
Bainbridge Island, WA
206-780-9303
www.rubysonbainbridge.com

Run of the River
9308 E Leavenworth Road
Leavenworth, WA
509-548-7171 / 800-288-6491
www.runoftheriver.com

Santiago's Gourmet Mexican
Cooking
111 E Yakima Avenue
Yakima, WA
509-453-1644

Sazerac
Hotel Monaco
1101 Fourth Avenue
Seattle, WA
206-624-7755

The Shelburne Inn
4415 Pacific Highway S
Seaview, WA
360-642-2442
www.theshelburneinn.com

The Shoalwater
4415 Pacific Highway S
Seaview, WA
360-642-4142
www.shoalwater.com

Silverwater Cafe
237 Taylor Street
Port Townsend, WA
360-385-6448

Skagit Bay Hideaway
17430 Goldenview Avenue
La Conner, WA
360-466-2262 / 888-466-2262
www.skagitbay.com

Spice Jammer Restaurant
852 Fort Street
Victoria, BC
250-480-1055

Splitz Grill
4369 Main Street
Whistler, BC
604-938-9300

Stephanie Inn
2740 S Pacific Street
Cannon Beach, OR
503-436-2221 / 800-633-3466
www.stephanie-inn.com

Toad Hall
12 Jesslyn Lane
Sequim, WA
360-681-2002
www.toadhall.tv

Tojo's
202-777 W Broadway
Vancouver, BC
604-872-8050
www.tojos.com

Tulio
Hotel Vintage Park
1100 Fifth Avenue
Seattle, WA
206-624-5500
www.vintagepark.com

Turtleback Farm Inn
1981 Crow Valley Road
Eastsound, WA
360-376-4914 / 800-376-4914
www.turtlebackinn.com

Typhoon!
2310 NW Everett Street
Portland, OR
503-243-7557

Villa Isola
5489 S Coles Road
Langley, WA
360-221-5052 / 800-246-7323
www.villaisola.com

The Vintner's Inn at Hinzerling Winery
1524 Sheridan Avenue
Prosser, WA
509-786-2163 / 800-727-6702
www.hinzerling.com

West (formerly Ouest)
2881 Granville Street
Vancouver, BC
604-738-8938
www.westrestaurant.com

Whitehouse-Crawford
55 W Cherry Street
Walla Walla, WA
509-525-2222

White Swan Guest House
15872 Moore Road
La Conner, WA
360-445-6805
www.thewhiteswan.com

Wildwood
1221 NW 21st Avenue
Portland, OR
503-248-9663
www.wildwoodrestaurant.com

The Willows Inn
2579 W Shore Drive
Lummi Island, WA
360-758-2620 / 888-294-2620
www.willows-inn.com

Woodstone Country Inn
Georgeson Bay Road
Galiano Island, BC
250-539-2022
www.gulfislands.com/woodstone

Yarrow Bay Beach Café
1270 Carillon Point
Kirkland, WA
425-889-0303
www.ybbeachcafe.com

Potato and Goat Cheese
Stuffed Peppers with
Spicy Tomato Sauce,
44–45
Salmon and Potato
Pancakes, 107
Yukon Gold Potato and
Goat Cheese Soup with
Sheep's Sorrel and
Garlic Croutons, 90–91
Prosciutto
Chicken Breasts with
Prosciutto and
Cambozola, 175–76
Pudding
Budino, 220–21
Pure Gold, 239

Q

Quail
Grilled Tamarind-Glazed
Quail, 47–48

R

Rainier Cherry–White
Chocolate Crème Brûlée,
192–93
Raspberries
Lavender Cream Scones
with Raspberries, 6–7
Raspberry and Almond
Tart, 206–7
Ravioli
Blue Cheese and Basil
Ravioli, venison with,
146–48
Ray's Boathouse
Artichokes Stuffed with
Herbed Cream Cheese
and Bay Shrimp, 62–63
Lemon Mousse with
Strawberries, 194
Razor Clam Chowder with
Turnip, Truffle, and Thyme,
84–85
Relish
Apple-Onion Relish, for
Smoked Pork Loin,
156–57
Eggplant Jam, 100
Onion Marmalade, for
tuna, 144–45
Rhubarb Relish, for
Grilled Scallops with
White Asparagus and
Mâche Salad, 64–65
See also Chutney

Rémoulade
Celery Root *Rémoulade,*
for Smoked Salmon
Cakes, 49–50
Rhubarb
Rhubarb Compote,
Stilton Cheesecake
with, 202–3
Rhubarb Crisp with
Crème Fraîche Ice
Cream, 222–23
Rhubarb Relish, for
Grilled Scallops with
White Asparagus and
Mâche Salad, 64–65
Rice
Four Onion Risotto,
104–5
Salmon Kedgeree, 31–32
Wild Mushroom, Leek,
and Wild Rice Cakes,
163–64
Rice pudding
Budino, 220–21
Ricotta and Hazelnut
Croustillants, with Poached
Anjou Pears and Red Berry
and Rosemary Compote,
226–27
Risotto
Four Onion Risotto,
104–5
Roasted Oysters with Hazelnut
Butter, 41–42
Roasted Red Pepper and
Artichoke Sandwich, 113–14
Robin Hood, The
Mussels in Lavender-
Garlic Broth, 53–54
Rock Springs Guest Ranch
Granola, 10
Honey Peppered Salmon
with Tomato Ginger
Sauce, 184–85
Rolls
Martha's Rolls, 125–26
Rosemary
Toasted Rosemary
Walnuts, 132–33
Rub
Five-Spice Rub, for Five-
Spice Duck, 128–29
Ruby's on Bainbridge
Braised Lamb Shanks,
177–78
3-Carat Ruby, The, 238
Rum Sauce, for Warm Bread
Pudding, 204–5

Run of the River
Pure Gold, 239
Rye bread
Swedish Rye Bread,
109–10

S

Sablefish (black cod)
about, 169
Seared Sablefish with
Burnt Orange
Emulsion, 173–74
Salad
Asian Pear Salad, 102–3
Blood Orange Salad with
Hazelnuts and Point
Reyes Blue, 111–12
Dungeness Crab and Fuji
Apple Salad with Curry
Mayonnaise, 98–99
Green Bean Salad with
Mint Vinaigrette,
121–22
Grilled Beef with Grapes,
143
Grilled Romaine Salad
with Sun-Dried
Tomato Vinaigrette,
115–16
Shrimp with *Togarashi*
Spice and Asian Pears,
102–3
Spicy Eggplant Salad,
123–24
Salad dressing
Mint Vinaigrette, for
Green Bean Salad,
121–22
Sherry Vinaigrette, Blood
Orange Salad with
Hazelnuts and Point
Reyes Blue, 111–12
Spicy Lime Dressing,
Spicy Eggplant Salad,
123–24
Sun-Dried Tomato
Vinaigrette, for Grilled
Romaine Salad, 115–16
Salmon
about, 180–81
Cedar Smoked Salmon,
179–80
Grilled Salmon with
Stone Fruit Compote,
136–37
Honey Peppered Salmon
with Tomato Ginger
Sauce, 184–85

Cynthia C. Nims is a lifelong Northwesterner who reveled in growing up surrounded by great food–both in her mother's kitchen and exploring the region with her family, whether grilled oysters on a San Juan Island beach or huckleberry pancakes while backpacking in the Olympic Mountains. After graduating from the University of Puget Sound with a Bachelor of Science degree in mathematics and a second major in French Literature, Cynthia followed her dreams and went to France to study cooking at *La Varenne Ecole de Cuisine.* After receiving her *Grand Diplome d'Etudes Culinaires* and working on numerous cookbooks with the school's president, Anne Willan, Cynthia returned home to Seattle. She became the editor of *Simply Seafood* magazine, where she worked for seven years. Today, Cynthia is food editor of *Seattle Magazine,* local editor of the *Zagat* restaurant survey, a cookbook author, and freelance food and travel writer. She is a member of the International Association of Culinary Professionals and Les Dames d'Escoffier.